# THE HISTORY OF THE GLIDER PILOT REGIMENT

# THE HISTORY OF THE GLIDER PILOT REGIMENT

by
CLAUDE SMITH

with a Foreword by
General Sir John Hackett
GCB CBE DSO★ MC MA

With illustrations by
Alan Richards, DFM

LEO COOPER
LONDON

First published in Great Britain in 1992 by
LEO COOPER
190 Shaftesbury Avenue, London WC2H 8JL
an imprint of
Pen & Sword Books, Ltd,
47 Church Street, Barnsley, South Yorkshire S70 2AS
Reprinted 1992, 1996

A CIP catalogue record for this book is available
from the British Library

ISBN: 0 85052 326 5

Typeset by Yorkshire Web, Barnsley, S. Yorks.
In Plantin 10 point

Printed by
Redwood Books,
Trowbridge, Wiltshire

DEDICATED
TO THOSE 553 MEMBERS
OF THE REGIMENT
WHO GAVE THEIR LIVES
FOR THEIR COUNTRY

# CONTENTS

# ILLUSTRATIONS

## in the text

## by Alan Richards, DFM

# MAPS

# PREFACE TO SECOND EDITION

This Preface affords me the opportunity partly to correct a serious omission in the list of squadron commanders during 1945 given in Appendix III of the first edition. I must confess to a feeling of guilt that not one ex Royal Air Force squadron commander is shown there, and this was quickly highlighted by Squadron Leader Kenneth L. Ashurst OBE (Retd) who commanded 'M' Squadron at Gt. Dunmow.

Indeed it was with difficulty that the list of army squadron commanders was compiled, and my efforts to obtain the names of the ex RAF ones proved unavailing. It is now possible, however, to add the following:- S/Ldr J.R. Patient DFC, who preceded S/Ldr Ashurst in command of 'M'; S/Ldr S.C. Kent, 'D' and 'L' Sqdns; S/Ldr Reynolds, 'F' and 'I' Sqdns; S/Ldr Avery, 'J' Sqdn; S/Ldr Huntley, 'K' Sqdn; and S/Ldr White, 'E' and 'N' Sqdns.

C.A.S.

Gt. Massingham,
Norfolk,
August, 1992

# ACKNOWLEDGEMENTS

I am indebted to a lot of people for help in the writing of this book, primarily to Lieutenant-Colonel R.W.G. Nicholls, MBE, and David Brook, without whose guidance it would certainly not have reached the publication stage. Their advice has resulted in the revision of much of the subject matter and its presentation.

Colonel S.M.W. Hickey, MRAeS, Major John Cross and Harry Foot of the Museum of Army Flying at Middle Wallop, and the staff of the Public Record Office at Kew, all supplied the efficient and cheerful service one always receives at such establishments.

One of the greatest pleasures experienced during the writing has been the contact made with so many other ex-members of the Regiment, all of whom have supplied me with much information: Major T.I.J. Toler, DFC, TD; David Hall (whose lists of all glider sorties from the UK, in such detail, can be studied at the Museum of Army Flying); Major 'Andy' Andrews, DFM★; Colonel M.F.V. Willoughby; Bill Mackenzie; Arthur Rigby; Sidney Bland (for locating numerous relevant files at the Public Record Office for me to peruse); Alan Richards, DFM; Squadron Leader F.C. Aston, DFC, TD; Ian Blackwood, MM; Richard Clarke; Lt.Col B.H.P. Jackson, DFC; Len King; John Lister; Major W. McNeill, Lt.Col J.W. Place, DFC; and Denis Cason.

That General Sir John Hackett, that great soldier and historian, has written the Foreword is a source of immense pride.

I have been more than fortunate in that Alan Richards agreed to design the book cover and draw the plans of the landing-zones, as well as make available for inclusion his admirable sketches.

I have also made free use of many articles which have appeared in past numbers of the Regimental Magazine *The Eagle*.

It was a great pleasure to make contact with Doctor R.P.G.A. Voskuil of Oosterbeek, who supplied the details regarding the sighting of the glider evidence at Wolfheze in 1955 by a KLM photographer.

James Moore, publisher, author and historian, perused the manuscript with a professional eye, and I am thankful for his valued advice.

Lastly, to my wife for living with it over the past months, and to the Regiment for being the provider of it all.

# FOREWORD
## by
## General Sir John Hackett
### GCB CBE DSO* MC MA

THOUGH NEVER A GLIDER PILOT myself I yield to no one in respect and admiration for the British glider pilots of the Second World War and the Regiment that embodied them. I did not come across them personally until early in 1943, when the Fourth Parachute Brigade, which I had been raising and training in the Canal Zone, joined up with the First Airborne Division in North Africa and we looked forward to following up the expulsion of the Axis from Africa with the invasion of Italy. Thereafter I saw a good deal of them, learning early on how very good they were as fighting soldiers and glad later on to have a good number under my command in 'Market Garden'. Indeed it was on a visit to a GP position in Oosterbeek that I received the wounds which put me out of the fight and was happy to be allowed by Roy Urquhart to hand over command of the shrunken remnants of my brigade to one of the best of them all, Lt-Col Iain Murray. The invitation to become Patron of the Glider Pilot Regimental Association a year or two ago was one that I accepted with great pleasure.

Churchill's order, given just 50 years ago on 22 June 1940, to raise a force of 5000 British Airborne troops, in which powerful parachute and gliderborne components would be embodied, was what began it all. The techniques of delivering troops on to the battlefield in towed gliders, or dropped by parachute, had for some years been under study in several countries. Britain now developed them with vigour. From very early on the concept dominating the selection, training and use of British glider pilots was that having brought in their loads in vehicles now no longer of any use they should be put into the battle as infantry and for this they had to be as fully capable as for piloting gliders. The concept emerged of 'the total soldier'. That great fighting airborne general, the American Jim Gavin, used to complain that his glider pilots after they had landed were little more than a nuisance. They were willing enough to help but had no idea at all what to do. It was otherwise with the members of the GPR, officially established in the order of battle by an order of 21 December, 1941, as the First Glider Regiment. These glider pilots, all officers or NCOs, usually of the rank of Sergeant or Staff Sergeant, knew well what to do when they got into the battle and were superbly trained to do it. I shall always treasure the memory of their performance in 'Market Garden', in which the proportion of their officers and men who were killed in action was far higher than that in any other part of the First Airborne Division, and I speak as commander of a brigade that dropped in nearly two thousand strong and came out less than two hundred. It was Jim Gavin, incidentally, who observed that if attacking airborne troops cannot be put down on or very near the target the plan should be reconsidered and perhaps cancelled. It was a pity our masters had not hoisted that one in before 'Market Garden', though the use of 6th Airborne Division in Normandy and the subsequent triumphant success of the Rhine crossing in March, 1945, showed that some, at least, understood it.

This book, the story of one of the smallest and shortest-lived Regiments in the British Army, and one of the very finest and deserving to be among the most famous, had to be written. It has been most meticulously researched and impeccably presented. Names crop up in it of outstanding importance, above all that of George Chatterton. It was George who chiefly carried the torch of the GPR through its great days, the contrary winds of doubt as to whether gliders should remain with the Army or go to the RAF, and into the last stages of its life, when at war's end it was clear that big gliderborne operations were now a thing of the past, and the flame began to flicker. It is from here that the narrative, most faithfully discharging its duty as a necessary record, begins to lose the splendour of its earlier chapters. Where the spirit of the GPR lingers on most strongly is now not so much in the periodic convivial meetings of ageing brothers-in-arms as in the fervent study of aerial and land/air warfare today, in the age of helicopters and swift general technical advance in warlike method. It will always, however, be the quality of the members of the Glider Pilot Regiment, their union of skills at a very high level in most aspects of airmanship, and in the fighting of the land battle, and the courage, fortitude and discipline which marked them out everywhere that has earned the GPR an enduring place among this country's fighting regiments.

Personal memories are inevitable in any mind reflecting upon great events, even those nearly half a century old, in which there had been a personal interest. For the ill-fated airborne invasion of Sicily in July 1944, successful but none the less tragic, Gerald Lathbury's 1 Para Bde and the 1st Airlanding Bde under Pip Hicks, were to go in, with my own 4 Para Bde held in North

Africa in Divisional reserve. General Hopkinson, the Divisional Commander, was going over too, which left me at Sousse as acting Divisional Commander. I saw Hoppy off, towed by a Texan Lt-Col of US Troop Carrier Command, who in several previous months of liaison and joint training in Palestine, with US C47s, had become a close friend. 'With Willie here pulling you', I said to the Divisional Commander, 'whatever happens to anyone else you will get there'. But Hoppy's glider was cast off by the tug pilot with no hope at that distance, against adverse winds, of getting ashore and he was later picked up out of the sea by the Royal Navy, a wet and pretty angry Major-General. The Navy dressed him in the only spare dry clothing the little wardroom could find, the Maltese messman's second white drills, and he went ashore like that to spend a day or so following his Division's battle. Meanwhile, at base in North Africa, I was finding angry glider pilots, also picked up, prematurely cast off in an operation in which we lost some three hundred and fifty men drowned, coming ashore in fury looking for a tug pilot's throat to cut. The trouble was that the US Troop Carrier Command was largely manned by Civil airline pilots, mostly trained on Randolph Field, who flew their C47s impeccably but knew nothing of navigation. None of them, except in the lead ship, had a map and they flew on the lead ship as the next best thing to their accustomed beam. Moreover, with no knowledge at all of what happens in battles, they were flying into their first taste of combat in aircraft with neither armament nor armour and even without self-sealing tanks. Little wonder that so many shed their gliders and stood for home when the stuff from the ground started coming up.

I deeply understood, and shared, the feelings of our Glider Pilots, but I knew that we had largely to rely on the US Troop Carrier Command for the rest of the war. They would learn, and a bust-up now would be fatal. So I confined all returning Glider Pilots to camp. Days later, after congratulatory parades had been held in TCC camps and medals given, it was safe to let our pilots out. These were great people: they knew the form and responded.

General Hoppy was a few weeks later to be killed in Italy. He did not die from a sniper's bullet, as current accounts claim, and as appeared in the narrative before us, though this is now corrected. He was brought down by a burst of German machine-gun fire in September 1944, while following up an attack of my own 10 Para Bn near Massafra, against a German parachute rearguard. I was beside him at the time and Johnny Goschen, the Grenadier AAMC of 1 Airborne Division (who had even less excuse than the GOC then to expose himself) and I between us carried him out of the battle. This was another great gliderborne soldier. Those who went into battle in gliders (far more hazardous, it always seemed to me, than parachuting) and above all those who got them there, the Glider Pilots, deserve our enduring esteem. This book, with its careful and balanced account of what was done, and its wonderfully complete record of those who did it, will do much to ensure that it gets this and keeps it.

# INTRODUCTION

THE CONCEPT OF CONVEYING elite troops and heavy equipment, including tanks and artillery, by air straight to unprepared landing-zones miles behind enemy lines to prepare the way for the advance of conventional ground forces was not the overnight brainchild of some military genius. The first nation to awaken to the possibilities of the use of airborne forces on a large scale was Russia, who began to develop parachuting and gliding, first as a national sport soon after World War 1 and then, by 1935, by the creation of a body of parachute troops carried in gliders. The Poles then set up a parachute training school at Le Gionowo near Warsaw in 1936 on similar lines to the Russians, and by 1939 the French had formed two companies of *infanterie de l'air*.

Germany had been prevented from openly developing such aggressive formations by the terms of the 1919 Treaty of Versailles. However, it had not taken military-minded persons in that country long to seize upon the fact that, contained in the skills inherent in the sport of gliding enthusiastically being pursued by thousands of young Germans, lay the source of pilots of powered aircraft for the future Luftwaffe being planned in defiance of the Treaty. The sport soon became a state-controlled activity, and in 1935 thousands of young glider pilots rushed to join the Luftwaffe, which had become a reality. The knowledge that by that year Russia had produced a towed glider capable of carrying eighteen passengers had not been lost on Hitler. He then announced that Germany no longer recognized the validity of the Treaty.

The other Western Powers did nothing to stop Germany's rapid rearmament programme, being preoccupied with a policy of appeasement, and the development of the troop-carrying glider was a natural consequence of the build-up of German airborne formations. These forces were to form an important part of her military planning, which inevitably led to the outbreak of hostilities on the 3rd of September, 1939. Britain's attitude to all this is summed up in one sentence contained in a report of the Inter-Services Training and Development Centre concerning the question of this new-fangled nonsense in which the foreigners were dabbling; it affirmed: 'and it is for consideration as to whether the present is the time to direct effort to the production of a weapon which may never be used'. This was six months before the start of the most devastating war waged by the human race.

It is interesting to note that as early as 1931 a young woman in Britain, in collaboration with two RAF officers, had designed a towed glider capable of carrying cargo. The 'young woman' was Barbara Cartland and the glider, specially built for the project, was air-towed from Manston to Reading on 20 June, 1931, where it landed to deliver mail. Later that year the glider (the 'Barbara Cartland') carrying a passenger, raced an express train from London to Blackpool – winning easily. While other nations were soon to see such flights as the opening of a new epoch in air travel the aero-towing of gliders was banned in Britain as being too dangerous!

The dynamic force in Germany behind this new method of warfare was Luftwaffe Colonel Kurt Student. Such was the success of his drive and ability that he was able to respond to Hitler's orders in late 1939 to prepare airborne troops for a surprise attack against Belgium, Holland and France so that at 0415 hours on 10 May, 1940, it was possible for ten DFS230 gliders conveying 78 army engineers to take off from Cologne for an attack on the Belgian Fort at Eben Emael situated at the confluence of the River Meuse and the Albert Canal near Liège. This fort promised to be a formidable obstacle to the German Panzer forces which were to be let loose on the unsuspecting Belgians. It had been completed in 1935 and its heavily-armoured turrets held six 120mm and eighteen 75mm guns. Machine-guns and anti-tank guns covered all the approaches, and numerous anti-aircraft guns were sited within its massive concrete walls, all of which were controlled from an underground command post and were manned by over 1,000 troops. Its capture, together with the three adjacent bridges over the River Meuse was, therefore, vital to the rapid forward movement of Germany's Panzers.

Hitler himself conceived the plan for the airborne assault. He realized that ground forces would probably take two weeks to capture the fort, and he had been the first to notice that inside the impregnable walls a flat, grassy plain was open to the sky and formed a perfect landing ground. He therefore ordered that assault parties were to land in gliders, one of them directly on to this meadow and with their armour-blasting hollow explosive charges destroy the gun emplacements and set about the capture of the fort by surprise, while others were to secure the three bridges at Veldewezelt, Vroenhoven and Kanne. Preparations for the first glider-borne assault in the history of warfare began in November, 1939, and when the gliders took off for the operation, towed by Ju52 aircraft, every detail had been worked out meticulously.

The force followed a forty-five-mile-long string of beacons to the German border where the gliders released 12 miles from the objective at a height of 8,000 feet just as daylight was breaking. By midday on the following day they had captured the fort and its defenders at a cost of only six killed and twenty wounded, and had secured two of the bridges at a cost of fifteen killed and thirty-nine wounded. The third bridge was blown up as they arrived. Glider-borne assault troops had made a spectacular debut and their primary purpose, that of preparing the way for ground forces, had been so successfully demonstrated that long German tank columns were soon passing the fort, which until then had been thought impregnable, and were crossing the River Meuse with impunity. The operation was quickly followed by other parachute and glider-borne assaults in Holland, carried out with equal success, and Student's *Fallschirmjäger* were eventually to expand to a strength of about 4,500.

As intelligence of the outstanding achievements of the German airborne forces began to register in other countries, so the potential of this new form of warfare was realized. The British Expeditionary Force in France soon found itself surrounded in a pocket at Dunkirk as a result of the rapid advance made by the German Army, and in the eight days following 26 May it was taken off the French coast and carried back to England by 848 ships ranging from destroyers to private motor cruisers. The German forces continued to swarm across France and their success was so complete that on 17 June, 1940, the French government asked for an armistice, which was granted on the 22nd. On that very day Winston Churchill addressed a Minute to the Combined Chiefs of Staff in London directing that an airborne force of 5,000 paratroops, and a proportionate glider force, was to be raised in England by the Spring of the following year, ending in true Churchillian fashion with the phrase, 'Pray let me have a Note from the War Office on the subject'.

In those few words (dictated at a time when Britain had been left to face overwhelming odds alone, having very little resources with which to do so), the Prime Minister showed a remarkable degree of faith in his country's power to fight back, and in the people who in the coming years were to do such great things. A not insignificant part in those achievements was to be played by the Glider Pilot Regiment.

The Germans intended that their airborne troops should next spearhead the invasion of England. A rather alarmist cablegram from the United States dated 18 June, 1940, addressed to the Chief of the Imperial General Staff in London, General Sir John Dill was worded, 'Report here is fifteen thousand gliders armed with machine-guns being built in Holland to attack England silently. Be on the alert.' The Air Ministry was asked for its views concerning Germany's use of gliders and reported that unconfirmed stories had been received to the effect that the Germans had used them to assist in the capture of Fort Eben Emael and a photograph had been seen showing ten small gliders on the ground near the fort. The Ministry went on to say that reports had also been received from Sweden alleging that the Germans had about 200 gliders in Denmark and Norway which constituted a threat to England. As an illustration of the naivety prevailing at the time, the rest of the Report is worth quoting in full: '(there is) no knowledge that Germans or Russians have conceded any real military value to the glider. It is thought that gliders could be detected by R.D.F., negating any idea of a long silent approach, and that to have a long glide it must be towed to a height at which provision of warm and heavy clothing and oxygen for troops become necessary. In addition it would be completely dependent upon wind, and from such a height could easily make a negative ground speed, thereby landing further away from its target than it was at the moment of release. It is noteworthy that the Germans themselves claim that their capture of the fort was a triumph for their parachute troops and have published photographs proving this to be so. A glider large enough to carry even five men would need so great a wing-span and so big a fuselage that it would probably need an assisted take-off. Finally it may be pointed out that a commander who has sufficient tanks and motor-cycles to move his troops does not mount them on tricycles. Why then should the Germans put their trust in gliders? It is most improbable that they will.' The reference to the Germans' claim, *backed up by photographs*, that paratroops had captured the fort, shows that even Higher Command could fall victim to Germany's efficient propaganda machine; they had indeed circulated the parachutist story, wishing to keep secret their use of gliders. The initials RDF in the report referred to Radio Detection Finding, the original name for radar.

However, it was not destined that England should be the next target for the German airborne forces. In November, 1940, Greece successfully repulsed an attack made on her by Italy, and this embarrassment to the Axis powers was aggravated when British and Anzac troops moved into that country from North Africa in March, 1941, under the command of Lieutenant-General Sir Henry Maitland Wilson. Apart from the fact that British bombers based in Greece were within range of the Rumanian oil fields, the exploitation of which formed an important part of Hitler's plans for the invasion of Russia in May of that year, he had no intention of permitting British troops to establish a foothold on the European mainland. All thoughts of attempting an invasion of England had long since been abandoned, and Hitler therefore decided to postpone the assault on Russia and drive the British out of Greece first. Consequently he invaded that country on 6 April, 1941, and proceeded to carry out his intention.

Just before daybreak on 26 April, following a heavy bombing attack by German aircraft, three DFS230 gliders containing thirty-six German paratroops landed at both ends of the Corinth Canal bridge which was being used by the British and Anzac forces retreating to the South. These were followed by paratroops dropping around the bridge, which was quickly taken, only to collapse immediately afterwards, possibly as the result of a chance projectile triggering off the demolition charges previously placed in position. The bridge was all that linked the Peloponnese with the Greek mainland and this lucky chance enabled 50,662 British and Anzac troops, who had already crossed the bridge, to be evacuated from the Peloponnese to Crete. From this Greek island, only 160 miles south of the mainland, British bombers would still be able to reach the Rumanian oil fields, but Hitler at first decided to ignore the threat and press on with his Russian adventure. Student, however, persuaded him that Crete could be captured by his airborne forces on their own, and as Suda Bay on its north-west coast formed the largest natural harbour in the Mediterranean and was extensively used by the Royal Navy, perhaps too much persuasion was not needed. The occupation of the island by the Axis would threaten the allied convoy route between Malta and Alexandria; plans for its seizure were therefore put in hand.

The Allied Commander in Crete was Major-General Bernard Freyberg, VC, and intelligence reports had left him in no doubt that German airborne forces were to be expected. He had only arrived on the island three weeks before, but soon had his forces disposed so as to meet this threat in the best possible way. He had not long to wait. At 0715 hours on 20 May, 2,000 German aircraft started to arrive over the island's northern coastline. Firstly bombers, Stuka dive bombers and fighters concentrated their attack on Maleme airfield and silenced all the anti-aircraft guns sited there. Then thirty-two DFS230 gliders landed around Maleme and nearby Heraklion. As the occupants of the gliders emerged they were met by the combined fire of automatic weapons and within seconds whole platoons of Germans had been wiped out. The paratroops, who started to arrive at 0745 hours, were also subjected to the same punishment, and hundreds of them were killed before they could get out of their harnesses.

Fighting was still in progress at Maleme when more gliders and paratroops arrived at two other airfields, Heraklion and Rethimnon, and German casualties there were also extremely heavy. By the end of that day the 7,000 German airborne troops had been reduced in number by 40 per cent, but a large number of the survivors had established themselves near Maleme. The airfield was eventually taken when more aircraft brought in a force of 650 mountain troops and 550 more paratroops the next day, and yet another 2,000 mountain troops on the 22nd. The battle raged for six days until the defending troops were forced to admit defeat and were evacuated to Egypt by the Royal Navy.

As promised by Student, Crete had been captured entirely by airborne forces − but at a price. 5,140 of the 13,000 Germans taking part had been killed, wounded or were missing, and 220 aircraft had been destroyed. The assault also resulted in a vital seven weeks' delay in the German invasion of Russia, and the loss of so many of his elite troops, which it had been intended should form a part of that invasion, caused Hitler to resolve never again to employ airborne forces as such. They were, however, kept intact and used as ground forces until the war ended. Allied leaders, nevertheless, took cognizance of the fact that a lightly-armed airborne force had flown 200 miles and successfully attacked a heavily defended island, capturing it in six days. They were unaware of the extent of the casualties inflicted, or of Hitler's decision, and were left with the resolve that their own airborne forces must be built up as rapidly as possible.

# I

## EARLY DAYS

ON 21 JUNE, 1940, the day preceding Winston Churchill's Directive that a force of 5,000 parachutists and gliderborne troops was to be raised in England, an Establishment had been formed at RAF Station, Ringway, near Manchester, controlled by the Director of Combined Operations at the War Office. The Establishment was given the title 'Central Landing School', and its directive was to investigate the technical problems associated with parachuting and the carriage of troops by glider. A search for volunteers with pre-war experience of flying sailplanes, or with an interest in parachuting, brought together there a small group of Service personnel and civilians under the command of Squadron Leader L.A. Strange; the officer in charge of the army involvement was Major J.F. Rock, Royal Engineers, who had been posted from Scotland where he was serving as a Brigade Major.

It had been agreed between the Air Ministry and the War Office that the responsibility for airborne operations from the time of emplaning to deplaning must be a Royal Air Force one, and four obsolescent Whitley aircraft, together with some Tiger Moths and Avro 504's, were supplied to the Unit. The Air Ministry and War Office drew up specifications for four types of military gliders, and were eventually to place orders for the production of prototypes with General Aircraft Company Limited, Airspeed Limited and Slingsby Sailplanes. A Glider Training Squadron was formed, commanded by Squadron Leader H.E. Hervey, MC, and various experiments were immediately entered into using BA Swallow light aircraft with the propellers removed to simulate gliders. These were used to experiment with multiple tows, two or three of them being towed behind one Whitley using tow ropes of differing lengths.

A nation-wide search produced an assortment of sailplanes from private gliding clubs. The first four models, three of which had been made in Germany, arrived by road at the beginning of August, and these were used to train RAF gliding instructors, tug pilots and ground crews. These four models were soon joined by others until the Establishment possessed a Minimoa, a Rhonbusard, a Condor, a Viking and several Kirby Kites. Accidents were fairly frequent during these early days at Ringway, mainly caused by the hemp tow rope breaking, but this cause was largely eliminated when nylon tow ropes arrived from America.

Who could have visualized then the ultimate airborne operation of the war just 56 months ahead, when, within a space of 63 minutes, two complete airborne divisions would be landed on German soil? The British contribution to that massive undertaking would comprise the employment of 440 tug/glider combinations carrying into battle over 4,800 men and a vast quantity of weapons and equipment including an Airborne Armoured Reconnaissance Regiment. But all that belonged to the future, and during the brief but at the time seemingly endless period separating present and future there would be encountered much trial and error and frustration, a vast amount of effort, and valour and dedication far beyond the normal call of duty.

Two other units were set up in addition to the Glider Training Squadron; a Technical Development Unit and a Parachute School, and Major Rock lost no time in making his first parachute jump, which he achieved on 14 July. He was to be promoted to Lieutenant-Colonel in October of that year.

On 6 August, 1940, the Chiefs of Staff informed the Prime Minister that of 3,500 volunteers, 500 specially selected men were being trained as paratroops, a piece of intelligence which prompted him to point out that his requirement had been for ten times that figure. However, he was told that limitations in training equipment and, above all, in aircraft availability, made it impossible for the time being to go beyond the figure of 500 and that the need for a rapid development of the Bomber Force made the provision of squadrons solely for the purpose of dropping parachute troops out of the question. The Air Ministry also informed him that they believed the use of paratroops was a clumsy and obsolescent method of delivering men on the ground and that there were far greater possibilities in the use of gliders. The Prime Minister growled that if this was considered to be the case it should be taken up seriously, and asked for a full report on what had been done about gliders.

On 9 September a report was submitted to Winston Churchill from the War Office which detailed the types of raids for which airborne troops could be used, and calculated that about 1,000 men would be required for such raids, of whom 100 would be paratroops and 900 glider-borne. The PM was told that plans had been made for three such forces to be ready by the Spring of the following year, plus 200 parachute saboteurs. The total airborne force envisaged was 500 parachute troops, 2,700 glider-borne troops and 360 glider pilots. Mr. Churchill accepted this on the basis that the resources available at the time would not permit anything larger. At the time the threat of German invasion was very great and priority was being given to the defence of the United Kingdom. No one was prepared to give much thought to the creation of a force which could not exert any influence on the war for some time to come. The RAF in particular was looking for fighter aircraft to defend the country and bombers to attack Germany. There was a desperate · shortage of everything and the provision of an airborne force was well down the list of priorities.

However, Ringway was getting on with its job to the best of its ability. On 18 September it was renamed Central Landing Establishment, and Group Captain L.G. Harvey assumed command, assisted by Wing Commanders Sir Nigel Norman and G.M. Buxton, Captains M.A. Lindsay (of Arctic exploration fame) and J. Lander, and a few RAF enthusiasts and ex-professional stunt parachutists. Technical trials and the practical testing of many theories were taking place there, and much of the credit for the success of the early experiments must go to Major Rock. On arriving at Ringway he had had no previous experience of parachute training, which was his particular responsibility, but his unfailing courage and determination was an inspiration to everyone.

The Establishment was placed under the command of 70 Group of RAF Army Co-operation Command, and much valuable work was done in those early days without which the later expansion of airborne forces would not have taken place. An excellent rapport was also built up between the two Services involved, greatly contributing to the success of future airborne operations.

On 26 September the Duke of Kent watched a demonstration at Ringway involving two towed gliders and four live parachute drops, and this was followed in October by a night tow of five miles by two Avro 504s towing four sailplanes. Then, on 13 December, five sailplanes were towed to Tatton

Park, five miles south-west of Ringway, where they were landed simultaneously with sixteen parachutists dropped from two of the Whitleys, within a radius of 200 yards. Tests were also carried out into the effect of landing sailplanes on water, using the lake at Tatton Park.

The original policy, which had been laid down in September, 1940, was that the personnel to be trained to fly the gliders would be obtained from the army, and the following month sixty-six men from No. 2 Commando with previous flying experience were selected. No. 2 Commando was part of a Commando Force which had been recruited from Independent Companies formed to take part in the British intervention in Norway. On 9 April, 1940, Germany had invaded Norway and Denmark in order to protect its supply route for Swedish iron ore, and Allied forces, including British, had responded by sending a force into Norway between 15 and 18 April. The Allies had everywhere been repulsed, and the last of them were evacuated early in June.

On returning to England, No. 2 Commando had been converted to parachute duties as the nucleus of airborne forces, and was re-designated 11 Special Air Service Battalion on 21 November, 1940, with Parachute and Glider Wings. The sixty-six men from No. 2 Commando were attached to Army Co-operation Command squadrons for preliminary training prior to conversion as glider coxswains (at that stage CLE always referred to them as coxswains), and when the Glider Wing was formed the following month they were held on its establishment. The Parachute Wing was later to become 1st Battalion, the Parachute Regiment.

On 11 November, 1940, the Deputy Director of Plans at the Air Ministry forwarded to Group Captain Harvey the draft of a Minute he was proposing to put forward, and asked for his comments. One of the items raised was to become a recurring subject of contention between the Air Ministry and the War Office throughout the war years – should the men chosen to fly the gliders be drawn from the army or the RAF? Extracts from the draft Minute were worded as follows:-

'Hitherto it has been presumed that the training and technical requirements necessary for operating gliders are relatively simple matters. It appears now that this is not the case and that the glider pilots for such operations as are envisaged will require many hours' flying experience before they can be considered reliable and that their training must include a number of apects of flying not previously thought necessary for glider pilots. They will be required, in effect, to make spot landings in swift succession and in order on unknown places with a dead stick in large engineless aeroplanes, having been released from their tows over some unknown place, possibly in twilight. This is no task for a beginner in flying who is primarily a soldier.

'An airborne operation must surely be an air operation from the time of assembly of the forces until their disembarkation. The GOC and the AOC must make their plan together, but it must be for the AOC to execute the air operation before the Commander of the Landing Force again takes over his command. As in naval landing operations the crews of all craft are naval crews under naval control and experience, so in air landing operations the pilots and crews would appropriately be airmen (RAF or seconded) unless there are strong reasons to the contrary.

'The pilots must be experienced flyers: as such they could not and should not be allowed to lie fallow as unemployed pilots in the prolonged intervals before and between airborne operations. They should be kept employed on flying of one sort or another − i.e., within the RAF.'

Group Captain Harvey's reply dated 14 November presented his views thus:-

'I have always understood that the spheres of responsibility had been precisely defined, and that the army would take over from the air force at the moment of casting off of tows. It has been represented to me that the naval precedent is one to be avoided, and that by developing, in the glider coxswain, a class of man half airman, half soldier, the execution of an operation involving both an air plan and a ground plan would be simplified. There should be created that close co-operation between pilot and piloted that has often been lacking in sea landings and has contributed to their failure.

'Moreover, the naval analogy is not in fact exactly applicable. Naval responsibility ceases on touching the beach. The glider coxswain on touching down will be the only man present who will know exactly where the landing has been made and in which direction the troops should go. He has the best forward view, he is highly trained in map-reading and studying ground from the air, and he will have noted the lie of the land to the objective. Even if only a Corporal, he will be the one to lead the other 23 officers and men to the right place.

'While there is a strong argument for glider coxswains to be employed on other flying, I think the suggestion that they be used on flying of one sort or another with the Royal Air Force is bound to lead to confusion. They can be kept in flying practice by using a certain number of large gliders for quick lift work

behind bombers of obsolete type. It is in my opinion imperative
that they should wear a distinctive uniform or badge. This would
in no way preclude their acting under air force control.'

The final word, for the moment, was given by the then Deputy Chief of Air
Staff, later to become Air Chief Marshal Sir Arthur Harris. At a Meeting
held at the Air Ministry on 11 December, chaired by Harris and attended
by War Office representatives, he declared that the policy to use army
personnel was wrong and should be changed to trained RAF bomber pilots,
on the grounds that flying the large 25-seater gliders then at the design stage,
and which would be as large as a bomber, would prove to be an even more
skilled task than flying a bomber itself. Only the most fully trained and
skilled RAF bomber pilots should be selected for the job, being trained to
fly gliders and then returned to Bomber Command until required by the
army for airborne operations. Harris expressed reservations about the
proposed use of 'semi-skilled, unpicked personnel – even infantry corporals
have I understand been suggested – to fly gliders.' The future
Commander-in-Chief of Bomber Command was known to hold entrenched
beliefs and to trust only in orthodox views.

It was further stated by Sir Arthur that a primary consideration in the
raising of airborne forces must be to ensure that, as far as possible, the
expansion of the bomber force should not be prejudiced by channelling
instructors and pilots into the airborne force organization until there was an
airborne operation in view. However, he affirmed, it was necessary to
produce a structure which would be capable of providing rapid training as
soon as such an operation was envisaged.

Harris's reservations about the use of army personnel resulted in a
memorandum from Headquarters, Army Co-operation Command, to the
squadrons concerned to the effect that there would probably be no more
army pupils sent to them, and that the future of those already undergoing
instruction was to be carefully reviewed. It recommended that those who
were considered not likely to make satisfactory glider pilots should be
returned to their units, and the memorandum stressed that the standard of
flying required of glider pilots would be comparable to that of the pilot of a
heavy bomber.

On the 1st of November, 1940, Group Captain Harvey had produced a
Paper headed 'Provision of an Airborne Force' in which it was proclaimed
that 'the reasons for the creation of an airborne force were (i) to prepare a
high-speed striking force to be used as the spearhead of offensive operations,
or for a counter-offensive; (ii) to contain a large enemy force on defence of
vulnerable points; (iii) to develop a knowledge of a form of warfare that
must inevitably be of great importance in future and may at any time be
used against us, and (iv) to provide by towed gliders a means of air transport

of troops and equipment using pilots that can at all other times form part of the operational bomber force.' It was made apparent in the last few words of the Paper that Harris's views, soon to be asserted, were official policy.

The Paper contained the information that it would be possible to have available 360 glider coxswains and 500 trained paratroops by March, 1941, and that 1,000 lightly-equipped glider-borne troops could be employed by day by September, 1941. It continued, 'The main characteristics of a 25-seater glider have been decided and an order for a prototype can shortly be placed. Experiments for train-towing are in progress, and an order for an 8-seater was placed in July in advance of precise knowledge of military requirements, and production up to 400 has been ordered. A design for a tank and transport carrying glider with capacity up to 9 tons is being studied.'

The Paper then discussed the training of glider coxswains (the word 'pilot' at (iv) had been used conjunctly with their role as bomber pilots) and contained the ambitious statement that 'at the conclusion of their training the glider coxswains must be able to undertake a successful tow of 500-1,000 miles in conditions of fog or darkness'. It soon became apparent that the estimates given in this Paper, and in the War Office Report of 9 September, regarding the size of the airborne forces which would be available by March, 1941, were also on the optimistic side.

The order for the 400 8-seater gliders had been placed with General Aircraft Company Limited, but it was realized at once that there were tactical objections to 8-seaters on the grounds that from a military point of view it was desirable to land men compactly in larger numbers than eight, that the numbers of towing aircraft required would be uneconomical, and that the towing of gliders in tandem in darkness and through cloud would be difficult. The development of a 15-seater, in addition to the 25-seater and the tank-carrying glider, was given the go-ahead, with the proviso that the development of the larger types should not be allowed to delay the production of the small ones, which in any case would meet the requirements of training. Specifications for the 25-seater were handed to Airspeed Limited, while that for the 15-seater went to Slingsby Sailplanes.

General Aircraft lost no time in designing and developing their glider, which they named the Hotspur. The prototype took to the air on 5 November, 1940, and Ringway received its first model on 6 February, 1941, and promptly began trials towing it behind a Boulton & Paul Overstrand aircraft. The Hotspur was, in fact, the model on which all glider pilots were to receive their initial gliding instruction, and its rapid progression from drawing board to production was remarkable. As specified, it was designed to accommodate eight fully-armed troops and had the ability to carry a cargo weighing 1,880 lbs. That it was only ever used in a training role was certainly no criticism of it. Its specification had matched it with the tug planes which were available at the time – the Hawker Hector, Hawker Hart and Miles Master – and although, after the decision had been made to produce larger gliders, it was visualized that the Hotspur *might* have to be used operationally, there were objections to its use for such purposes, as already stated.

The Hotspur accommodated an instructor and pupil sitting in tandem. It had a wing-span of 45ft, 10¾ins, a length of 39ft, 3½ins, and its weight fully-loaded was 3,598lbs. 1,015 of them were to be built during the war, and, being made of wood, they utilized a section of industry not previously involved in war production to any significant extent, namely furniture manufacturers.

Airspeed's design, the Horsa, was also accepted and an order for 400 was placed in February, 1941. The prototype was to make its first trial flight behind a Whitley on 12 September. It was at first estimated that Airspeed's order could be completed in England by July, 1942, and investigations were made into the possibility of producing a further 400 in India. However, on 1 April, 1942, the Indian Defence Department was to report to the War Office in London that as there was no suitable indigenous timber available in India it would be necessary for it to be imported. This would have resulted in a prohibitive price for the gliders and the idea was abandoned.

Had it been possible for the Indian Horsas to have been produced they would have gone to the Middle East as, at that stage, it had been decided to confine airborne forces in India to paratroops. In any event there were not likely to be any glider pilots or tug aircraft available out there for some time. Be that as it may, another report was on its way to the War Office from India in April, this one from the Commander-in-Chief, General Wavell. He reported that operations were being planned to take place in Burma that autumn and asked for information about the prospects of obtaining 200 American Waco gliders. This resulted in a cypher message from the Ministry of Aircraft Production in London to the British Air Commission in Washington dated 31 August which was worded: 'Decided to abandon scheme to make Horsas in India. 20 Wacos and 10 glider pilots required to arrive India by early 1943 in order to allow India to develop planning of glider-borne force. Further 200 Wacos to arrive India June, 1943.' A decision had been made that gliders were a necessity for the purpose of carrying supporting arms for the paratroops and by mid-1944, 500 Wacos, together with American glider pilots, had been delivered to the Far East.

We shall return to the Waco glider in greater detail in Chapter 4, and to India in Chapter 10 when the Regiment's presence there was beginning to materialize, but let us return now to 1941 and the United Kingdom. In view of the fact that the Horsas for the Middle East would not be forthcoming from India, Airspeed's order was increased and the first production model appeared in June, 1942. By the end of the war Airspeed would have produced over 5,000 of them. The Horsa was of vast proportions in comparison with the Hotspur and it accommodated first and second pilots side by side in a roomy, perspex-covered cockpit. It was originally designed purely as a means of conveying a body of troops which could be delivered on the ground as a compact fighting unit as opposed to the rather scattered arrival of paratroops. Alternatively it doubled the number of paratroops which a bomber could carry on its own, and for this purpose it was fitted with two passenger doors, one on each side of the fuselage, widely separated for their simultaneous exit. The doors could be opened in flight by sliding them upwards inside the fuselage in order that they could also be used as Bren-gun positions, and apertures were fitted on the top of the fuselage in the centre of the wing, and in the tail, for the same purpose. This means of engaging the enemy was never to be used in practice.

If the Horsa had ever been used to convey paratroops they would have attached their static lines to small rails over the doors as they approached them prior to jumping, and supporting arms and supplies would have been dropped in containers carried in wing cells. The only vehicle ever intended to be carried inside the Horsa was a solo or combination motorcycle. The undercarriage was designed to be jettisoned after take-off, but once the Horsa was adapted for carrying heavy supporting arms for the air-landing troops and paratroops it became normal practice to retain the undercarriage in position, which permitted greater control after touch-down. A rectangular door was then fitted to the port side just aft of the nose, and this was hinged at the bottom, so that when lowered it formed an unloading ramp. In order to avoid damage to the ramp during the loading of heavy equipment, separate loading channels were used which spanned the space from the ground to the glider's floor. An arrester parachute system was developed to shorten the landing run by using a pair of fourteen-foot parachutes stowed under the tail. A fully-loaded Horsa could be stopped in less than 100 yards in this way. This was designed for use when *coup-de-main* assaults were undertaken as will be seen later, and twelve Horsas received this fitting.

The Horsa's wing-span was 88 feet, its length 67 feet, and its weight fully-loaded was 15,250 lbs. The tow-rope on the Mk1 version formed a 'Y' at the glider end which was attached under the leading edges of the port and starboard wings. Both glider and tug were provided with tow-rope release mechanisms so that the tug was able to drop the rope after the glider pilot had cast off. It was an understood rule that the tug pilot would never release the glider from his end except in a case of dire emergency. The central pedestal in the cockpit housed the compass, elevator trim-tab control, flap control, tow release and undercarriage jettison lever. The brake lever was attached to the first pilot's seat, and later, in the Mark II version, on his control column. Air-pressure gauge, airspeed indicator, altimeter and turn-and-bank indicator were fitted in the instrument panel. Communication between the glider and tug was by means of a telephone cable woven into the tow rope.

The glider's production was a triumph of organization and improvisation, and its design and the construction of the prototype were carried out in only ten months. General Aircraft were later to build the Hamilcar to comply with the requirement for a glider capable of carrying vehicles, artillery and tanks or, alternatively, 40 troops.

Slingsby's model, the Hengist, was to appear in May, 1942. As intended, it had only been developed as an insurance against any failure of the Horsa 25-seater, and only eighteen were ever built. One other model to be produced was the twin version of the Hotspur, designed by General Aircraft in an attempt to introduce an interim 15-seater glider by joining two Hotspur fuselages 12 feet apart by means of a new wing centre-section, the outer wings being standard Hotspur. A prototype was built but proved unpopular with pilots and the project was dropped.

But to return to the Glider Training Squadron. On 28 December, 1940, it moved from Ringway to Haddenham, near Thame, in Oxfordshire, its aircraft at first comprising five Tiger Moths and five Kirby Kite and Falcon III sailplanes. By January, 1941, fifteen members of the RAF with pre-war experience of flying sailplanes had been found and posted there as gliding instructors. They quickly discovered that they had to train themselves not only to undertake the role of instructors for the glider pilots but also to double as tug pilots. In April, 1941, Haddenham was re-named No.1 Glider Training School and the airfield was henceforth known as Thame. Its first Hotspur arrived by low-loader in September of that year.

The first twelve army pupils had completed their preliminary flying by the beginning of February, 1941, and the following month they were posted to Haddenham (as it was then still called) to begin their gliding instruction, initially on the civilian sailplanes. They were joined by sixteen RAF bomber pilot volunteers. The army personnel included Corporal Strathdee, formerly of the 1st Dragoon Guards, who was destined to be killed in the first operation involving the use of gliders, Major Lander from the Ringway staff, formerly of the Royal Corps of Signals and later to command 1st Independent Parachute Company, and Second-Lieutenant Oxenford, formerly of the Durham Light Infantry, later to lose his life at Arnhem.

It was immediately apparent that none of the army trainees had received anything approaching the hours of instruction on light aircraft which he should have had, and it was necessary for them all to carry out a complete course before progressing to gliders. Their training at the Army Co-operation

Squadrons had been on a casual, part-time basis given by pilots who were not qualified instructors.

The introduction to the syllabus for this Glider Training Squadron Army Course No.1, which was to be of six weeks duration, pointed out that it must be regarded as being an experimental one because of the wide variations in the pupils' previous flying experience and the non-availability of troop-carrying gliders. The flying programme on light-powered aircraft comprised 2 hours 40 minutes general dual flying, 2 hours formation flying, 4 hours instrument flying, 5 hours 20 minutes map reading, and 4 hours formation pin pointing. The glider training comprised 1 hour 45 minutes general dual, 2 hours 55 minutes flying practice, 1 hour 20 minutes duration towing, 1 hour 45 minutes formation flying, 2 hours 20 minutes dive approaches, and 2 hours 55 minutes timed approaches; a total of 31 hours. The ground subjects covered flying regulations and procedure, principles of flight and glider pilotage, Link-trainer exercises, airframes, navigation, meteorology, and signals.

Five of the twelve army trainees were sent from Thame to Ringway to stage a demonstration of glider towing for the Prime Minister on 26 April, 1941. All five of the Kirby Kite sailplanes which were used, towed behind Tiger Moths, finished their landing runs wing tip to wing tip within a few feet of the distinguished spectator and his party of senior officers and eminent civilians.

Two days later, on 28 April, Churchill was enquiring about the build-up of the paratroop and glider force, and asking for a timetable of expected results. In its reply the Air Ministry reiterated the view that 'flying a glider as large as a Stirling (bomber) requires the same order of skill as is required in pilots of heavy bombers, therefore for airborne operations experienced operational pilots must be used in gliders'. The reply continued, 'The intention is to pass a continual flow of operational pilots through the glider training squadron and thence into the bomber force. Once the minimum number of glider pilots are available in squadrons a process of conversion could be carried through in a short time when such a force is required.' (It is to be noticed that the five men chosen for the Ringway demonstration on 26 April at Thame had been taken from the army personnel!)

A Glider Exercise Unit was set up at Ringway in June, 1941, and succeeded in giving its first demonstration in September with three Hotspurs. And then in November a fully-loaded Hotspur was released at 10,000 feet and managed to arrive back at Ringway from a distance of twenty miles. The Unit was busy finding answers to many formidable but realistic questions which Rock was putting to it about glider tactics. He had already produced a list of roles for the employment of Airborne Forces and had designed special clothing and equipment for them. The flying training programme was to consist of a twelve-week course on light powered aircraft, completing 80 hours day and 8 hours night flying on Tiger Moths and Miles Magisters, which would include dual and solo cross-country flying, aerobatics, and ground subjects. This would be followed by the Glider Training Squadron course which, without the need for light powered aircraft flying training which had been inserted into Course No.1, would last for four weeks. To complete the training a four-week course at a Glider Operational Training Unit would be undertaken, when the first live loads would be carried and much more night flying carried out.

Harris's policy of using RAF personnel to fly gliders had been adopted during 1941, but it had not been a success. The one hundred RAF pilots initially involved in the scheme had quickly become disenchanted with gliders, and then on 28 August of that year a meeting at the Air Ministry, chaired by the Director of Plans, averred that it was not now considered necessary to provide trained RAF bomber pilots to fly gliders. It was also agreed that they could not be spared for detachment to Airborne Forces as and when required, so it would be an advantage if the army would supply their own glider pilots.

On 29 September the Army Council agreed to this proposition provided the necessary men could be taken from the 5,000 army personnel who had already applied for transfer to the RAF for aircrew duties. These applications had been invited under Army Council Instruction No.1520 of 1940 because of the great expansion taking place in the RAF, but such transfers had been suspended in 1941. It was mainly from this source that the initial members of the Regiment were to be obtained. The switch from RAF to army personnel explains the inclusion of the twelve weeks pre-glider flying course which would be necessary now that trained bomber pilots were not to be used. All the RAF pilots who were already being instructed on gliders were eventually returned to normal RAF duties by October, 1942.

The Air Ministry's *volte-face* had been brought about as the result of a conference held there on 22 August to discuss the provision and training of flying personnel for Airborne forces. All present opposed the employment of bomber pilots as glider pilots on the grounds that it would immobilize a large number of bomber aircrew for the period required for training and for any operation. With regard to the provision of tug pilots, the AOC of No.70 Group told the conference that their training had been *very carefully considered and everyone was of the opinion that this was quite simple and would consist of only two or three hours flying* (author's italics). Everyone at the conference appeared to favour whatever course involved the minimum expenditure of effort from Bomber Command, and as the training of tug pilots was considered such a simple matter it could be left until just before an operation was planned!

Urgent meetings were held at the War Office following the Air Ministry's recommendations, and a crop of memoranda resulted. All this activity resulted in the Army Council approving, on 21 December, 1941, the formation of the 1st Glider Regiment, initially of 624 all ranks all of whom were to be trained to fly Horsas by 31 December, 1942. There had been much discussion concerning the composition of the new unit. It was at first suggested that other ranks should have a minimum rank of corporal with additional pay of three shillings a day when qualified, but it was finally agreed that the minimum rank should be sergeant and that they should receive two shillings a day special pay. This would result in a qualified sergeant receiving eight shillings a day, exclusive of war pay, with an increase after six months' service in the rank bringing his pay to nine shillings and six pence a day, exclusive of war pay. This compared with the twelve shillings and six pence a day received by RAF sergeant pilots, and was almost equivalent to that of an infantry lieutenant, indicating the relative importance of the two jobs. After a further six months' service, on his Commanding Officer's recommendation, one in three of the sergeants would be eligible for promotion to staff sergeant, bringing their daily pay to eleven shillings and six pence exclusive of war pay. Officers were to receive two shillings a day additional pay.

A certain amount of haggling then followed, but the proposed structure was finally accepted on the basis that those selected for the unit would need to be of an exceptionally high educational and medical standard, in fact embryo officers, who would have very little chance of obtaining commissions within the unit in which it would be essential to hold them after their training for piloting duties. The Treasury was therefore asked on 12 November, 1941, to give its early sanction to the proposals in order that volunteers could be obtained in sufficient time to enable training to begin on 1 December, 1941. On 21 November the process of calling for volunteers for the new unit was set up, the first batch to comprise five officers and forty other ranks who would be required on 31 December.

The Air Ministry had agreed to the War Office suggestion that army personnel who had already been accepted for transfer to the RAF for flying duties should be given the opportunity to volunteer, and it was agreed that succeeding batches were to be obtained from the same source and then from other volunteers. A twenty per cent regular element should be aimed at. A headquarters would be formed by 1 January to act as a holding unit and for shaking down each batch of volunteers for a month prior to commencing flying training. The original army glider pilots already under training were to be taken into the new unit.

In a letter to the General Officer Commanding, London District, dated 11 December, the Director of Organization, War Office, wrote: 'As the new unit will consist of young and high-spirited personnel it is considered that the senior staff should consist at least partly of warrant officers who have been trained up to the standard of the Brigade of Guards. I am to request that volunteers for the appointments of RSM and 3 CSM's may be called for from WO's of the Brigade of Guards.' There is in this more than a hint that the high-spirited young men would need breaking in, and it would soon be apparent that this was indeed the intention.

Regular officers of the army had been debarred from applying for transfer to the RAF for flying duties, and in order that the twenty per cent regular element of the unit should extend to all ranks applications for secondment to it were invited from regular officers. The Conditions of Service within the unit were circulated to all Army Commanders on 3 December with a call for volunteers.

The setting-up of the formation was published in a War Office Memorandum dated 24 November which ratified its establishment. It was to consist of five companies, each with five platoons split into two sections. Towing aircraft were to be provided from bomber squadrons, and volunteers would be examined by RAF Aircrew Selection Boards who would apply to them the same general intelligence, educational and medical standards as for RAF pilot trainees. The glider pilots would be trained by the RAF and would qualify after successfully completing the flying training, which had been laid down by the Glider Exercise Unit at Ringway. The NCOs would then be promoted to sergeant, and after six months' service as a qualified pilot would be elegible for promotion to staff sergeant. Officers would be promoted to fill vacancies in the Establishment. The manner in which these army pilots, many of whom had been 'even infantry corporals', conducted themselves in the battles to come was such that they upheld the highest traditions of the Service.

By now the initial period of airborne forces experimental thinking was drawing to a close, and Brigadier F.A.M. Browning, then commanding 24 Guards Brigade was appointed Officer Commanding the British 1st Airborne Division on its formation on 1 November, 1941. The creation of the Division had been ordered by the Prime Minister, and it comprised 1st Parachute Brigade, commanded by Brigadier Richard Gale, and 1st Air-Landing Brigade, commanded by Brigadier H.E.F. Smyth, soon to be succeeded by Brigadier G.F. Hopkinson. The 1st Parachute Brigade comprised two battalions located in the Manchester area, and the 1st Air Landing Brigade was formed from 31 Independent Brigade Group stationed in South Wales.

The War Office memorandum announcing the formation of the Division affirmed that the target date for its ability to operate had been set as 31 July, 1942, depending, in the case of the Air Landing Brigade, on the production rate of gliders and glider pilots. 'It must be accepted,' the memorandum noted, 'that gliders must be looked upon as expendable stores, but this is very far from the truth in the case of pilots. The glider pilot will be a highly trained airman both in power aircraft and gliders; in addition to which he must be highly trained as a fighting soldier having landed. It is probable that later, when pilots and troops become trained, the RAF Command with whom the Division works will be Bomber Command and not Army Co-operation Command.'

The memorandum listed the weapons and equipment which would be issued to the Division: 2-pounder and 6-pounder anti-tank guns and 20mm Hispano guns, specially modified for carriage in gliders (with the publication of this memo, the first of many future modifications to the Horsa became necessary as the composition of the loads which it was required to carry diversified); and Vickers machine guns, Bren guns, anti-tank rifles and two- and three-inch mortars, all modified for dropping with paratroops. It also listed the issue of special clothing, equipment and rations for airborne troops: sleeping bags, windproof water-resisting smocks to eliminate the need for ground-sheet and great-coat, string vests for wearing under the usual woollen underclothing, neck-cloths, frame pattern rucksacks of Norwegian design, 48-hour rations of light weight and small volume suitable for any climate.

31 Independent Brigade Group was a formation of regular units recently returned from India, which had just completed mountain-warfare training in Wales and was already trained to operate in a light role. It was re-named 1 Air-Landing Brigade Group and was composed of the following units: 1st Battalion the Border Regiment, 2nd Battalion the South Staffordshire Regiment, 2nd Battalion the Oxfordshire and Buckinghamshire Light Infantry, 1st Battalion the Royal Ulster Rifles, 31st Independent Reconnaissance Company, 223 Anti-tank Battery RA, 9th Field Company RE, 31 Independent Infantry Brigade Ordnance Workshop and Field Park, RAOC, one company troop-carrying vehicles RASC, 181 Field Ambulance RAMC, Brigade headquarters and Signals section. The role it was expected to perform had been expounded to all Army Commanders in another War Office memorandum dated 10 October in which it was stated that its basic air transport would be the Horsa, and an appendix showed specimen loads based on experience to date.

223 Anti-tank Battery RA, subsequently renamed 1st Air Landing Anti-tank Battery RA, was commanded by Major T.I.J. Toler who was later to command 'B' Squadron, the Glider Pilot Regiment. In November, 1941, Major Toler took one of his 2-pounder anti-tank guns to Ringway which, on 1 September had become 'Airborne Forces Establishment' (on 15 February, 1942, it was again to be redesignated 'Airborne Forces Experimental Establishment'). The jeep had now arrived on the scene from America and trials were to be made to find out if it was possible to fit one

into a Horsa, together with a 2-pounder gun. The jeep promised to answer the need for a light-weight towing vehicle, so that the conveyance of a gun which could be immediately manoeuvrable when landed by glider appeared to be a feasible proposition.

Major Toler had already demonstrated the jeep's capabilities by using it to tow one of his guns across a ploughed field before a gathering of senior officers of the Division, and he now proceeded to carry out the necessary loading trials at Ringway using a Horsa mock-up. The trials were successfully accomplished, and the jeep was destined to form a vital part of future glider tactics.

This was one of a series of trials which were being carried out at Ringway following a meeting there on 18 November at which it had been decided to ask 1st Airborne Division to provide one of each type of vehicle or other item which it was proposed should be carried in gliders, so that experiments could be made using the Horsa mock-up. At first the Chief Designer protested that his glider had been designed to accommodate only the maximum load hitherto agreed with the army — twenty five troops or a motorcycle combination. However, the necessary modifications were carried out and the Horsa from then onwards was capable of carrying not only the weapons listed in the War Office memorandum announcing the formation of the Airborne Division, but also their motive power, which was a significant step forward.

Many other alternative loads, consisting of mobile arms and equipment weighing up to 7,000 lbs, were soon to be added to the list, necessitating the fitting of the hinged ramp already mentioned. As we shall see, the later Mark II Horsa had a hinged nose which made it unnecessary to negotiate an awkward 90° turn with such loads before driving them out.

The success of the trials involving the 2-pounder and its jeep (so named by the Americans from the vehicle's official name, G.P. or General Purpose) had revolutionized the concept of the use of gliders since it was now accepted that artillery and other heavy equipment complete with towing vehicles could be landed in quantity by gliders ready for immediate deployment. It is interesting to note that in the early War Establishment for an Air Landing Anti-tank Battery, RA, a glider pilot was designated as the driver of the jeep, and also that motor cycles were provided for the glider pilots carrying the guns.

Much thought was given to this new use of the Horsa for the purpose of delivering heavy weapons to support paratroops and air-landing troops, instead of using it merely for the purpose of carrying personnel only, particularly when they were out of range of fighter aircraft cover and friendly artillery. The British 25-pounder gun weighed nearly two tons and would require major modifications to fit it into a Horsa, but this was finally achieved by designing a new Mk III carriage for it. However, the artillery piece most widely carried by the Horsa was going to be the American 75mm pack howitzer which had been developed before the war for transportation by animals. It had a short barrel, pneumatic-tyred wheels, a folding box trail, and it could be carried complete with its ammunition and jeep. It could also be broken down into nine loads for parachuting if required.

# II

## FORMATION OF THE REGIMENT

FOLLOWING QUICKLY upon the decision to create a unit of army glider pilots, the War Office decided that it should be formed into a separate corps which it was suggested should be called the Army Air Corps. The question of the inclusion of parachute battalions was raised and it was agreed that this should not be implemented for the time being. If it was decided to do so later, the Corps could be split into two units — a glider wing and a parachute wing. A certain amount of correspondence then followed as to whether the name of the glider unit should be 1st Glider Pilot Regiment or 1st Glider Regiment and it was eventually agreed to adopt the former.

The Army Air Corps was authorized by Royal Warrant dated 24 February, 1942, promulgated by Army Order 21/1942 dated 27 February. This announced that 'the Corps will consist of such units and personnel as may be decided from time to time by the Army Council. Initially it will comprise only the 1st Glider Pilot Regiment whose personnel will be found from volunteers already serving in the army'. The formation of the Glider Pilot

Regiment with effect from 24 February, 1942, was published in Army Order 128/1942, and a further War Office memorandum (undated) set out that it was considered that personnel of parachute battalions should belong to one regiment and that it had been decided to form a new regiment, to be called the Parachute Regiment, as part of the AAC. The above-mentioned Army Order therefore confirmed the formation of the Parachute Regiment with effect from 1 August, 1942. Later, Army Order 42/1944, announced the formation of the Special Air Service Regiment with effect from 1 April, 1944, as a unit of the AAC.

On the date of its formation the Regiment acquired as a training depot a deserted airfield at Tilshead on Salisbury Plain, which had until recently been the base for 225 Squadron RAF, with its twelve Lysander aircraft. The airfield had been in use since 1925 as a base for Army Co-operation Squadrons, and the small cluster of wooden huts there did nothing to convey the fact that a Regiment unprecedented in the British Army was being formed. However, the windswept group of buildings had the impressive designation of Training Depot of the 1st Battalion, the Glider Pilot Regiment.

Rock had been appointed to command the Regiment and, on 1 January, 1942, he had been sent to No. 16 Elementary Flying Training School at Burnaston near Derby, so that as Commanding Officer designate he could start flying training before the first forty-five volunteers for the Regiment arrived. Burnaston had been set aside for the initial flying training of glider pilots on light aircraft on 31 December and all its six flights were to be employed to that end.

Major G.J.S. Chatterton was appointed Rock's Second-in-Command, and on 24 February he took up his appointment at the Regimental Depot ready to receive the first of the volunteers who would undergo a three-week probationary period before being accepted. Chatterton was especially suitable for a commanding role in such a regiment. After serving as a naval cadet at Pangbourne he had become a fighter pilot of no mean ability in the RAF before the war. Joining in 1930 he became a member of the famous No.1 Squadron, but had later been involved in a mid-air collision and received injuries which resulted in his transfer to the Reserve of Air Force Officers. At his annual medical examination in 1938 he was classified Category 'C' and told that in the event of being called up for service it would be for ground duties. This he could not contemplate and he applied for a transfer to the Territorial Army, and joined the 5th Battalion, Queen's Royal Regiment. By the end of 1941 he had reached the rank of Major when he seized upon the opportunity to return to flying by volunteering for the new glider unit.

Chatterton had very definite ideas about discipline which he promptly put into practice, with the aid of two Brigade of Guards Warrant Officers, CSMs

Briody and Cowley, who had responded to the call for volunteers. He did not wish to take into account the fact that the men joining the new Regiment were already trained soldiers who had, moreover, been subjected to the rigorous selection procedure of the RAF Aircrew Selection Boards, but instead paid special attention to the War Office affirmation that great care should be exercised over the selection of senior NCOs.

It is a matter of debate whether or not an undue emphasis was placed on spit-and-polish at Tilshead. Undoubtedly a certain amount of it was necessary so that the volunteers, with their diversity of previous training standards, could be forged into a homogeneous unit in which only the highest standards would be tolerated. The men accepted had to become not only skilled pilots on whose flying ability depended the lives of the high-calibre troops they carried, but they also had to be capable of taking their place alongside those troops once on the ground, and act as infantrymen, gunners or sappers, proficient in the handling of all airborne weapons and vehicles. Contained in that concept lay much of the distinct character of the Regiment which was being formed. The instantaneous transposition from one role to the other required an acute mental adjustment which the members of the Regiment had to learn to take in their stride, but this ability was to stem more from the natural intelligence of the type of man selected than from an excess of military drill. At Tilshead outstanding men were perhaps unnecessarily lost to the Regiment simply because they committed minor infringements of turnout.

What kind of men were volunteering for this new unit which was very much an unknown quantity at that time? Clearly there were many reasons behind their applications for transfer to it over and above a desire to fly. It was apparent that there was a very good chance of this particular desire resulting in an early departure from this earthly life. It was, in fact, made clear to them at their interviews that they would be required to fly troops and equipment into enemy-held territory on what could possibly be a 'one-way ticket'. One reason, probably applicable to many, was a burning desire to hit back. Certainly this was the thought which motivated Reg Dance, whose beautiful young bride of three weeks had died in his arms as a result of a bombing raid on London. Many were impelled by a desire to defy fate and engage in whatever perilous activity presented itself (clearly Iain Murray fell into this category; he was to see to it that he never missed an operation). Many lesser reasons existed, of course: a desire to get away from an unhappy unit or leave a blotted copy-book behind, or possibly a death-wish following a broken marriage.

Whatever impulse had caused their arrival at the Regimental Depot, the sobering effect was that they were required to remain there for a period of six weeks. Only then were those who had managed to avoid the ignominy of being returned to their former unit as unsuitable material posted to what, after Tilshead, was the sheer bliss of Elementary Flying Training School.

On 15 January, 1942, 38 Wing of the RAF Army Co-operation Command had been formed, with its headquarters at Netheravon and with Ringway's Sir Nigel Norman in command. Its role was that of lifting 1st Airborne Division into the air. On 16 April the Prime Minister was given a demonstration of paratroops and gliders at Netheravon in which the maximum number of aircraft at the disposal of 38 Wing were used: twelve Whitleys for the paratroops and nine Hectors each towing a Hotspur. The PM directed the Chief of Air Staff to make proposals for increasing the number of discarded bombers which could be made available for the use of Airborne Forces, and to give serious thought to the possibilities of implementing a suggestion originally propounded by Sir Nigel Norman, that a self-contained force of aircraft should be formed to consist of four squadrons with a total of 96 aircraft, whose specific task would be to tow the gliders.

In fact it appears that note had already been taken of Sir Nigel's views as the PM's directive was quickly followed by an Air Ministry Report dated 18 April regarding the provision of pilots and crews for heavy glider-tugs. It pointed out that, although the policy until then had been not to allocate bomber aircraft specifically for this work but to divert bomber squadrons successively to glider towing for a limited period, it had now been realized that this policy would be wasteful. Much time-wasting would inevitably occur while the handover from one squadron to another was taking place, during the time that it took for the new squadron's aircraft to be fitted with the removable fittings necessary for towing, and while the members of the new squadron were being trained for tug duties. In connection with the latter consideration the Report affirmed, 'We cannot afford to have learners on both ends of the tow-rope'. This was a great stride forward; it had at last been accepted that the previous policy was impracticable.

Sir Nigel Norman now had the rank of Group Captain, and his headquarters was alongside that of 1st Airborne Division. Netheravon, together with nearby Shrewton, became the base for the Glider Exercise Unit which moved there from Ringway on 1 February, 1942, and had become 296 (Glider) Squadron. It was this Squadron and the others of 38 Wing, which were to give the glider pilots their final operational training and tow them into action, together with squadrons of 46 Group which were to join them later.

The Horsas were now beginning to arrive from Airspeed's factory in large numbers, and were soon parked all around Netheravon airfield with, at first, very few tugs to tow them. Training in the handling of them was, therefore, necessarily limited. The first night flying exercise with gliders did take place there on 29 July, however, and highlighted one important need – that a suitable tow-cable indicator was urgently needed for use during night flying or in cloud when the tug aircraft disappeared from the glider pilot's view. This Cable Angle Indicator was soon developed and given the nickname of 'angle-of-dangle'.

The first Halifax tow of a Horsa had been carried out in February, 1942, during the extensive trials conducted by Airspeed, and the arrival on the scene of this combination pointed the way to the great achievements to come. Ringway had also received its first Horsa in February.

38 Wing expanded steadily during the summer of 1942. Its paper strength of four operational squadrons, each with thirty Horsas, was materializing and by July two of them, 296 and 297, had moved from Netheravon to Hurn. They were both up to strength with full complements of Whitleys and had made themselves proficient in paratroop dropping and glider towing.

The Whitleys had been found suitable for paratroops as the underneath gun position could easily be adapted to enable the paratroops to drop through. It had also been found suitable for towing unladen gliders as its Merlin engines possessed a reserve of power which prevented them from overheating under the extra strain.

A third squadron, 295, was still at Netheravon and had reached half strength. The fourth, 298, formed at Thruxton and intended to include a flight of Halifaxes, necessary for towing a fully laden Horsa, and the Hamilcar, which was being developed, was disbanded when a series of crises to the Allies' war effort caused a change in priorities. So for a long time the Wing was left with a total strength of sixty Whitleys, which were useless for operational purposes or even for exercises using fully laden gliders.

In June a decision was made to allocate the Albemarle for use as a tug. General Browning had reported to GHQ, Home Forces, on 4 February: 'I understand 500 Albemarles have been produced and are not required for bombing operations; their construction is mainly of wood and their production interferes little with construction of bombers in operation by Bomber Command. I suggest that they be made available for the Airborne Division.'

No RAF command did, in fact, want the Albemarle as its speed was too low, its range restricted, its bomb load inadequate, and its gun defences unsatisfactory. The performance of the three which were loaned to 38 Wing in August was mildly encouraging and these 'unwanted' aircraft were gladly accepted into the airborne family on the basis that they were better than nothing.

A different proposition was the American C-47 aircraft, whose timely arrival during the following winter was providential. This machine had been flying since 1934 as the passenger-carrying DC3. It was to do sterling duty during the war both with paratroops and as a glider-towing aircraft for the Waco/Hadrian, but its drawback in operations was its vulnerability. However, without it the scale of the Allies' airborne operations of 1944 and 1945 would have been impossible as it became the main workhorse of Airborne Forces. Over 2,000 were delivered to the RAF alone, the British giving it the name 'Dakota'.

Apart from its ability to tow gliders, the Dakota could carry a normal payload of 2½ to 3 tons or 14 to 18 fully-equipped paratroops, and could take off with such a load from a dirt strip less than 3,000 feet long. Its maximum range with extra fuel tanks was 1,500 miles, and when dropping paratroops it could safely fly as slowly as 110 miles an hour, the slipstream at that speed posing little problem. It became the only allied plane used for the major paratroop operations of the war, no British machine being able to compare with it for that purpose, although Stirlings, Halifaxes and Albemarles were all modified for paratrooping.

A wise policy adopted at this time was that of also modifying all British bomber aircraft coming off the production line for glider towing by the addition of fittings which strengthened the rear of the fuselage, thus making it unnecessary for later modifications to be made on those used for this purpose. When 38 Group, as it was to become, took over two squadrons of Stirlings from Bomber Command in December, 1943, the wisdom of this policy became immediately apparent.

Initially pupils leaving No.16 Elementary Flying Training School were divided into two parties, half going to No.1 Glider Training School at Thame and the other half to No.2 GTS which had been opened at Weston-on-the-Green on 20 November. The first 35 army pupils, including Lt-Colonel Rock, arrived at these two stations on 15 April, 1942. They then passed on to 101 and 102 Glider Operational Training Units at Kidlington and Shobdon.

The GOTUs had only the use of the Hotspur with Hector tugs at first, as no other aircraft was yet available, but nevertheless they can be considered as the first serious training schools for military glider pilots. A really thorough syllabus was prepared, based on Ringway's theories and experience, and tactical exercises were carried out, together with night flying.

Two Heavy Glider Conversion Units were then formed, No.21 at Shrewton on 29 June, 1942 (which later moved to two of Brize Norton's satellite stations) and No.22 at Fairford on 15 October to which the members of the Regiment were posted from the GOTUs. As already stated, the syllabus and standard of training required had been fully worked out at Ringway in 1941 and, on 3 July, 1942, it was decided to transfer the Glider Schools from 70 Group to RAF Flying Training Command. A further GTS (No.3) was formed at Stoke Orchard, whilst Thame moved to a larger airfield at Croughton. Eventually the GTS and GOTU courses were combined, and 101 and 102 GOTUs became 4 and 5 GTSs respectively.

In order to meet the Regiment's requirement that its 624 members should be fully trained to fly Horsas by 31 December, 1942, it was necessary that the total capacity of 18 EFTS Flights be made available for the purpose of providing the elementary (pre-glider) flying training, and 21 EFTS at Booker was opened to trainees from the Regiment on 13 May, 1942, followed by No.29 at Clyffe Pypard on 21 May and No.3 at Shellingford on 25 July. Ample facilities were now available for initial training on light powered aircraft and advanced flying on gliders.

On 28 June Rock completed his flying training and assumed command at Tilshead, and on 3 July the first course of trained pilots arrived there from Kidlington. The Regiment's No.1 Squadron (as the 'companies' were called from the beginning) was formed under Major R.W. Roe, and was organized into three Flights.

An interesting legal point cropped up at this time when a member of the Regiment disobeyed flying orders while flying a glider at one of the GTSs by landing on the wrong side of the flare path and colliding with another aircraft. As he had not been posted to the RAF unit, it was found to be impossible to deal with him under Section 39a of the Air Force Act which covered all offences committed by RAF personnel such as low and dangerous flying. The case was therefore handed to the Army to deal with, only for the discovery to be made that there was no appropriate section in the Army Act. This anomaly was quickly rectified by a ruling that in future all glider pilots attached to the RAF for training must be officially posted, but once trained, even though flying gliders, they were to be subject to Military Law.

Rock informed a conference held on 24 July at Headquarters Airborne Division to discuss the flying training of glider pilots in relation to exercises with troops, that by the end of August one Flight of glider pilots (24) would be qualified in night flying with live loads in Hotspurs and would be ready to take part in semi-operational exercises with 296 and 297 Squadrons at Hurn.

The War Office now required 764 operationally trained glider pilots to be available by 1 April, 1943, 912 by 1 June and 1,064 by 1 July. A minimum of 30 hours flying every six months had been estimated as necessary to keep glider pilots in practice and to allow for their training to operational standard. Their advanced training was to be organized into four phases leading up to tactical exercises at Hurn where personnel of the Air-Landing Brigade would be carried.

On returning to the Regimental Depot Rock had been quick to show his disapproval of Chatterton's severe disciplinary methods and he made it plain that he would like them modified. He wanted to create a smart and well turned-out regiment, but 'a clear eye coupled to steady, light flying hands controlled by a quick-thinking mind' was his model for a glider pilot, and he had quickly sensed the eagerness and inner discipline of the men who were beginning to join the Regiment. Being fully aware that the object of military drill was to ensure instant compliance with orders, he believed that there was no place for this concept in flying a glider and that too much drill would probably result in a ham-fisted pilot. In view of their different outlooks in this respect, it was fortunate that he and Chatterton separated when the 2nd Battalion was formed on 17 August, 1942, and Chatterton was appointed to command it with the rank of Lieutenant-Colonel. He had been faced with a routine medical examination just before the appointment when he had been passed Category 'A' – fit for flying duties!

A tragic loss then occurred when Lieutenant-Colonel Rock was involved in an accident during a night flying exercise at Shrewton on 27 September and received injuries from which he died in Tidworth Hospital on 18 October. Rock had envisaged two main roles for gliders: in *coup de main* assaults, and for the rapid reinforcement of ground already taken and held by friendly troops, either paratroops or conventional forces. He had been against using gliders in direct assaults in the face of the enemy, which he had described as 'about as futile as charging the enemy in a fleet of RASC three-tonners'. Whether or not it would have been possible for him to have carried into practice his views that massed landings should only be made into secure landing-zones is another matter.

It was in conformity with his practice always to lead from the front that, when the flying accident occurred, Rock was practising the use of a *coup de main* night landing system which had been devised by the Commander of No. 2 Squadron, Major Maurice Willoughby, who at the time was at the Heavy Glider Conversion Unit at Brize Norton. The system consisted of three dim lights supposed to have been clandestinely placed in position, and it was while coming in to land that Colonel Rock's Hotspur hit an obstacle. His death was a very great loss to his country and to the Regiment. He had been through Staff College and spoke four languages. He had come out of France through Dunkirk. While at Ringway, carrying out such valuable experimentation into the use of airborne forces, he had spent six weeks in hospital following an accident during a parachute jump in a high wind. At EFTS the engine of his aircraft had failed on one occasion, resulting in the aircraft turning over on landing while he sustained a black eye; and he had passed out at Thame on Hotspurs with an above-average rating. His obituary in the *Daily Express* read:

> 'Lt-Col John Frank Rock, pioneer of British Paratroops and Airborne Forces, has given his life for his work. After surviving a number of narrow escapes in experimental parachute jumping

and glider work he died in a military hospital from injuries received in a glider crash. He always tested the risk himself before asking his men to do it, and such was the force of his example that we gladly followed where he had led.'

Lieutenant-Colonel Chatterton assumed command of the Regiment and formed a Regimental Headquarters at Tilshead; Major Willoughby took command of the 1st Battalion and Major I.A. Murray of the 2nd Battalion. Major Murray had been a former member of the Auxiliary Air Force and of the Grenadier Guards and was destined to lead his battalion (by then renamed No.1 Wing) during the Normandy landings, the Arnhem battle and the Rhine crossing. Major Willoughby was a regular officer and, at his interview after applying for secondment to the Regiment, he had been invited by the Commander 1st Airborne Division to become Second-in-Command of the Regiment, only to receive a letter from General Browning a week later to the effect that Major Chatterton, who was his senior, had received the appointment.

# III

## OPERATION FRESHMAN

IN FEBRUARY, 1942, Allied Intelligence was alerted to the fact that the Germans had ordered the output of heavy water at the Norsk hydroelectric power plant at Vermork in Norway to be tripled. Heavy water (deuterium oxide) is an element which is essential for research into making atomic bombs, so it appeared that the Germans might well be building an atomic pile, a supposition which was supported by the knowledge that they had already prohibited the export of uranium from Czechoslovakia. The plant was situated in a deep valley in central southern Norway, the thickly forested sides of which rose almost vertically from a narrow river bed to over 3,000 feet, the water power for the turbines being drawn from the slopes of the 5,400 feet Gaustal Fjell which overlooks the valley.

The dislocation of the German experiments was considered to be of such importance that a decision was made, following talks between the Prime Minister and President Roosevelt, to destroy at all costs their existing stocks of heavy water, which was extremely difficult to produce in any large quantity. In the summer of 1942 the British War Cabinet presented the task to Combined Operations Headquarters as one with the highest priority and various meetings and discussions took place at which possible methods of attack were considered. Heavy bombing raids were ruled out from the start because of the possibility of casualties among the Norwegian work force, although, as will be seen, this method had to be resorted to later. A landing of commando troops in Catalina flying-boats was impractical due to the fact that there were insufficient days left before the lakes in the vicinity of the plant became frozen over. It was considered that demolition equipment dropped with a parachute force would be too widely scattered in such terrain, in addition to which the arrival of such a force would quickly become common knowledge in the vicinity of the drop. Another alternative was the use of glider-borne troops, and the nearest suitable landing-zone (hereinafter in this book referred to as LZ, or DZ for paratroops' dropping zones) was at Mosvatnet, a five-hour approach march from the target. It was this method which was decided upon.

Special Operations Executive had been called into the planning at an early stage as their help would be needed in the placing of Norwegian agents in the vicinity of the plant to feed back information to England before the landings took place and to guide and assist the attacking force throughout.

From the first it was clear that the operation was not going to be easy. Both Major General Sir Colin Gubbins, Chief of SOE, and Colonel J.S. Wilson, who headed its Norwegian Section, have subsequently stated that they objected to the plan on the grounds that 'it was ill conceived and susceptible to too many failures at too many stages in its operation'.

Of all countries Norway has the least suitable terrain for glider operations. The 500-mile tow, to be made during the hours of darkness, was longer than any so far attempted even in daylight. The weather prevailing in that part of the world at the beginning of winter was unpredictable and mostly unfavourable, and it was essential that the glider landings be made during clear conditions. Nevertheless, the necessary planning went ahead as a matter of urgency.

The employment of two gliders each carrying fifteen army airborne engineers of 9 Field Company (AB) RE, and 261 Field Park Company (AB) RE, was decided upon, each tug/glider combination to act independently of the other. Following the demolitions the two parties would break up into twos and threes and make good their escape by walking a distance of 200 miles into Sweden. They were to wear normal army uniform with civilian ski-ing kit underneath.

Because of the distance the gliders would have to be towed, the only aircraft capable of carrying out that task with full loads were four-engined Halifaxes and difficulty was now encountered procuring them. At that stage of the war Halifaxes were in extremely short supply; only twelve squadrons of RAF Bomber Command were equipped with them and, of these, seven had only received them during recent months or even weeks. But eventually three machines were made available at Netheravon. The first one arrived on 24 October, 1942, having been obtained from the Royal Aircraft Establishment at Farnborough devoid of all movable fittings.

The Officer Commanding 38 Wing was left with the task of converting some of his own crews on to the Halifaxes and providing them with the necessary training in towing fully-laden Horsas. Each of the chosen tug-pilots subsequently completed 59hrs 30mins flying in them before the operation. This demanded of the ground staff tremendous servicing effort and it is to their great credit that they made such an achievement possible.

It was decided not to call for volunteers from among the glider pilots but to choose the best four available, and Major Willoughby picked Staff Sergeant M.F.C. Strathdee, who had been the first to solo on a Kirby Kite at Thame, with Sergeant P. Doig as his second pilot. Both were excellent pilots, although their glider training to date had necessarily been all too brief, certainly not sufficient preparation for the impending operation. However, they were both reported to be 'as keen as mustard' for it. The other glider was to be flown by two RAAF pilots, Pilot Officer Davies and Sergeant Fraser, who were both bomber pilots converted on to gliders.

The training was carried out at Brize Norton and included night flying — taking off in daylight and landing at night on minimal flare-paths — and practice in jettisoning the undercarriage with a parachute apparatus during the flight to reduce drag. This in-flight parachute release was necessary to obviate any possibility of the undercarriage bouncing and striking the glider if released without a parachute during take-off. Some of this training was carried out behind Whitleys and altogether 44hrs 20mins glider flying was completed.

The glider pilots were given special briefing and ground training in connection with the operation and the escape. Local intelligence was provided by Combined Operations Headquarters with photographs of the objective and certain neighbouring areas, and Norwegian maps of the area were supplied. Very detailed information concerning the LZ was made available by Norwegians living in England.

The thirty sappers were given strenuous training carrying 80 pounds of equipment, explosives and sleeping-bags, culminating in a four-day trek over the mountains in Snowdonia, instruction in the effective use of their explosives at a hydro-electric plant in Scotland, and special commando training. A large model of the Vermork plant was studied so that the sappers and glider pilots could locate every item of equipment it contained. The positions of all doors and windows, and the beats and routines of the German sentries were committed to memory. Lastly the escape equipment was issued including documents to facilitate the crossing of the Swedish frontier.

It was realized that it might be difficult to locate the LZ, and the use of Rebecca/Eureka navigational aids was decided upon. Eureka was a radio-beacon device set up on the ground at any given target, and Rebecca was carried in the aircraft: it emitted a signal to which Eureka responded, thus providing directional information. The fitting of Rebecca into the Halifaxes was carried out at Netheravon, and on 18 October four Norwegian SOE agents were parachuted into Norway in order to set up Eureka and flares on the LZ and then to join up with the demolition parties.

It was known that the German forces guarding the power-plant numbered about 64 men and it was also believed that members of the Gestapo were stationed in the nearby town of Rjukan. Intelligence sources also reported the existence of mines and barbed-wire fences around the factory. The landings would have to be made by moonlight and as the next full moon would appear on 19 November, 1942, that was the date fixed for the operation, which was given the codename Freshman. The departure point was to be Skitten, a satellite of Wick in northern Scotland. To have mounted it from the Shetlands would have been ideal, but a runway of at least 1,600 yards was necessary and none of that length existed farther north than Skitten. The aircraft, gliders, and personnel involved moved there just before the operation was due to take place.

The Halifaxes carried out a leaflet-dropping flight to Oslo on the 18th, with the 1st pilots of the gliders as passengers, in order that the ground and target could be examined and to give much-needed navigational training. One aircraft reached Oslo without encountering opposition either in the form of fighters, anti-aircraft fire or even searchlights, and all on board were able to view the target. The second aircraft was forced to return without having carried out its test flight due to engine failure.

The next day a coded message was received from the four Norwegians, 'Sky clear with moonlight. Beautiful weather'. At Skitten there was unbroken cloud and rain and by the time last-minute difficulties had been overcome darkness had fallen.

During the entire day on the 19th the Meteorological Officer at Skitten had considered the weather to be unsuitable for gliders. A strong westerly airstream prevailed over Scotland and the northern part of the North Sea and, in addition, the regular meteorological flight from Wick had been cancelled because of unserviceable aircraft.

The glider pilots had not attempted a night take-off with full loads before and were given the option of postponing the operation until the next day, but they decided to go. One combination took off at 1745 hours and the other at 1800 hours. In both combinations the inter-communication systems were inoperative from the start and therefore the glider pilots and tug crews were out of touch with each other. So that the heavily-laden combinations could maintain height, it would be necessary for the tugs to be flown at almost full throttle, and because of the distance of the tow the route had to be as direct as possible which made steering around clouds out of the question.

One can only imagine what that journey must have been like for the glider pilots, none of whom had previously sat at the controls of a glider continuously for longer than an hour or so. They had taken off into a dark, stormy night and for hour after hour were forced to concentrate on a dim row of lights on the tug in order to maintain a correct station in the turbulent conditions with the constantly see-sawing gliders. They would gradually have become numb with the intense cold as the height increased. No doubt they were anxious at the thought of being responsible for the safe delivery of a body of highly-trained troops on to some outlandish spot among the mountains at journeys end. Their difficulties were exacerbated by lack of communication with the tug crews, and an inability to see anything whatsoever beyond the cockpit perspex but those dim lights for ever on the move. Conditions would have been that much worse for the troops sitting in the darkness of the body of the glider with nothing to do but submit to the violent movement, and with the ever-present feeling of nausea which was an inescapable accompaniment.

As the combinations approached the Norwegian coast a snow-storm was raging. The glider pilots had stayed on tow for four and three-quarter hours and Strathdee's combination had reached a height of 13,000 feet. The maps in possession of the Halifax Navigator, although the best available, were of poor quality and it proved impossible to identify any landmarks, in addition to which the Rebecca in the aircraft failed. After circling for an hour over the correct LZ, a fact which was not realized, it was decided to turn for home as the fuel level was already marginal for the return journey. Strathdee managed to stay on tow while the combination gradually lost height due to ice forming on the aircraft, but eventually the tow rope broke under the weight of the ice and the glider crashed among the mountains at Fylgjesdal overlooking Lysefjord, north-east of Stavanger, killing eight men and injuring four others.

At 2355 hours a signal was picked up at Skitten from the Halifax, 'Glider released in sea'. This signal had also been received at another station and by intersection of bearings the position of the aircraft was found to have been over the mountains of southern Norway. When the Halifax returned to base at 0300 hours this position was confirmed by a check of times and course. The glider had come adrift just over the coast nowhere near the target.

The other Halifax had apparently been unable to identify the correct LZ and the glider cast off and crashed on to a rocky, snow-covered slope approximately 2 miles north of Gasetjern, also on the coast of Norway south of Fylgjesdal. Three men were killed and six injured. The Halifax itself crashed into a mountain-side at Helleland, about five miles to the south of the glider crash. All seven crew members were killed.

On 21 November the German wireless made the following announcement: 'On the night of 19-20 November two bombers each towing a glider penetrated southern Norway. One bomber and both gliders were forced to land. The sabotage troops in the gliders were engaged and killed to the last man.' The truth of the matter was that all members of the two glider parties who had not been killed outright in the crashes were captured and eventually murdered by the Germans acting on direct orders from Hitler. This atrocity was as criminal as any perpetrated by the German armed forces during World War II and is ample proof that such savage acts were not confined to the concentration camps.

The severely wounded from Strathdee's and Doig's glider were taken by the Germans to a prison at Stavanger where they were given what were intended to be lethal injections, following which they were strangled to put an end to their groaning. Their bodies were disposed of at sea. The uninjured were taken to Grini concentration camp near Oslo and, on 18 January, 1943, were shot by firing squad in the Trandum Forest. The men from the other glider were shot by firing squad at the German barracks at Slettebo near Egersund the same day. Before the arrival of the Germans at the scene of the crashes the local Norwegians had performed prodigious feats in succouring the survivors, but they were powerless to do anything to prevent them falling into the hands of the enemy.

When troops of 1st Airborne Division Engineers flew to Norway on 10 May, 1945, the story of the fate which had befallen the two glider parties gradually emerged as a result of painstaking investigations. The bodies of those not committed to the sea by the Germans were exhumed from the communal graves in which they had been unceremoniously buried and were reburied by men of their own units with full military honours, some in the cemetery at Eiganes on the outskirts of Stavanger and some in the military section of Vestre Gravlund cemetery, Oslo. The crew of the Halifax bomber were exhumed and reburied in Helleland churchyard.

The Germans involved in the murders carried out at Stavanger prison were eventually brought to trial before a War Crimes Tribunal at Oslo in August, 1945, and after a lengthy summing-up by the Judge Advocate of the evidence which had been given, the President of the Court sentenced two of them to death and one to life imprisonment. The officer commanding the local German forces in the area was tried before a military court at Hamburg in May, 1946, for being concerned with the shootings by firing squads and was found not guilty. The officer commanding all German forces in Norway at the time was brought to trial at Brunswick in July, 1946, and was found guilty. He was sentenced to life imprisonment and was released in 1953 because of ill-health.

The Regiment had lost its first two members killed in action, but mercifully they had both been spared the horrors awaiting the survivors of the disastrous landings as they had both been killed in the crash.

In the end the Germans were prevented from making use of the heavy water from Vermork. After the unsuccessful Freshman operation six Norwegian members of SOE were dropped by parachute from England and succeeded in temporarily destroying the heavy water plant with explosives after joining forces with the four Norwegians who had waited in vain for the airborne troops' arrival on 19 November. An attack on 16 November, 1943, by the American 8th Air Force resulted in partial damage to the plant which had by then been repaired. Then in February, 1944, came the *coup de grace* which was carried out by three Norwegian members of the local resistance groups. It had been learned that the Germans had decided to remove all the existing stocks of heavy water, and certain machinery necessary for its production, to a safer location in Germany. This provided an ideal opportunity, and the railway ferry, carrying the vital consignment across one of the numerous Norwegian lakes, was blown up and sunk by explosives which had been placed in position by the Norwegians acting on instructions from London.

# IV

## ASSAULT ON SICILY

AN OUTLINE OF THE operational flying training programme has been given in Chapter I but in the early days this was rather more the intention than the reality. During the second half of 1942 it was virtually at a standstill. A top secret letter from Sir Arthur Harris proposed limiting post-training flying to seven hours a year, a notion which, if adopted, would have been disastrous for the Regiment.

Members of the Regiment were generally becoming so despondent at the lack of progress in their training that one of them, 20-year-old Staff Sergeant Alec Waldron, took the risky step of calling to see Mr D.N. Pritt, KC, the Socialist MP for North Hammersmith, at his Chambers in Middle Temple early in 1943. The KC was told about the unsatisfactory situation and despatched a letter to the Prime Minister, which was placed before him on 4 March. The letter was highly critical of the RAF's failure to supply suitable aircraft for towing gliders, and its apparent lack of drive in providing proper glider maintenance and training facilities for glider pilots. As a result reports were called for by the Prime Minister from the Secretaries of State for War and Air.

The Report from the Secretary of State for War, dated 17 March, drew attention to the fact that an RAF Wing under Army Co-operation Command had been attached to the Airborne Division. It affirmed that there was not the slightest grounds for any suggestion of lack of co-operation, or of any lack of maintenance as the RAF tradesmen concerned had no responsibilities for maintenance of other aircraft. Neither was there a shortage of gliders although it was a fact that the number of tug aircraft was not yet up to scale.

The Report continued that, regarding the plans made in 1942 to train 1,064 glider pilots by 1 July, 1943, and thereafter at a rate of 90 per month, the 1st Battalion (624) was now nearly up to strength, but the 2nd Battalion (450 at present) was not able to carry out any glider training due to the decision to cut down on the number of gliders produced; they were therefore continuing their military training. (It is fact that the Prime Minister himself had directed in December, 1942, that the production of Horsas should be curtailed).

It then went on to point out that the Air Staff would only agree to continue the programme of initial training for glider pilots, so those who had already passed through Glider Training School could not, therefore, keep in practice. The Secretary of State agreed that the standard of discipline demanded was undoubtedly high, 'as we cannot afford to train unsatisfactory men as glider pilots, who must be highly trained and disciplined'. He concluded the Report: 'There is, however, a divergence of views on Airborne Forces generally and I cannot pretend that I am satisfied with the position'.

The Secretary of State for Air's Report dated 18 March, set out the current facilities available for training 'which have been provided on the agreed scale with the exception of the three exercise squadrons which are still some 30% below strength [the reasons for this being] first the special priority given to Bomber Command for the period of the 50 squadron plan; second, the fact that the Whitley, on which these squadrons have relied, has proved unsuitable for towing gliders. Search for a suitable replacement is proceeding urgently but so far the Ministry of Aircraft Production has been unable to clear the Albemarle which is the type that No.38 Wing would themselves like to employ. If the Albemarle is proved satisfactory the 3 squadrons can be built up to full strength fairly rapidly. The suggestion that the RAF maintenance people give preference to their own machines is devoid of foundation. Training for the Airborne Division is in the hands of self-contained units which have their fair share of personnel. In November, 1942, you decided that the establishment of the Airborne Division should be fixed at two parachute brigades plus a small glider-borne force ... and it was decided to keep some 600 glider pilots in training. This programme was smaller than that to which the Air Ministry had worked prior to your decision and already about 1000 potential pilots had started their basic training ... it was considered expedient to complete the training of all the pupils who had already been entered. The thought behind this arrangement was that, if subsequently it were decided to enlarge the programme, it would be easier to arrange a refresher course for pilots who had completed their glider training than to start training ab initio. Meanwhile the balance of pilots not required for flying duties would continue their military training. These circumstances may account for the uncertainty in the minds of the glider pilots and may possibly be responsible for some of the complaints which have reached Mr Pritt about the lack of a definite policy.'

At the time of Waldron's productive visit to Mr Pritt, and completely unaware that it had been made, Major Willoughby had spoken to Vernon Bartlett, a BBC war commentator, on the same subject after taking him night flying from Shrewton. It was well known that Bartlett had the PM's ear and Major Willoughby was told that Mr Churchill would be made aware of the facts. The result of this lobbying by two members of the Regiment, carried out quite unknown to each other, was that the PM called Sir Arthur Harris to a meeting and, after listening to his explanation that no more bombers could be deployed for glider-towing, left him in no doubt that the necessary tugs for 38 Wing must be found. Thereafter operational flying training for members of the Regiment improved.

To emphasize further the unsatisfactory state of airborne forces generally at that time General Browning had sent a report to GHQ, Home Forces on 11 January, 1943, in which he pointed out that there were only 48 aircraft available for dropping paratroops or towing gliders, none of which was capable of towing a fully-loaded Horsa.

He complained that it was not possible to drop a complete parachute battalion in one lift, or to tow one single air-landing unit complete with its equipment. He also pointed out that little had been done to implement the agreement made in April, 1942, that 38 Wing should have 96 aircraft by November of that year, and that the situation 'further deteriorated when through unwarrantable negligence on the part of those responsible it was discovered that such aircraft as had been issued to 38 Wing were unsuitable for towing a fully loaded Horsa, which information was not forthcoming until at least 4 months after flying trials had been in progress'.

He further stated, 'Bomber Command display no interest and carry out no training in parachuting or towing,' and later in the Report gave as his opinion that 'the writing on the wall has been painfully obvious in N. Africa where months of hard fighting and grievous losses lie ahead; this for no other reason than that aircraft were not available at the right place and time to accomplish the capture of Tunis which, in the circumstances, was a practical certainty by Airborne troops up to 23 November, 1942 – how many thousands of valuable British lives will be lost during the next year due to the practical non-existence of suitable aircraft?', and again, 'the resources at the disposal of 38 Wing can only keep 150 glider pilots employed and in practice. As he is responsible for piloting a Horsa with a valuable load of troops and their weapons, it is quite impossible with present resources to give him more than 15 hours a year which renders him quite unfitted to perform this responsible task.'

All this uncertainty and contention two and a half years after the Prime Minister had decided that an airborne force should be raised appears incomprehensible until one considers just how unprepared Britain was in 1940 even to participate in conventional warfare, let alone its more sophisticated aspects.

But at least someone in the Regiment had realized that, as military training appeared to be necessarily taking precedence over flying training, due to delays in finding places at EFTS and to the shortage of tug aircraft, there were more advantages to be gained from battle courses than from an excess of 'spit-and-polish', and a Battle School for the Regiment was set up early in 1943 at Southbourne near Bournemouth. 2 Squadron was billeted there, and Sergeant Richards and five other NCOs were sent from Tilshead to help get the Battle School off the ground. The officers were: Major Hamish O'Malley – Commandant (later replaced by Major Ian Toler), Captain John Morrison – Chief Instructor, and Lieutenant 'Peggy' Clarke. In common with all the members of the Regiment, they were desperate to obtain some glider flying but anything was an improvement on the unimaginative Tilshead routine, and the new project was entered into with enthusiasm. It proved a great success and provided valuable training.

*Some* flying was obtained during this period, resulting from a rather unconventional idea of Sir Nigel Norman's. 296 Squadron moved from Hurn to Andover on 25 October, 1942 and Sir Nigel saw in this an opportunity to give the glider pilots practice in carrying live loads, and the RAF personnel experience in operating a glider unit. Forty members of the squadron and seven tons of equipment were moved by lightly loaded Horsas, which also moved out the squadron that was making way for 296.

It was decided that this service could be extended, and over a period of seven months 1,500 men and 230 tons of equipment belonging to various squadrons were moved to new quarters in this manner. This was hardly the role members of the Regiment had envisaged for themselves but it was a means of providing some useful lessons to glider pilots, tug pilots and ground crews.

In January, 1943, Chatterton had put forward a proposition that the Regiment's formations be called 'Wings', 'Squadrons' and 'Flights' instead of retaining the army designations of 'Battalions', 'Companies' and 'Platoons', and his suggestion had been put into effect from 25 January. During this renaming period the 2nd Battalion, under the command of Lieutenant-Colonel Iain Murray, became No.1 Wing, and the 1st Battalion, under the command of Lieutenant-Colonel John Place, became No.2 Wing. A Wing corresponded with a lightly armed infantry battalion and was equipped with 38 small arms, 12 Bren-guns, 12 Thomson sub-machine guns and 192 rifles. An anti-tank capability was later provided by the PIAT (Projector, Infantry, Anti-tank). Each of the squadrons had four operational flights and a Headquarters flight each with four officers and forty other ranks.

The wearing of the maroon beret by all airborne forces had been sanctioned early in 1942, and deliveries of this distinctive headdress began on 12 June of that year, so that by now it had been issued to all members of the Division. It was not to be very long before the Axis forces would be made aware of this item of uniform and refer to its wearers as 'Red Devils', as the British 1st Parachute Brigade formed part of the Allied forces which had invaded French North Africa on 8 November, 1942, under the command of General Eisenhower, taking part in Operation Torch. Eisenhower was soon appointed Supreme Allied Commander in the Mediterranean theatre of operations and, in February, 1943, the Allies set up a special Joint Planning Staff to work out the next move against the Axis once they had been removed from North Africa.

Following much persuasion from the British, Sicily had been chosen as the stage for this, as it was assumed to be fairly certain that a successful assault there would knock Italy out of the war and open up the Mediterranean to allied shipping.

As we have seen, Browning had affirmed in a report on 11 January, 1943, that had sufficient aircraft been available it would have been possible for Tunis to have been captured by British airborne forces by 23 November, 1942. This remark had been prompted by Germany's swift reaction to Operation Torch. On 23 November they had responded by beginning to invest Tunis with their forces from Crete. Hitler had realized that the possession of this strategically positioned peninsula afforded the best means of denying the passage of the Mediterranean to the Allies, and he intended to stake everything on its defence. It was also clear that its possession would provide the Allies with an ideal base from which to mount an invasion of Axis-dominated Europe, and by Christmas Day, 1942, German strength in Tunisia had reached 50,000.

However, not having recourse to such airborne forces, Eisenhower incurred Winston Churchill's displeasure by asserting that he did not consider the Tunisian battle would be over by the end of April, 1943, thereby leaving insufficient time for mounting the invasion of Sicily during June as the Prime Minister was demanding.

The PM had written in a Personal Minute to the Chief of Staffs' Committee on 13 February, 1943: 'It is absolutely necessary to do this operation in June. We shall become a laughing stock if, during the spring and early summer no British and American soldiers are firing at any German and Italian soldiers'. This comment could only be meant to apply to the interval between the close of the Tunisian Battle and the assault on Sicily and was rather a speculative one as the date when the Tunisian fighting would end was necessarily an unknown factor on 13 February. Nevertheless, Churchill's wish prevailed and the preparation and training for the Sicily operation undoubtedly suffered in no small degree from the shortage of time available for it because of the PM's insistence on a June date (it was, in fact, to take place early in July).

The Regiment found itself involved in this hasty preparation and training and received orders to accompany 1st Airborne Division to North Africa in order to take its part in the operation. By now it could produce fifty crews who had completed their EFTS, GTS and OTU courses, and it was agreed with the American Troop Carrier Command stationed in North Africa that sixty additional crews who had not completed these courses could also be sent out to make use of such resources as the Command could provide in order that their training could be continued.

Chatterton was concerned that the Regiment was not prepared for action. However, he set forth with 2 and 3 Squadrons of No.2 Wing, which had been augmented with elements of 1 and 4 Squadrons. They sailed in a Dutch ship, *Niew Holland*, from Gourock on 13 April, 1943, and arrived at Oran in Algeria on the 26th. From there the squadrons were conveyed a distance of sixty miles to Tizi on the Mascara Plain where the remainder of 1st Airborne Division was concentrated together with 51st Wing of the American Troop Carrier Command.

The Division's 1st Parachute Brigade rejoined it at Mascara on 10 May, and the 4th Parachute Brigade, commanded by Brigadier J.W. Hackett, would also be joining it on 10 June from Haifa. The Division would then comprise three parachute brigades and one air-landing brigade.

At Tizi the glider pilots were provided with quarters in a temporary prisoner-of-war compound which the Americans had constructed. This was hardly a distinguished start and did little to improve morale already affected by the circumstance that all rank insignia and flying badges had had to be removed from uniforms for security reasons before leaving the UK. Chatterton, whose headquarters had been established at Mascara, was notified that training would be provided by the Americans as agreed. As the only suitable tug aircraft in North Africa in any appreciable quantity were American C-47s and the only gliders were the American Wacos, any airborne effort would be carried out with the use of these aircraft. The glider pilots would be British.

Major-General G.F. Hopkinson, who had previously commanded 1st Air-Landing Brigade, had been appointed to command 1st Airborne Division. A second Airborne Division, given the title '6th', had been formed in England under the command of Major-General R.N. Gale, and Lieutenant-General F.A.M. Browning had been placed in command of all British Airborne Forces. Chatterton was summoned to General Hopkinson's headquarters in Algiers and Operation Husky was revealed to him.

The British 8th and the American 7th Armies were to land in southern Sicily and the British landings, at Cap Passaro, were to be spearheaded by 1st Air-Landing Brigade. The Brigade was required to seize the Ponte Grande over the Anopo Canal and, should little opposition be encountered there, the port of Syracuse. This would pave the way for the 8th Army's advance to Messina together with the Americans who were to land farther west.

The Regiment's task was to convey the Brigade, which was commanded by Brigadier P.H.W. Hicks, and comprised 1st Battalion, the Border Regiment, 2nd Battalion, the South Staffordshire Regiment, 9th Field Company RE and 181st Field Ambulance, to Syracuse and land it there by moonlight between 2210 hours and 2330 hours on 9/10 July. Twenty-four hours later it was to land anti-tank guns on to the Catania Plain forty miles farther up the east coast, also by moonlight at 2353 hours, in support of the British 1st Parachute Brigade, under Brigadier G.W. Lathbury. Their task was to capture the Primasole Bridge over the Simeto River, which was the only crossing over this obstacle and controlled the exits on to the Catania Plain.

Aerial photographs of the LZs at Syracuse revealed that they were rock-strewn and wooded, and consisted of small fields enclosed within stone walls. Chatterton has written in *The Wings of Pegasus* that after he had expressed concern to General Hopkinson that the LZs looked far from ideal, and that his pilots had had no experience of flying the American Waco, he received an ultimatum from the General that if after studying the photographs for half an hour he still considered the glider operation to be too difficult he could consider himself relieved of his command. Left with his own thoughts for the stipulated half an hour, he concluded that there was nothing to do but accept the situation and prepare his pilots for the forthcoming task with every means available.

He was now faced with the task of getting his glider pilots converted to the Wacos; but the difficulty was that there were no Wacos in evidence, until four of them eventually arrived, having been flown from Accra on the Gold Coast by the Americans. Members of the Regiment then lost no time familiarizing themselves with the American gliders, and before long Chatterton had carried out a moonlight landing with one, taking off from

1. The first Glider Pilot Regiment solo in a Kirby Kite, Haddenham, March, 1941. S/Sgt Malcolm Strathdee CFI (killed in Norway on Operation 'Freshman'). *Left to right:* Strathdee, S/Ldr Saffrey, S/Ldr Tim Hervey, O.C. Haddenham, F/O Sproule.

2. Hotspur demonstration for Winston Churchill.

3. Two Hotspurs in free flight just after cutting loose from their tugs. The
Hotspur carried two pilots and seven troops.

4. A Corporal pupil in the cockpit of a Hotspur.

5. The Tiger Moth was the basic powered trainer for all glider pilots.

6. The Mk II Horsa with glider pilot crew, showing the hinged forward opening cockpit for unloading.

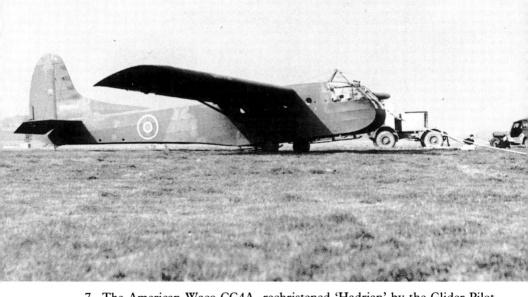

7. The American Waco CG4A, rechristened 'Hadrian' by the Glider Pilot Regiment.

8. Halifax tug and Mk II Horsa preparing for take-off.

Thiersville, one of the airstrips at Mascara, releasing over Mascara and gliding the eight or nine miles back to Thiersville for a perfect landing without the use of a flarepath.

The fighting which had been in progress in North Africa since September, 1940, ended on 13 May, 1943, when the last of the Axis forces on that Continent surrendered. Their presence became untenable once they had been squeezed into a pocket around Tunis by the British 8th Army attacking from the east, and the British and American armies which had taken part in Operation Torch, from the west. Eisenhower's prediction had therefore been proved to be correct, and very little time was left before the invasion of Sicily was to be mounted.

It was now urgently necessary to get at least some Horsas out to North Africa in order that the Regiment would be able to deliver the anti-tank guns complete with their towing jeeps, and other supporting weapons, to the paratroops at Catania. The Wacos would not be able to accomplish this task satisfactorily. They could carry thirteen fully-armed troops, or an anti-tank gun *minus* its motive power, the jeep; whereas the Horsa could carry both gun and jeep, which was a distinct advantage when landing in action. 295 Squadron at Netheravon was therefore given the task of ferrying forty Horsas out to Sale in Morocco, an operation which was given the codename Beggar, or as it was usually referred to unofficially Turkey Buzzard.

At first this was considered an impossibility because of the distance involved, but a 1,500 mile test flight around the UK with a Halifax/Horsa combination proved that it could be done, provided the Horsas' undercarriages were jettisoned first to reduce drag. 295 Squadron had an establishment of one flight of Halifaxes and two flights of Whitleys. All aircraft belonging to 'A' Flight, which had the Halifaxes, required extensive modifications before the operation could be undertaken, including the fitting of extra fuel tanks in the bomb bays. In order to carry out the required training for the ferrying task the squadron moved firstly to Holmsley South on 1 May and then to Hurn towards the end of June. This was necessary as Netheravon was unsuitable for night flying.

The members of 2 Wing who had not been included in the North African draft had moved to Fargo Camp on Salisbury Plain near Larkhill, which had become the Regiment's new Depot on 11 December, 1942, and twelve officers, one Squadron Sergeant-Major and eighty-seven NCOs were now moved to the RAF stations at Thruxton, Netheravon and Hurn to stand by for training for the ferrying. The Movement Order signed by Major Willoughby stipulated: 'These personnel will not be touched or interfered with except under direct orders from Headquarters 38 Wing or Airborne Division. They are on three days notice to move overseas and should not be given more than 48 hours leave.'

A conference was held at 38 Wing Headquarters on 21 May at which it was stated that the necessary modifications to the Halifaxes were going ahead as quickly as possible, together with the training of the crews. It was not possible, however, to delivery forty Horsas *and* give the crews the thorough training required, and as the priority was to have ten fully-trained Halifax crews with their aircraft in North Africa by 21 June it might be possible to deliver only fifteen Horsas by that date.

The operational order for the flight, from Headquarters 38 Wing to OC 295 Squadron, dated 22 May, specified that the Halifax/Horsa combinations were to depart from Portreath in Cornwall, and the Halifaxes were to return to the UK on the day following their trip in order to prepare for the next one, unless the weather was unsuitable, in which case they would tow the Horsas on to Mascara. In any case no more than six gliders were to be allowed to accumulate at Sale at any one time.

The operational order included a plan of the airfield at Sale which, it was pointed out, was controlled by the Americans. Its runways were of inter-locking iron plates laid on sand, and an area 150 yards by 1,700 yards near one of the runways, and plainly marked on the ground, was suitable for the gliders to land on. Captain Clarke was the Regiment's liaison officer there. It was the intention that after the ferrying had been completed the Halifaxes should remain in North Africa to tow the Horsas during the Sicily invasion.

Following an exhaustive eleven weeks of preparation and crew training, during which four crashes occurred and three Halifax pilots and ten crew members were killed, while one other Halifax pilot was seriously injured, twenty-seven of the thirty-one Horsas which left England were safely ferried from Portreath to Sale, a distance of approximately 1,400 miles, between 3 June and 7 July. Of the other four, one was missing, two had been forced to ditch, and one had been taken back to base following an engine failure on the tug.

The Horsas had been prepared for the trip to North Africa by a Heavy Glider Maintenance Unit at Hurn and were then towed to Portreath by Whitleys in order that the Halifaxes could be kept in peak condition. This maintenance work was seriously handicapped by the fact that 'A' Flight had had to send fifty key RAF personnel to North Africa by sea at the beginning of May to attend to the Halifaxes on arrival there.

Twenty-three of the combinations were provided with Beaufighter escorts by 248 Squadron (and on 7 July with Mosquito escorts) for the first three hours of the trip until the Bay of Biscay was reached, where the escorts had to return to base before their fuel ran out. The escorting pilots insisted that while they were present everyone kept as low as 500 feet so that they (the escorts) could avoid interception on the return flight. The Beaufighters were grounded for modifications when the other eight trips took place. For the Halifax crews not returning to the UK after arriving at Sale a further flight of 350 miles to Froha on the Mascara Plain was necessary, with no intermediate rest except for the time it took to fit the spare undercarriage which each Horsa carried.

Froha was another of the airstrips at Mascara, and during this leg of the journey two gliders were dropped in the desert when the tugs developed engine trouble. The odyssey then continued for a further 580 miles without break to the base in Tunisia which was to be used for the forthcoming operation, crossing the Atlas mountains at a height of 7,000 feet. The first Horsa arrived at Kairouan in Tunisia on 28 June, just twelve days before the invasion of Sicily began, and during this last phase of the journey, five Horsas were released in the air due to mechanical failures in the tugs.

Because of the length of the tow from Portreath to Sale three glider pilots were provided for each Horsa. While taking his turn at the controls of one of the first gliders to set out from Portreath, Major Alistair Cooper was forced to ditch in the Bay of Biscay when the tow-rope broke. The three pilots then drifted in their rubber dinghy for eight hours until picked up by a Royal Navy corvette. Major Cooper was back at the controls of another Horsa within 48 hours and this time arrived with it at its intended destination in Tunisia. The other two glider pilots, Staff Sergeants Hall and Antonopoulos had teamed up with Staff Sergeant Conway for their second trip and they were once again forced to ditch in the Bay after an attack by German Focke Wulf Condor aircraft. This time they were adrift for eleven days before being rescued by a Portuguese fishing boat.

Staff Sergeants Jenks, Atwood and Flynn, who had taken part in the 1,500 mile test flight around England, finished their take-off run at Portreath with the undercarriage embedded in the wing of the glider after it had bounced back on being jettisoned. This made handling difficult, and the use of flaps at the end of their journey impossible. It was also apparent that the first part of the glider to make contact with the ground would be not the skid, but the leg of the undercarriage protruding from the wing. However, it was decided to worry about that later, and, being a one-time jazz trumpeter in the Highland Light Infantry Dance Band, Jenks, never without his trumpet, entertained both crews by playing it over the intercom. While coming in to land at Sale the undercarriage parachute suddenly opened, successfully pulling the undercarriage out of the wing but bringing it into contact with the tailplane. The glider pilots effected repairs themselves after what was necessarily a rough landing. During the ferrying and the training for it five members of the Regiment lost their lives.

At the beginning of May the Wacos started to show up in North Africa, although that is perhaps an inappropriate term as the first consignment to arrive were neatly packed in wooden crates on La Senia airfield at Oran. The glider pilots decided not to wait for someone to start assembling the gliders, however, and a party of six officers and sixty-two NCOs moved to La Senia on 8 May and uncrated and assembled them, living in the empty crates on the airfield during the process. In ten days, with the aid of two American fitters, they had erected fifty-two, which were flown to Froha and Thiersville by C-47s.

A further 500 Wacos had been shipped from the US at the beginning of May and as soon as they began to arrive at various North African ports their urgent assembly was undertaken by the Americans with their customary efficient organizational ability, although many problems were encountered. The crates in which they had been shipped had been unloaded haphazardly so that the sets of five crates which contained the parts to make up one complete glider were in disarray and scattered among the various ports, and vital instruments were sometimes missing altogether. However, by 13 June three hundred and forty-six had been completed and delivered to 51st Wing, but on the 16th most of them had to be grounded for repairs, and by the 30th so many had developed weaknesses in the wire bracing of the tail unit that all were grounded for three days. The intercom sets between glider and tug were not to be seen until the operation was imminent.

The Americans had not even considered the glider for military use until February, 1941, and a contract for the supply of the Waco CG4A was not signed until June of that year. The first one was delivered in April, 1942, and by the end of the war almost 14,000 were produced, 750 being handed over to the British, who named it the 'Hadrian'. It had a wingspan of 83 feet 8 ins, a length of 48 feet 3¾ ins, and a weight fully-loaded of 7,500 lbs. Unlike the British gliders, it was constructed of steel tubing covered with fabric.

The American 51st Troop Carrier Wing had been fully engaged in Operation Torch, but was now assigned to 1st Airborne Division for Sicily, and had set up its operations room at Mascara in May, 1943, in order to co-ordinate the American and British activities. The Wing formed part of the American Troop Carrier Command which had been established in the United States in April, 1942, for the movement of the American airborne forces, and its headquarters had arrived in Scotland on 1 September, 1942, to take command of the US Troop Carrier Groups already in the UK which were to take part in Torch — the 60th, 62nd and 64th. Of these Groups, 62nd, now based at Matmore, which was another of the Mascara airstrips, was the least experienced, its pilots not having graduated from their training courses, or flown solo, until midsummer of 1942, and its first echelon only arrived in the UK on 22 September of that year. 60th Group's first echelon arrived in the UK in June, 1942; it was considered the best of the three, although it possessed only thirty-six of its entitlement of sixty navigators, and all but one of these had received only about 50 hours' navigational training. This Group was now at Thiersville. 64th Group, which arrived in the UK in late July, 1942, did not compare with the 60th but was fractionally better trained than the 62nd. It was not now stationed at Mascara, having been attached temporarily to the American 52nd Troop Carrier Wing which had arrived in North Africa in May, 1943, and had been allocated to the American 82nd Airborne Division for the Sicily operation.

Every opportunity was made at Mascara by the RAF's 38 Wing representatives who had flown out there to make available British experience of methods and procedure in airborne matters which had been developed by the Wing at home, but the offering of suggestions, usually unsolicited, was found to require considerable tact and was mostly ignored. This situation undoubtedly would have improved following the expected arrival of Sir Nigel Norman, a man whose charismatic presence it would not have been easy to ignore. It was a bitter blow to all the 38 Wing personnel awaiting his arrival at Mascara, where the senior RAF officer was Squadron Leader Lawrence Wright, when it became known that Sir Nigel had been killed on his flight out.

However, in the three weeks following 29 May an intensive training programme was carried out at Froha, where the Regiment's No.2 Squadron was based, and at another airstrip at Mascara named Relizane, which had become No.3 Squadron's base. During this three-week period 1,363 daytime lifts and 510 nighttime lifts were carried out.

51st Wing's C-47s were based at Thiersville and Matmore under the command of Colonel R.A. Dunn. Before the training period commenced, the Wing had had no previous experience of glider towing, having been engaged with paratroops during Torch and the subsequent fighting, flying them the 1,100 miles from the UK. Throughout the winter since November its aircraft had been kept fully occupied with the movement of men and supplies because of the lack of an adequate road and railway system in North Africa. Certainly no time had been available during the winter for training in its primary function, that of operating with Airborne Forces. It must have been foremost in the minds of everyone who took the trouble to think about it that only three week's joint training for the Wing and the airborne troops, previously without knowledge of one another, was ludicrous. But faced with Churchill's insistence on an early date for the operation, such thoughts had to be thrust to one side. Immediately before and during the training period not only had the majority of the Wacos then in use been assembled by members of the Regiment but also maintained and handled on the ground by them.

At Relizane and three of the other airstrips were 111 American glider pilots who had been sent there in March to familiarize the British glider pilots, when they arrived, with the Waco which had very different landing characteristics from the British gliders. Lift-spoilers were fitted instead of flaps, giving it a long flat glide, thus making a pin-point landing difficult. These American glider pilots had even less flying experience than the members of the Regiment, having graduated from flying school only at the beginning of 1943. Late in March they had managed to obtain a few French gliders and had attempted to tow them with jeeps, but the gliders had achieved only 'ground hops'. The Americans, who had originally belonged to 316th Troop Carrier Group, had landed at Suez on 1 February, 1943, when they had immediately been pressed into service as second pilots on C-47s, being used to help supply the British 8th Army. Twenty-four of them eventually volunteered to fly as co-pilots on the gliders taking part in the Sicily operation when it was found that there were insufficient British glider pilots, and the nineteen who survived the operation were later given permission by Colonel Chatterton to wear the Regiment's first pilots' wings.

The Americans had requested that they should be allowed to become members of the Regiment, but Colonel Chatterton had replied in a letter dated 2.11.43: 'After forwarding to the War Office a request made by you that certain officers of your squadron should become members of the Glider Pilot Regiment, we have had the following answer:- "It is impossible that the officers concerned become full members of the Regiment." However, I should be most delighted if those officers would consider themselves honorary members of our Mess. This is an English custom which makes the officers concerned honorary members of the Regiment. It is, however, impossible under British Military Law to post officers of another nation in our orders. We enclose as requested, six pairs of wings. Permission for wearing these must, however, be granted by the United States Army.' Verbal permission was given on 22.12.43 by Brigadier-General Paul L. Williams, Commanding General, XII Troop Carrier Command, U.S. Army, for the nineteen Americans to wear the wings.

Other glider pilots from the 316th Troop Carrier Group had been sent to Accra in March to assist in the assembly of the Wacos which had arrived there.

Co-ordinated planning for the forthcoming operation was made extremely difficult by the fact that the headquarters of General Alexander, who was in overall command of all ground forces taking part, was in Algiers, more than 200 miles from the American Troop Carrier Command headquarters and training bases. Other headquarters involved in the planning were scattered from Morocco to Egypt.

The Regiment's first full-scale exercise with 60th and 62nd Groups took place on 14 June, by which time both Groups were beginning to get their quota of gliders. Fifty-four Wacos, each fully laden with members of the Air Landing Brigade, were towed for 70 miles, all to land back at Froha within a space of 20 minutes in an area 1,000 yards by 300 yards.

The paratroops also managed to put in·much useful practice during this training period, altogether doing 8,913 jumps, with liaison between them and 51st Wing improving all the time, as indeed it was with the Air Landing Brigade. Then, on 20 June over seventy Wacos were flown a distance of 100 miles, again without mishap. 296 Squadron had now arrived from Hurn with its Albemarles and placed under the command of 51st Wing; they also took part in this latter exercise.

The following night eleven gliders took off and all landed within a marked area away from their airstrips. The conditions at the North African airstrips were such that, on take-off, the glider pilots found themselves enveloped in a thick cloud of red dust which completely obliterated their view of the tug until they were both airborne.

By the time the training period ended all the members of the Regiment at Mascara had received, if not an abundance of Waco flying, at least sufficient to make them reasonably competent to undertake the task ahead of them. One of them, Staff Sergeant 'Andy' Andrews, has written that, being one of the North African draft to have completed his EFTS, GTS and OTU courses in the UK, he arrived in North Africa with 68 hours' day and 3 hours' night flying in gliders, or 185 day lifts and 16 night lifts. At Mascara Andrews accomplished 6 hours 40 minutes on Wacos as first pilot and 4 hours 45 minutes as second pilot during daylight, and 1 hour during night-time, or 16 day lifts and 6 night lifts. He affirms that he considers the training received by the majority of the British glider pilots prior to the Sicily invasion was more than adequate. The Americans had referred to them during the training period as 'fast learners'.

The tug pilots had also received at least some glider-towing practice. One factor which was to have a serious effect on the forthcoming operation, however, was the absence of practice landings on to LZs in the coastal area from releases made a short distance off shore, which would have been of considerable help in preparing for the Sicily invasion. The art of judging distances under such circumstances was, therefore, not mastered, and there was certainly insufficient time to organize mass off-shore glider releases at night.

It had at first been the intention that 52nd Wing of the American Troop Carrier Command, which had been trained in glider towing in the US, would be assigned to 1st Airborne Division for the operation, whilst 51st Wing would fly the American 82nd Airborne Division, but the roles were now reversed.

The 51st had by now experience of working with the British, and the 52nd

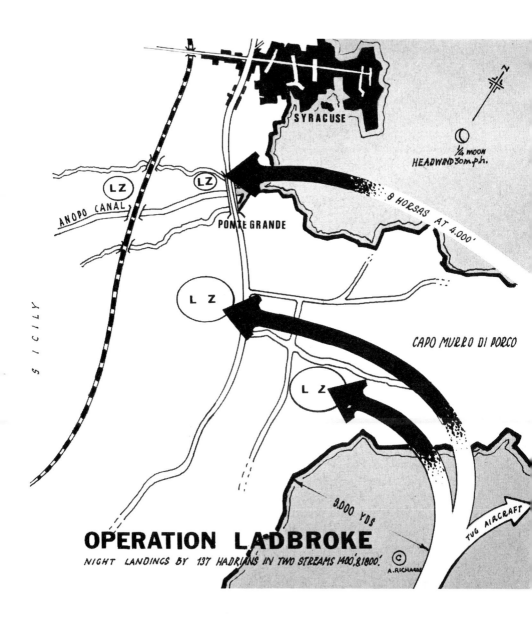

OPERATION LADBROKE

NIGHT LANDINGS BY 137 HADRIANS IN TWO STREAMS 1400' & 1800'

had been training with the 82nd Division in the US for the three months prior to leaving for North Africa, so this switch was logical. Another consideration was the fact that the C-47s of 51st Wing had been modified for use by the British paratroops taking part in Torch. However, 82nd Division's participation in the Sicily invasion was to be confined to paratroops, while the British airborne division's involvement would include the use of gliders, the towing of which was a new experience for 51st Wing. The decision also appeared to lose more of its logic when the task of towing the gliders from Mascara to the operational base in Tunisia was, in fact, given to 52nd Wing.

At the beginning of June Colonel Chatterton flew to Malta so that from there he could be taken over Sicily in a Beaufighter to observe the target area for the operation. Standing between pilot and navigator as they flew up and down the Sicilian coast line at 50 feet was an enjoyable experience, but from his awkward observation post he could not make out anything in the dark mass below which would be of any help in planning how best to come to terms with those rock-strewn, enclosed 'fields'. They did manage to strafe some shipping on the way back to Malta, but he returned to North Africa in, if anything, an even more apprehensive mood. The Regiment's task to be undertaken in a month's time was formidable in the circumstances.

The American C-47s which were to tow the majority of the gliders to Sicily, were slow and extremely vulnerable, being unarmed and unarmoured and without selfsealing tanks. Because of this, on the night of 9/10 July the glider pilots would be required to cast off 3,000 yards out at sea; this the Americans had insisted upon in order that the expected coastal anti-aircraft fire could be avoided. It would be necessary for those release points to be judged by the combinations' apparent distance from the dark, unfamiliar shore for which, as has been said, no practice had been given. As the aircraft would be needed for follow-up operations this was perhaps understandable but was to have tragic consequences.

The intended approach to the LZs was not one which would enable the glider pilots easily to pick up the target, but it had also been dictated by the C-47s' vulnerability to flak. The chosen approach was to be north-eastwards parallel to the coast line between Cap Passaro and Cap Murro di Porco so that the release points would enable the tugs to turn seawards and so avoid the worst of the flak at Syracuse.

As outlined above, 1st Air Landing Brigade's task following the night landing on the 9th/10th was the capture of the Ponte Grande over the Anopo Canal one mile south of Syracuse, which was to be held until relieved by the seaborne forces coming in seven hours later. The bridge was first to be seized by *coup de main* by two companies of the South Staffordshire Regiment carried in eight Horsas which were to be landed into fields near the bridge. These Horsas would be towed by 295 Squadron's Halifaxes.

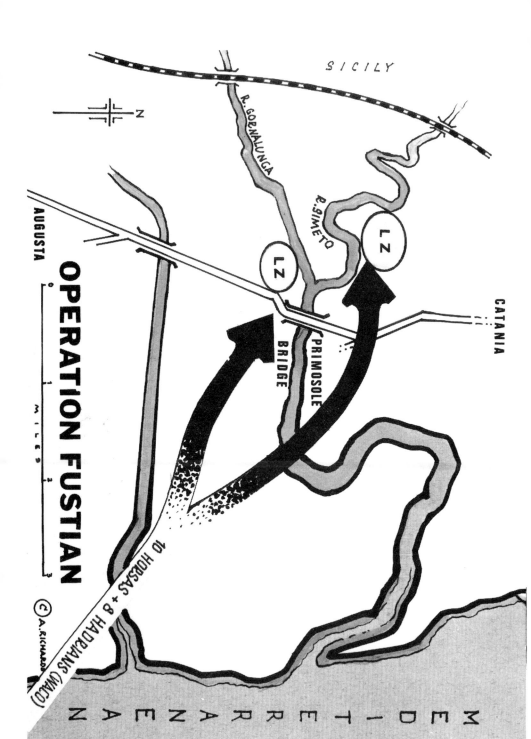

**OPERATION FUSTIAN**

SICILY

N

AUGUSTA

CATANIA

R. GOERNALUNGA

R. SIMETO

LZ

LZ

PRIMOSOLE

BRIDGE

10 HORSAS + 8 HADRIANS (WACO)

MILES
0 1 2 3

© A. RICHARDS

MEDITERRANEAN

The remainder of the Brigade's troops, carried in Wacos towed by 296 Squadron's twenty-eight Albemarles and one hundred and nine C-47s flown by the Americans, were to release 3,000 yards out at sea for their LZs west of Penisola Della Maddalena. They were to advance to the bridge and consolidate the position, with exploitation into Syracuse if possible.

The gliders would also carry six 6-pounder anti-tank guns, ten 3 inch mortars and seven jeeps. Coinciding with the advance to Syracuse by the Border Regiment, fifty Wellington aircraft were to bomb the town. Altogether a fleet of one hundred and forty-five gliders would be required for this part of the operation, which was given the codename Ladbroke.

For the operation two days later in support of 1st Parachute Brigade, a further eleven Horsas and eight Wacos would be needed to land the anti-tank guns and jeeps at 2353 hours. All the gliders for this operation, codenamed Fustian, would be towed by 295 and 296 Squadrons' Halifaxes and Albemarles.

The American airborne tasks would also be split into two separate operations. One hour after Ladbroke two hundred and fifty C-47s would drop 3,405 paratroops of 82 Division five miles north-east of Gela, which is about 55 miles west of Syracuse, in order to block any movement of enemy reserves, which were located at Caltagirone, towards the American beachhead. This would be followed the next night, after the seaborne troops had established beachheads, by another parachute drop.

1st Airborne Division's War Diary at the time contained the entries: 'The landing of gliders by moonlight is a perfectly feasible operation and the casualties from crash landings are unlikely to be excessive. The glider pilots will have little difficulty in locating the landing area'. Regarding the Primasole Bridge operation the diary was rather more perceptive: '... increases in anti-aircraft positions in the area are a little disturbing and there is the reported arrival of 104th Italian Division ... the conditions under which I believe the operation might well be launched remain as before, but I feel myself that the chance of achieving these conditions have been reduced by the latest developments in the enemy's preparation for defence.'

Just before the operations were due to take place the required one hundred and forty-five Wacos carrying 1,200 men of 1st Air Landing Brigade and 296 Squadron's ground crews were ferried the 570 miles from Froha, Thiersville and Matmore to five airstrips near Sousse and Kairouan on the Tunisian coast named El Djam Base, El Djam I, El Djam II, Goubrine Base, and Goubrine II, to join forces with the nineteen Horsas at Goubrine I which had successfully completed the Beggar operation. The American paratroops were to be lifted from another nine airstrips nearby.

As a consequence of the punishment suffered by the Halifaxes during the towing operation, and the need to undertake seventeen modifications which were found to be essential, only seven of them were to be available for Ladbroke. The eighth Horsa for the *coup de main* party would have to be towed by one of 296 Squadron's twenty-eight Albemarles which had also been flown on to Tunis.

296 Squadron had also taken part in the ferrying of the Wacos to the forward area, and during a period of six days, twenty-eight lightly loaded Wacos carrying a total payload of 11,200 lbs had been towed by their Albemarles. The choice of the training area for the division having been at Mascara instead of much further east nearer to the operational base was primarily so that security could be preserved. Had it been located in eastern Tunisia the target for the forthcoming operation would have been indicated as Sicily or Italy.

Many of the gliders had not been test-flown and in lieu of this each tug made a circuit at Froha and the other airstrips in order that the glider pilot could judge the airworthiness of his charge. None of the glider pilots had previously flown continuously for more than an hour and they were now faced with a difficult trip, including the 7,000-foot crossing of the Atlas mountains, in air which was so rough that a drop of 300 or 400 feet in the turbulence was common. Only one fatal crash occurred during the move and that was as a result of a glider's tail falling off. Both glider pilots and all twelve troops being carried were killed. Two other Wacos made forced landings on the way.

At Sousse the waiting period was enlivened by a series of explosions which occurred on 6 July when an ammunition dump situated about three-quarters of a mile from the glider pilots' camp caught fire and thousands of tons of explosives blew up. Several men were hurt by flying fragments but there were no fatalities. All the tents and most of the small arms and equipment were destroyed, however, and much feverish activity was needed to replace all the essentials as the move to the take-off strip was due to take place the following day. By the 9th the Quartermaster's staff had, by some miracle, seen to it that all was in order.

But if this incident was not a sufficiently strong omen of bad times ahead, there was another in store in the form of an untypical thirty miles-an-hour wind which was blowing on the morning of Ladbroke, which persisted all day. This caused Chatterton, later in the day and too late for his decision to reach many of the combinations before they had taken off, to alter the cast-off heights for the gliders, which had been calculated for the still air which had prevailed during the training period. The Wacos were still to cast off 3,000 yards from the coast but the height was now raised 300 feet so that those bound for LZ1, the majority of which were to be towed by the C-47s of 60th Group, would be released at 1,800 feet; those bound for LZ2, the majority of which were to be towed by 62nd Group, would be released at 1,400 feet.

Chatterton has written in *The Wings of Pegasus*: 'I was perplexed to know what height I should give to the gliders to cast off for landing for to date we have been landing in dead-still air ... I felt desperately alone in trying to make my decision and I left it to the very last moment. The difficulty was that I had no telephonic communications with the six strips on which the gliders were stationed. Somehow or other the height would have to be put round by word of mouth. I have to admit that I could not decide whether to instruct the tug pilots to go much higher or to keep to a lower height than 2,000 feet.'

It would be interesting to know what advice he received on this point from others. The final decision had to be his, but Squadron Leader Wright who was 38 Group's adviser on all glider matters with the RAF title 'Air IC Gliders', was on hand and his views must have been sought, as were the commanders of the Troop Carrier Groups (albeit rather inexperienced in glider matters).

Both Colonel Dunn and Brigadier P.L. Williams, the commander of the Troop Carrier Command in North Africa, were to state in August: 'The fault lay in the planning and particularly in the release point set for the Waco gliders. Had that point been over the shore few could have mistaken it. Had it been 1,000 feet higher the gliders would have had sufficient range to compensate for the wind and for some misjudgement by the troop carriers.' Dunn was also to reiterate his views on the height question verbally as will be seen. The height increase meant that the eight Horsas were to cast off at a height of 4,000 feet for their two small LZs which were between a quarter of a mile and one mile west of the bridge, and at a distance of seven miles from it in order that they would arrive unannounced.

The route to be followed was due east from the Tunisian coast for 250 miles to a navigational check point at Malta, and then north-east for a 90-mile leg to the south-east tip of Sicily. As the tugs started up, the entire assembly was enveloped in the usual thick cloud of dust, but the armada was soon on its way with Chatterton flying the leading glider which included Brigadier Hicks among its passengers. Six Albemarles failed to take off due to faulty loading of the gliders.

In order to avoid the enemy's radar the C-47s flew below 250 feet at 120 miles an hour; the Albemarles flew at 350 feet at 125 miles an hour; and the Halifaxes kept to 500 feet and flew at 145 miles an hour. All were occasionally lashed with spray.

With the arrival of darkness each tug switched on a row of lights along the trailing edge of its wings to give a reference point so that the glider pilots could keep correct station. Approaching Sicily they started to climb to the cast-off heights, and the quarter moon came out; but despite its welcome appearance adverse circumstances then started to plague the tug/glider fleet and to create confusion among them with near disastrous results.

The strong wind which was still blowing was causing dust-storms on the ground, and the landmarks, so prominent in aerial photographs seen before take-off, were obscured in rolling clouds of dust, making it more difficult for the tug pilots to fix their positions or even to see the shore. Many combinations had been blown off course, and the air was crowded with tugs and gliders being flown in all directions. Most of the intercom sets between tug and glider were again ineffective, as they had been for Operation Freshman, and the complete lack of previous experience of anything approaching battle conditions began to tell.

Searchlights and a few anti-aircraft guns were soon in action, and in the disarray many of the gliders were released *by their tugs* far in excess of the stipulated 3,000 yards from the shore, putting a landfall out of the question, so that numerous gliders finished up in the sea. Those that did manage to reach land were scattered over an area twenty-five miles in extent, the majority having to land in unsuitable terrain.

Staff Sergeant Jack Caslaw had been amongst the first of the volunteers for glider training to be posted to Ringway in October, 1940. He was now flying one of the Wacos with Sergeant Anderson, and with a detachment from the Border Regiment as passengers. They were one of an element of four Dakota/Waco combinations. Caslaw remembers that as they skimmed the water on the way over from Tunisia, 'I said a little prayer to God, and to Saint Paul who had had trouble himself in those waters'; after which he had enjoyed the trip. That is until they were cast off by their tug far from the Sicilian shore. Caslaw flew on in free flight towards the moon which was where the land should be located, and Anderson went back to tell the passengers to get their kit on ready for landing. It quickly became apparent that the landing was going to take place in the sea, however, and the Borders were told to prepare for an emergency exit.

Caslaw held the glider off until the tail contacted a wave top, when 'she just swashed down into the water; no one even lost his footing'. He then showed his passengers how to climb out on to the port wheel and haul themselves on to the wing, just as Frankie Gross of Detroit, an Airframes fitter, had shown him when he had been assembling Wacos at La Senia.

It got windy and cold. Two men were washed away — the only two passengers Caslaw was to lose during six years of glider flying. Dawn exposed the peak of Etna, smoking peacefully with a cloak of cloud around her shoulders, and the wing continued to bear them up. They were eventually picked up by a Hunt Class destroyer at 0630 hours, by which time they were ankle deep in water. Caslaw describes as one of the minor tragedies of war the fact that he was unable to drink the naval rum presented to him, due to the fact that his mouth had become so raw!

The operation to capture the Ponte Grande, of such vital importance to the invading forces, was miraculously carried out successfully although only two of the eight gliders carrying the *coup de main* party arrived on the LZ. It had been only too obvious that the gliders would need to be flown with outstanding skill. A distance of seven miles had to be flown in darkness after cast-off one mile out at sea, and landings made into two fields just two acres in extent once they had been located.

One of the two gliders was flown by Staff Sergeant Dennis Galpin who was carrying No. 15 Platoon of 2nd Battalion, the South Staffordshire Regiment under Lieutenant L. Withers. Immediately after take-off, in the inevitable cloud of red dust, the Halifax had appeared to be in trouble and the pilot announced that he was returning as the aircraft had developed engine trouble. However, the engine picked up again as soon as they were back over the airstrip and they set off once more, well behind the others.

Just short of cast-off point the tug pilot told Galpin that he would take them to within five miles of the objective instead of seven miles as briefed because of the high wind, and to make certain they would have sufficient height to reach it he would take them up to 5,000 feet. Very little flak was encountered over the coast and, once the glider had cast off, the dim outline of Cap Murro di Porco could be seen. After flying on the predetermined course for several minutes they were exactly over their target at 2,000 feet. The glider was then caught in a searchlight beam and forced to take violent evasive action as quite a few guns began to give it their undivided attention. This took it out to sea again, still in the beam of the searchlight, and Galpin decided to go down low and approach the bridge with a little speed in hand, flying parallel with the canal. The searchlight followed the glider down to the ground and conveniently illuminated its approach on to the field, highlighting the bridge at the same time. Full flaps were applied and the glider touched down fairly smoothly. No time was lost capturing the bridge, but there was no sign of the other gliders. The second Horsa to arrive had been flown by Captain Denholm, and on coming in to land it hit the canal bank and a bangalore torpedo which it was carrying exploded, killing all on board.

The remainder of the night was fairly quiet for the glider pilots and South Staffords at the bridge, and around dawn a few more members of the Air Landing Brigade, as well as several more glider pilots began to arrive until the force amounted to eight officers and sixty-five other ranks. Apart from rifles and small arms, their armament comprised one 2-inch mortar and two Bren guns. The Italians had previously prepared the bridge for demolition but the charges were quickly removed. The small force was not to know at that stage of the operation that the majority of the gliders had been forced to land in the sea.

During the following morning the Italians mounted a heavy counter-attack with, at least, a battalion of infantry with field guns and mortar support. They soon had the bridge completely surrounded, but they were unable to drive the airborne troops off it until 1530 hours by which time the defenders had been on the bridge for eight or nine hours and had lost half their number killed while only nineteen of the others remained uninjured. They had also used up most of their ammunition. Even then a small force which was made up of sixteen glider pilots and four others, under the command of the Regiment's Lieutenant A.F. Boucher-Giles, held out near the canal mouth until their ammunition had been completely expended. They held this position against overwhelming odds for the best part of an hour until they were forced to give it up. The Italians did not hold them prisoners for very long. A patrol of the Northamptonshire Regiment appeared and disposed of the enemy, and the bridge was soon retaken by the Royal Scots Fusiliers coming up from the beaches.

Chatterton and his tug arrived at the target area at about 2200 hours and flew along the coast searching for the LZ, when flak started to come up from Syracuse, directed at the Wellington bombers which were raiding it. The C-47 suddenly started to turn away from the coast and dive, much to Chatterton's consternation, forcing him to cast off and turn back towards Sicily. He then entered a pall of dust which the gale was causing, and a sudden burst of tracer tore open the fabric of his port wing. Suddenly the sea was rushing up at him and he levelled out and splashed down, eventually emerging from beneath the water to see all around him the dark forms of his second pilot and passengers. A searchlight from the shore picked them out and more bursts of tracer were directed at them. Eventually the beam moved away and they decided to swim for it.

No sooner had they gained the shore than bombs began to rain down on them and, with a tremendous crash, an aircraft hit the water where they had just been swimming. The resultant flames spread over a large area. Before long a boat was heard approaching and a Royal Navy pinnace appeared, out of which jumped members of the Special Air Service, a unit which Chatterton and his group were only too pleased to join. For the remainder of the night they occupied themselves attacking strong-points and pillboxes, and by dawn they had captured some 150 prisoners.

The follow-up airborne landings on the Catania Plain due two days later were postponed for 24 hours to synchronize with the ground advance, and those participating in these landings were also subjected to a certain amount of harassment, some of it from an unexpected quarter. The Horsas, six of which were towed by Halifaxes and four by Albemarles (one had been prevented from taking part after its tow-rope had broken), and the eight Wacos were dispersed by intense anti-aircraft fire directed at them by the Allied fleet lying off Cap Murro di Porco. The one hundred and seven C-47s carrying the paratroops had also received the same treatment.

The fleet had been subjected to enemy air attacks and had just received a signal to expect enemy torpedo bombers, so were understandably trigger-happy. Certain specific rules had been laid down at a conference held at Tripoli on 4 June. They were that multi-engined aircraft should not fly within five miles of any naval convoy unless it was unavoidable, in which case they should give advance warning and fly at an altitude of over 6,000 feet. If such advance warning had not been given the navy stipulated that ships would be free to fire on aircraft flying within a radius of 12,000 yards of cruisers and battleships, 5,000 yards of other warships, and 1,500 yards of small escort vessels. These were difficult rules to be observed in darkness, although the intended aircraft routes had been chosen with meticulous care to comply with them as it was a well-known fact at that period in the war that naval anti-aircraft gunners fired at any aircraft approaching at night.

Four of the gliders were shot down by enemy gunners after releasing from their tugs, three made disastrous crash-landings, and seven others landed in the midst of strong enemy positions.

One of the Wacos, flown by Staff Sergeant Tommy Moore and Sergeant Garrett, carrying twelve members of the South Staffordshire Regiment with four handcarts and a Bangalore torpedo, had lost a perspex panel from the front of the cockpit shortly after take-off, resulting in an uncomfortably cold trip during which communication with the crew of the Dakota was virtually impossible because of the noise caused by the inrush of air. During the flight Moore's glider, together with another being flown by Lieutenant Whittington Steiner, became detached from the main stream, and they eventually arrived at the Sicilian coast some forty minutes after the estimated time of arrival, and well north of their intended LZ. Both combinations were caught in a searchlight beam and Moore's tug pilot dived almost to sea level to escape from it. Steiner's glider was still to be seen in the beam flying at about 2,000 feet.

Moore eventually cast off at 2,300 feet a mile and a half from the shore. With the strong off-shore head-wind they made slow progress and had insufficient height to take evasive action against the searchlights and flak. The coast was crossed at an indicated height of 300 feet but details of the terrain below were scarcely discernible in the absence of any moon. The ground came at them at an alarming angle, bringing the glider to a sudden halt against a boulder which penetrated the cockpit, breaking Moore's ankle and pinning his leg under his seat. The glider had landed on a rocky slope about 100 yards from the beach and 20 yards from an Italian pillbox. Garrett was unhurt and kicked his way out through the side of the cockpit.

The occupants of the pillbox lobbed grenades at the glider and within minutes the whole of the fabric was ablaze, pieces of it falling into the handcarts of ammunition, which included phosphorous grenades and mortar bombs. A series of explosions killed about half of the South Staffordshires; one who had managed to get out of the glider was killed by the exploding ammunition over a hundred yards away. Garrett was helping one man from the glider when he was hit by a piece of flying shrapnel which tore away most of his left elbow joint. He then struggled to the nose of the glider and, putting his right shoulder under it, managed to lift it a few inches. Moore knew it was his only chance as his seat was now beginning to burn, and he lunged forward and jerked his leg free, but in doing so he felt his leg break. Together they tried to rescue one of the men from the wreckage but without success; mercifully he was unconscious. From the shelter of some rocks they watched the glider being torn apart by explosives until it was finally scattered far and wide when the Bangalore torpedo ignited.

Moore used a puttee as a tourniquet on Garrett's arm, but it was soon apparent that he would lose it. Their hopes of being rescued rose at dawn when they could see the invasion shipping about three miles offshore forming a continuous line along the horizon. Soon landing barges were seen nosing their way into Avola about five miles away. These were attacked by German fighter aircraft which straffed the coastal area.

As the day wore on Garrett grew weaker and became, at times, delirious. It was obvious that he would not be able to survive another night in the open. Having now abandoned hope of help arriving from Avola, Moore decided he must try to reach the shipping. He dragged himself towards the pillbox and discovered a dead Italian holding the cap of a grenade, with which he had no doubt helped to set the glider on fire and cause the explosions which had killed him. Taking the Italian's carbine and bayonet, he found that together they would serve as a crutch to enable him to reach the sea. It proved to be a difficult journey as it was necessary to cross rows of barbed wire. On attaining his goal he rested in the sea, then strapped a piece of driftwood to his injured leg, took two benzedrine tablets, and set off to try and swim to the shipping.

He was forced to abandon the attempt when about a quarter of a mile from the shore, and returned to a solitary farmhouse which he could see alongside the coastal path. This proved to be deserted, but shortly after his arrival an Italian patrol was seen to be approaching, towing a machine gun on wheels. Moore hid himself under a pile of beans in the kitchen while the Italians made a cursory search before moving away.

Help from Avola arrived at last in the form of a Medical Officer and stretcher party. Moore lost no time guiding them to Garrett, who was found to be suffering from gangrene and loss of blood. His left arm was later amputated at the shoulder. Moore's leg was set three times to correct displacements, and when he eventually returned to the almost deserted camp at Sousse some four months later, it was to discover that he was still posted as missing. Far from that being a correct record, however, he was later to take part in Operation Market.

Only four Horsas on Operation Fustian had landed their 6-pounder guns close to the Primasole Bridge, and only two of those landed on the correct LZ south-west of the bridge. The first pilots of these two were Staff Sergeants Protheroe and White. The paratroops' numbers had been reduced to 200 because of the widely scattered drop, but nevertheless the bridge was captured and the demolition charges removed. Very heavy counterattacks during which they sustained heavy casualties, subsequently forced the paratroops off the bridge, but they were able to prevent the Axis forces from regaining possession of it until the arrival of 8th Army troops and tanks.

The one redeeming factor in the almost catastrophic glider participation in the landing was that the members of the Regiment proved their undoubted ability to take on the role of 'total soldier' once on the ground. Some operated anti-tank guns and others made good use of a captured German 88mm gun during the defence of the captured Primasole Bridge. Despite the fact that they were first and foremost pilots, they showed remarkable adaptability, courage and self-discipline which augured well for the future.

Several factors had contributed to the unsatisfactory outcome of the glider operations: the rock-strewn and wooded LZs which confronted those who did manage to reach them (296 Squadron's Report on the operation contained the information that some of their pilots had later visited the area and were agreed that its nature made a safe landing in quarter moon an impossibility. They found the surface to be rough, rocky and broken, riddled with large holes and intersected at frequent intervals by stone walls about 4 feet high and 3 feet thick); the Americans' insistence on the gliders releasing 3,000 yards from the coast and, in many cases, releasing the gliders themselves (entirely the wrong procedure) in excess of that distance; the switch from 52nd Wing tugs to those of the more inexperienced 51st Wing for the operation; the inadequate time allowed for training, and also for the final briefing (aircraft requirements, the detailed flight plan, time tables, and allocation of gliders to LZ's were made known only 24 hours before take-off); and the Americans' use of a follow-my-leader technique rather than the British method of individual navigation, so that only the leaders carried navigators, which probably made for confusion when approaching a defended shore under the stress of a first operation with gliders.

Of the one hundred and forty-five gliders which had taken part in Ladbroke only forty-nine Wacos and five Horsas landed in Sicily. Sixty-nine gliders had come down in the sea, sixty-four of them having been released more than 3,000 yards from the coast as later testified by survivors. In fact some of the C-47 pilots themselves accused their leaders of keeping too far off shore.

Another factor adding to the vulnerability of the C-47 was that it did not have self-sealing fuel tanks, although as it happened flak had been negligible. Of the remaining twenty-two gliders, seven had cast off for various reasons before leaving Tunisia (six of which were being towed by the Albemarles), four returned from Sicily without having cast off due to failure to locate their LZ, and eleven were unaccounted for.

55% of all tug pilots who left Tunisia had failed to reach the correct release points. 56% of the American-towed gliders finished their journey in the Mediterranean and only 34% landed in Sicily. Taking 38 Wing on its own, 36% of the gliders had not been taken to the correct release points and 23% had landed in the sea, while 49% had reached Sicily.

When the British Prime Minister was notified of these figures he called it a disaster. Could there be found anyone bold enough to tell him that the primary cause of the disaster was the shortage of time available for preparation and training?

General Browning in his report on Ladbroke, submitted on 24 July, wrote:

Although there was no flak within thousands of yards of the glider release-point, there is no doubt that inexperience of the pilots in flying near flak induced them to cast off too soon and too far out to sea. [He was not of course referring to the glider pilots.] Navigation generally was bad. This is proved by the small number of gliders which landed even reasonably close to the landing-zone. In the first assault it is estimated only twenty-five per cent of the aircraft reached the correct point for glider release and a number of these released too far out to sea to enable the gliders to reach land. The remaining 75 per cent released their gliders on a front of no less than 30 miles with the result that only a few of the force reached their objective.

The results achieved on this, our first glider landing, do not shake my confidence in the value of gliders for carrying airborne troops to the battlefield by night.

The advantage of gliderborne troops over parachute troops, wherever it is possible to use the former, have been demonstrated. Troops carried by glider land in formed, even if small, bodies, and can carry with them a more liberal supply of ammunition, transport and comparatively heavy weapons. They can land in most country that is suitable for parachute troops, but it is almost certain that in future small advance parties will have to land ahead of the gliders to mark landing-zones with small lights.

Major Lander has been mentioned before and is to appear again as the officer appointed to command the 1st Independent Parachute Company which was to be formed to undertake this marking role.

The potential of glider-borne operations had been shown and the Horsa glider had proved itself, having done all that was required of it. The Dakotas and Albemarles had also demonstrated their ability to tow fully-loaded Wacos a distance of 340 miles against a strong wind and to return to base without refuelling, and five of the Albemarles had towed fully-loaded Horsas the same distance. The Halifaxes had, of course, done their job admirably. However, the need for far more intensive training had been made apparent. Useful lessons had been learnt, but at a cost. Over 300 men had been drowned off Syracuse. Of the fifty-four gliders which had reached Sicily during Ladbroke many had been widely scattered. Of the eighteen gliders taking part in Fustian only eleven had made a useful contribution to the fighting. Fifty-seven members of the Regiment had lost their lives.

But, in spite of everything, the spearhead had completed its task on the ground. When the amphibious landings were made there were no enemy coastal defences to oppose them, and the bridges which were vital to their advance into Sicily were intact. General Montgomery stated that the airborne troops saved the seaborne armies seven days fighting, with all the casualties that would have entailed. The Commander of 7th Army stated that his swift and successful landings, followed by a rapid advance inland, would not have been achieved at such a light cost without the action of the airborne troops.

General Alexander in his report on operation Husky, dated 21 July, 1943, wrote:-

The recent operations have proved the value of airborne troops, and given us a peep into their great possibilities if they are properly organized, equipped and employed. I can say without hesitation that the early capture of Syracuse was largely due to the 1st Airborne Division which was dropped outside the town to seize the immediate approaches to the port, and later the important bridge across the R. Simeto, south of Catania.

The airborne troops themselves are excellent. Tough, fit, efficient and of high morale; I don't say they haven't a lot to learn which can only be done by Training-Experience-Training. The outstanding weakness in the set-up is the lack of trained air force pilots to transport them. Through no fault of their own, they are untrained for and inexperienced in the job. The RAF must produce the pilots if we are to develop this arm, which I am convinced we must do.

Personally, I believe that it is the best solution to the invasion of Europe across the channel — airborne troops in large numbers in conjunction with the attack on the coast from the sea. I look at the problem like this: Tactics are continually changing with the introduction of new weapons and new equipment. The side which can take advantage of this and develop its tactics accordingly before its enemy will keep the initiative and produce the surprises — both battle-winning factors. The land defences have few, if any, open flanks to get round and turn but there is one flank (if you can so term it) — the flank, or open door over the top which is always there. It is there wide open for the side which has the air superiority. What an opportunity for us, if we only see it and can seize it.

Therefore, I repeat, we must at once raise, organize, equip and develop an airborne force of parachutists and gliders — say a corps of two Divisions. The RAF pilots, crews and machines must be made available and put aside for this corps with whom they must live, work and train to the exclusion of everything else.

I know that the answer will be that it is quite impossible to afford the pilots and the aircraft. Well! it is a question of priorities and personally I firmly believe that with our growing air supremacy, priority No.1 is for the airborne Corps.

# V

## MEDITERRANEAN OPERATIONS

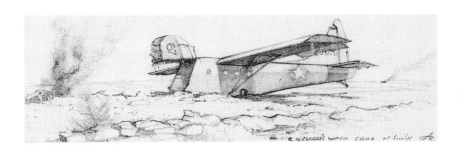

ONCE THE SITUATION in Sicily had stabilized, the survivors of the Regiment's 2 and 3 Squadrons were withdrawn to Tunisia and encamped between Sousse and Kairouan, where they managed to put in a certain amount of flying in Wacos while they regrouped. There they were rejoined by the remainder of the Wing's personnel who had started the move from Fargo Camp in June, and had sailed from Liverpool on HMT *Samaria*. They had arrived in Algiers without incident and remained in the harbour for two days before being taken on to Philipville in an American ship, eventually arriving at No. 5 Infantry Reinforcement Training Depot. There, despite frantic signals between 1st Airborne and Allied Force Headquarters in Algiers, they were lost sight of for twelve days, consequently missing the Sicily landings.

For a while the new arrivals were treated with a certain coolness by the battered remnants of 2 and 3 Squadrons who were understandably in a rather sombre mood, but this quickly passed off and they were soon being converted on to the Wacos. It was then that Colonel Dunn blurted out to Major Willoughby apropos the Sicily landings, 'We told you at the briefing that there was a 30 mph headwind blowing off Sicily and we wanted to put the release height up a further 2,000 feet, but your people wouldn't have it. We warned you our aircraft had no self-sealing tanks and we couldn't go in over flak, but you ignored our warning. Now we are being blamed for the fiasco.' Willoughby retorted that he was unable to comment as he had not been at the briefing.

Whether or not there had been time during the hectic few hours before the Ladbroke take-off, when the unexpected high wind materialized, for Dunn's alleged views to be conveyed to Chatterton is not known. We have already seen that insufficient time had been allowed for the final briefing. In any case it does not alter the fact that the majority of the gliders had not been taken sufficiently close to the shore for them to have had any hope of reaching it. Chatterton has stated: 'We could not put the gliders too far inland — and I didn't want them to overshoot,' a remark which, with benefit of hindsight, is not easy to understand.

Soon afterwards Major Willoughby and another officer who had arrived with the new draft, Major T.R. Mordaunt-Hare, were ordered to leave the next day for No. 5 IRTD. They were unable to discover the reason for this until they were shown reports that they had expressed views on the training and employment of the Regiment in such a way as to undermine the authority of its Commanding Officer. Willoughby explains: 'In fact we had kept what views we had to ourselves and had supported him at all times. We had told the C.O. that instead of sitting around doing nothing it was high time the pilots who had been on Husky should start doing some military training for the good of their own morale. This was met with a violent reaction.' However, Chatterton had obviously become aware of the criticism, and two senior officers were lost to the Regiment at a stage in its formation when every ounce of support was needed.

Chatterton was sent back to England in August by General Hopkinson, in order to make those in authority more aware of the proper use of gliders. He himself was determined that nothing remotely resembling the near-catastrophic Sicily landings should ever be allowed to happen again. In the certain knowledge that without any real backing any effort of his would be fraught with difficulties, Chatterton made use of the fact that the Wing temporarily found itself to be under the American Troop Carrier Command for organization and training and seized the opportunity to obtain as much support from that source as he could. The results of his efforts in that respect will be seen later. Before leaving North Africa he handed over command of the Wing to his Second in Command, Lieutenant-Colonel J.W. Place.

The Wing was now made aware that it was to accompany 1st Airborne Division during the part it was to play in the invasion of Italy. The Americans had been anxious to wind up operations in the Mediterranean theatre as soon as the Axis forces had been cleared out of North Africa, so that the Allies could concentrate on preparations for the decisive invasion of France. They were now even more reluctant, after Sicily, to commit their forces any longer in that area but, once again, the British view prevailed.

The Italians had asked for an armistice in August and it was the intention that the Allies' agreement to this would be announced twenty-four hours before the invasion of Italy. As part of that invasion General Hopkinson had been ordered to occupy the Italian naval base of Taranto, an operation given the title Slapstick. All the American aircraft, which had made 1st Airborne Division's participation in the Sicily landings possible, had now been switched to lift the US Airborne Forces to Italy and, therefore, 1st Airborne, including the glider pilots, would have to go by sea.

The British 8th Army was to cross the Straits of Messina from Sicily and land on the extreme south-west of Italy on 3 September. The American 5th Army, with their Airborne Forces under command, would land farther up the west coast at Salerno on the 9th. 1st Airborne Division's landings, also on the 9th, would be of a secondary nature, the object being to facilitate the escape of the Italian fleet to Malta on the same day.

Whilst in Tunisia the glider pilots received a visit from Lieutenant-Colonel Vladimir Peniakoff ('Popski'), the Commander of the redoubtable desert campaign Reconnaissance Force officially named Popski's Private Army. This Force was now attached to 1st Airborne Division and its Commander wanted ten glider pilots to be attached to it for a month during which time they would be familiarized with his own particular brand of warfare, and then fly him and his Force into the mountains in the toe of Italy. Popski was provided with his glider pilots and even insisted on being taught to fly a glider himself, but as it turned out the subsequent employment of the Force in Italy required a completely unheralded arrival which could not be guaranteed by glider even if carried out at night. In the event Popski used other means of transport.

In view of the role that the Wing was required to adopt in the forthcoming operation Colonel Place was now presented with the task of converting his six squadrons into an infantry battalion within a space of forty-eight hours. He had to obtain the complete scale of arms and ammunition which such a unit needed, with the proviso that only a bare minimum of baggage would be allowed, and no transport. Major A. Simpson was placed in command of the rear party to be left in Tunisia, and Colonel Place moved with his force of some 400 glider pilots sandwiched in a huge convoy of lorries carrying the rest of 1st Airborne Division to Bizerta, which was to be the departure point for their part in the invasion. Within a short time of arrival at Bizerta Major G.A.R. Coulthard with one squadron sailed for Italy on the Royal Navy cruiser *Aurora* with the advance party, to be followed shortly by the main party of glider pilots aboard *Princess Beatrix*.

Although it was known that the Italians had surrendered, there could be no guarantee that a friendly reception awaited them at Taranto, but little opposition was encountered as German forces in the area (mainly paratroops) were weak. A number of Italian submarines had been seen sailing on the surface towards Malta in order to surrender and, just before arriving at Taranto, an Italian battle fleet passed them heading in the same direction.

One hundred and thirty officers and men of 6th Parachute Battalion were lost when the ship on which they were being carried, HMS *Abdiel*, hit a mine in the harbour and blew up. The ship had also been carrying the Division's anti-tank guns and all the reserve ammunition. It was the intention that the glider pilots should thereafter be used in an infantry role. This would not be the first occasion during the Second World War, or any other, that men trained for a specialist job were to be used in a role which took no account of their expertise. Indisputably the glider pilots were competent infantrymen, but any justification for their deliberate use as such is somewhat negated by the fact that trained glider pilots were very much at a premium. In the event they were not even used as infantry, but in a variety of non-combative roles at Taranto.

The major part of the Wing was eventually withdrawn to Sousse in November and finally returned to England in piecemeal fashion during December, 1943, and January, 1944. No. 3 Squadron, under Major Coulthard, was left in the Middle East on attachment to 2nd Independent Parachute Brigade and renamed 1st Independent Squadron. Four officers, one warrant officer, and twenty-five NCOs under the command of Major P.F. Stancliffe went to India as the nucleus of the glider pilot force for the new 44 Indian Airborne Division being raised there. The activities of the Regiment in India are covered in a later chapter.

On 20 November the Independent Squadron left Putignano in Italy and between the 21st and 24th of that month arrived at Oujda in French Morocco which was the American Airborne Forces Training Centre. There they gladly took refresher courses on the Waco and did a certain amount of ferrying of newly constructed Wacos from Casablanca to Oujda. On 22 December the training centre moved to Comiso in Sicily and there, during the next few months, the Independent Squadron enjoyed a wealth of flying hitherto unknown. The American 5th Troop Carrier Command made available to them five Dakotas, and two of the Flights were sent to Gerbini and Ponte Olivio, whilst the third remained at Comiso. Very soon moonlight landings became routine.

They were joined during this period by the Pathfinder Unit of the British 22nd Parachute Brigade, so that it was possible to carry out training in the layout of LZs. As the invasion of southern France was by now well into the planning stage the opportunity to train with the Pathfinders was a great advantage. However, before that operation took place the Squadron was called upon to undertake another. It was to be its first as the Independent Squadron.

As a prelude to this operation, Staff Sergeant Morrison and Sergeant McMillan were flown to an airstrip in Tunisia in February, 1944, in order to pick up a Horsa, one of the three which would be needed for it. The glider was found to be just flyable, although the climate had taken its toll, and it was successfully flown back to Bari Airport on the Italian Adriatic coast to join the two others. The plan for the operation emerged. Under the codename Bunghole, the gliders were to convey a Russian Military Mission, which included two British radio operators and a French Canadian sergeant from the SAS who was to act as interpreter, from Bari to Marshal Tito's mountain headquarters at Petrovac in the foothills of the Dinaric Alps in Yugoslavia.

The American pilots who were to do the towing eventually decided that their Dakotas were not powerful enough to tow Horsas over the mountain range, the highest peak of which is 6,277ft, so Wacos were brought into use instead. Good navigation was essential to the successful outcome of the operation and three top navigators were called in from the Commonwealth Air Forces: a New Zealander, a South African and an Australian. In order to draw off enemy fighters which might interfere, a large fleet of Flying Fortresses was to attack targets where enemy forces were concentrated, and an umbrella of fighters would be provided to defend the combinations en route. A Sunderland flying-boat would patrol the route across the Adriatic to provide help in case of ditching.

The glider pilots discussed the best way to land in the deep snow which would be encountered at the end of the journey. A glider landing at speed and suddenly being brought to a stop by snow could very easily somersault, so it was decided to do a tail-down landing in order that the tail would act as a brake. With the Horsa the undercarriage could be jettisoned so that a landing could be made on the skid which was very like a large ski. The Waco had only two much smaller skids, with a fixed landing gear.

The distance across the Adriatic was roughly 150 miles, and as the Dalmatian coast was approached the vast fleet of Flying Fortresses was seen returning from their diversionary attacks. There were still a hundred miles to travel, and mists swirled around the Dinaric Alps obscuring the ground thousands of feet below, but the navigators brought them directly over the LZ. The combinations circled it to give the mist time to clear, and when it did so a hammer and sickle sign was to be seen roughly cut in the snow, together with smoke from signal fires.

The pilots of the first glider to cast off were Captain Turner and Sergeant Newman, followed by Staff Sergeant McCulloch and Sergeant Hall, and then Staff Sergeant Morrison and Sergeant McMillan. All three landings were accomplished with great skill and without mishap, and the party was greeted by rapturous partisans. The gliders were destroyed by burning, and the

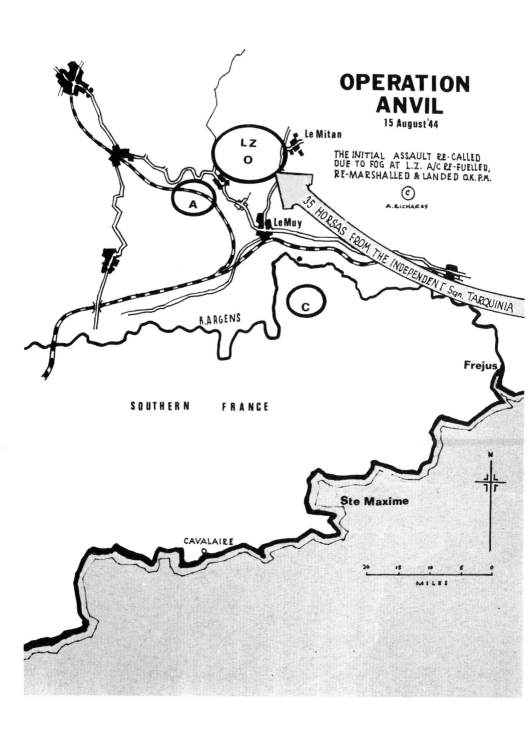

# OPERATION
# ANVIL
### 15 August '44

Le Mitan

THE INITIAL ASSAULT RE-CALLED
DUE TO FOG AT L.Z. A/C RE-FUELLED,
RE-MARSHALLED & LANDED O.K. P.M.

Ⓒ
A. RICHARDS

LZO

A

Le Muy

35 HORSAS FROM THE INDEPENDENT Sqn. TARQUINIA

C

R. ARGENS

Frejus

SOUTHERN FRANCE

N

Ste Maxime

CAVALAIRE

20    15    10    5    0
MILES

glider pilots were billeted with Yugoslav families during their stay, eventually to be flown out from a makeshift runway made on the snow by a Dakota flown into Yugoslavia for the purpose by Air Commodore Whitney Straight. Sergeant McMillan had volunteered to stay behind for liaison duties with the British Military Mission which was also there, and the other five were flown back to Bari and Comiso.

In April, 1944, it was agreed that the Squadron should change its Wacos for Horsas. Both gliders were capable of carrying loads equivalent to their own weight, which, in the case of the Horsa, was almost twice as much as the Waco, and included, as we have seen, the British 6-pounder anti-tank gun and its jeep, which had become an essential part of airborne forces equipment. A search party sent to North Africa for the purpose located fourteen Horsas which were being looked after by an RAF Maintenance Flight, and the gliders, together with the RAF personnel, were flown to Comiso. Two more Horsas had also been found and the sixteen were promptly taken into use for training.

New Horsas then started to arrive, having been shipped in crates from the UK to Naples, and in June, 1944, the Squadron moved once again, firstly to Guido in Italy to start training intensively with the units it was to take across to southern France, and then to Tarquinia airfield on the west coast of Italy where the runway pointed straight out to sea towards the invasion coast. Here the Independent Squadron was joined by C-47s of the American Troop Carrier Command which were to tow it to southern France.

Operation Anvil, later renamed Dragoon, the airborne part of the invasion of southern France, was to take place on 15 August, 1944. The intention had originally been that it should precede the Normandy landings, but at the time of the proposed date in April, 1944, most of the troops earmarked for it were locked in battle in Italy. The amphibious landings were to be made by the American 7th Army. The airborne forces for the operation were made up of Allied glider and parachute units then in the Mediterranean area which had been formed into the 1st Airborne Task Force under the command of Major-General R.T. Frederick, US Army. It included 2nd British Independent Parachute Brigade Group commanded by Brigadier C.H.V. Pritchard, 1st Independent Squadron, the Glider Pilot Regiment, and American paratroops and glider troops. 51st Troop Carrier Wing was to be joined by 50th and 53rd Wings to provide the aircraft, and the entire airborne force was accommodated on ten airfields just north of Rome.

The Allied forces would be opposed by the German 19th Army, comprising seven infantry divisions and one Panzer division. The airborne plan was that American and British paratroops would drop around Le Muy, some ten miles inland from the invasion beaches at 0445 hours, in order to prevent the considerable forces which the Germans were known to have in the area from getting through to the beaches, and to clear two LZs for the gliders which were to land later. The amphibious forces were to come ashore over a thirty-mile beachhead between Cavalaire and St Raphael at 0700 hours. Then at 0814 hours 35 Horsas flown by the British glider pilots and 26 Wacos flown by American glider pilots would start to land 64th Light Battery, RA, and 300th Air-Landing Anti-tank Battery RA, to reinforce the paratroops. The final phase of the airborne operation would come in the early evening when an American parachute infantry battalion would drop and 348 Wacos would bring in 2,250 American glider infantry troops, anti-tank guns, mortars and engineers.

Some 450 Wacos had been assembled in Italy and the American glider pilots to fly them had arrived there from the UK. At 0100 hours on 15 August Pathfinder aircraft carrying 1st Independent Parachute Company took off from Italy, and on arriving over the DZs at 0334 hours found a thick layer of fog obliterating all the landmarks, so they were forced to land blind and found themselves fifteen miles from the target. They were therefore unable to set up the navigational aids in the right place. The paratroops who started to arrive right on time also dropped through the fog from aircraft which had not had the benefit of those navigational aids, but the drop was accomplished with an 80% success rate.

The Wacos started to arrive at 0900 hours with 64th Light Battery, RA, and after circling their LZ for some time hoping for the fog to disperse, it did so, allowing the majority of the gliders to make successful landings. The British gliders had been recalled to Italy by the Commander of the Troop Carrier Wing when they had reached Corsica as he feared the heavily laden Horsas would suffer heavy losses landing on the fog-covered LZ. Two of them made forced landings in Corsica when their tug aircraft developed engine trouble. Back at Tarquinia they were hastily reassembled for a second take-off later, while the tugs were refuelled. This second take-off took place during mid-afternoon as part of the main airborne operation involving the 348 American-flown Wacos and the C-47s carrying the parachute battalion. By the time the Horsas reached the LZ the glider pilots had flown for seven hours that day, but all the gliders were landed intact in the right place, and delivered the 300th Air-Landing Anti-tank Battery, RA, with their guns and jeeps. The Horsas had not been expected back in Italy, of course, after their aborted trip. The chief credit for the speedy and efficient organization prior to their second take-off must go to the Regiment's Major W.H. Ewart-Jones who was on the spot.

The airborne task was accomplished successfully and the entire invasion was a complete success, the amphibious forces passing through the airborne men and linking up with the troops who had entered France via Normandy within one month of landing. The Regiment had lost just one of its members killed and the rest were withdrawn to Manduria in Italy on 9 September. There they carried out exercises with Wacos carrying bulldozers and other heavy equipment, which at first showed a tendency to fall through the floor until steel reinforcing sheets were fitted.

The Independent Squadron's next operation was as part of the occupation of Greece, codenamed Manna. It was mentioned in the Introduction that Hitler's decision to efface the embarrassment caused to the Axis powers by the British presence in Greece had resulted in a successful invasion of that country by German troops in April, 1941, and now it was apparent that they were about to release their hold on the country. The Allies therefore decided to occupy Athens as quickly as possible after the Germans had withdrawn from the city in order to bring supplies and relief to the Greek people and to maintain law and order in the vacuum which would be left by their departure. 2nd Independent Parachute Brigade Group and 23rd Armoured Brigade under General Scobie were given the task and on 8 September the airborne troops moved to a camp near San Pancrazio twenty miles east of Taranto, together with the American 51st Troop Carrier Wing.

The Germans did not, in fact, withdraw from Athens until October and the first Allied contingent to land in Greece on the 12th of that month were the Pathfinders whose job it was to sweep a lane clear of any mines the Germans may have left behind, and mark it for the glider LZ. An abandoned airstrip on the outskirts of Megara, a small town ten miles from Athens, had been chosen for the airborne landings. The Pathfinders were followed the next day by four Wacos flown by members of 1st Independent Squadron, which were carrying bulldozers needed for levelling the LZ for the rest of the squadron's gliders. The Germans who had been in the area until recently had moved on by the time the four Wacos arrived, and as soon as the LZ was levelled a signal was sent to the main airborne force that all was ready to receive them.

The paratroops of 2nd Independent Parachute Brigade then arrived in the C-47s of the American Troop Carrier Wing, closely followed by the gliders, all of which landed without opposition, and, having carried out their allotted tasks, the glider pilots found billets for themselves near the airstrip. Their temporary quarters eventually became a kitting-out centre for recruits to the Greek army when it began to rebuild itself.

With the exit of the German army of occupation from the scene, a power struggle was soon in progress between Greek royalists and left-wing factions supported by ELAS guerillas, pending the election of a government and the new Greek army recruits were considered by the left wing to be a potential threat to their political aspirations. They therefore adopted the expedient of relieving them of their British-made rifles as they left the kitting-out centre. These troubles eventually erupted into civil war and the members of the

Regiment were forced to maintain a strict guard on their gliders against possible damage, while the British forces were finding it difficult to maintain some semblance of order. The arrival of 4th Indian Division in November, and 4th British Division in December, as well as a conciliatory visit by Winston Churchill, resulted in the election of Archbishop Damaskinos as Regent. This put an end to the civil war, at least temporarily.

The precautionary guard placed on the gliders drew dividends when, on 5 December, 1944, it was possible to lift them all, with the exception of one irreparably damaged on arrival, and fly them back to San Severo near Foggia, where the Squadron was told to stand by for operations in support of Eighth Army. Twenty-seven Horsas had been flown from Fairford to Chiampino in Italy, via Istres near Marseilles, during 9/10 October, 1944, under the codename Operation Molten (the glider pilots carrying out the ferrying operation under the command of Major J.F. Lyne, returning to the UK later that month) and during the months following their return from Greece the members of the Independent Squadron were able to do a certain amount of flying on the Horsas. Some even managed to carry out a conversion course on an American Fairchild C61K four-seater high-wing monoplane. This powered aircraft was designed for cargo and troop-carrying, with a loading space 38 feet long, 8 feet wide and 8 feet high. It had a payload of 14,700 lbs and could accommodate forty-two troops or thirty-six stretchers.

No further operations were, in fact, carried out by the Independent Squadron, but it was to be June, 1945, before its 101 members arrived back in the UK, together with the rest of 2nd Independent Parachute Brigade Group.

9. a & b. Horsas showing full-flap dive approach.

10. Formation landing by Horsas, Brize Norton, 1943.

11. Tank-carrying Hamilcar showing the amount of space.

12. Halifax towing Hamilcar.

13. Airborne forces waiting for take-off in North Africa before the invasion of Sicily. The glider in the background is a Hadrian.

14. The Primosole Bridge, Sicily, 16 July, 1943.

15. S/Sgt Galpin's Horsa close to the Primosole Bridge, Sicily, 16 July, 1943.

# VI

## REORGANIZATION

AN INTRODUCTION to 1st Independent Squadron was made in the preceding Chapter and we have followed their activities right through. But we now rejoin Colonel Chatterton in England in August, 1943, where, soon after returning from North Africa, he obtained an interview with the then Director of Training at the Air Ministry, Air Chief Marshal Sir Peter Drummond, who was fortuitously an old friend of pre-war days. The ACM showed him a cable which had been dispatched to the Air Ministry and was worded: 'Give every assistance to Col George Chatterton, US Air Force. Make available a number of lectures and follow the advice of this officer on glider operations. Signed, Wigglesworth, Air Commodore for Gen Dwight Eisenhower.' The Director of Training wanted to know what Chatterton was doing as a Colonel in the US Air Force, but nevertheless he had got the message and promised that every assistance would be forthcoming.

Henceforth an entirely new attitude towards the Regiment began to be fostered just when it was needed. A further indication that the Regiment had 'arrived' had been manifested in the formation of the Regimental Association on 20 July, 1943, with the stated object of 'Promoting the welfare of all ranks of the Regiment, past and present, and their dependents, and enabling all ranks to maintain contact during post-war years by means of reunions and social functions'. It is a remarkable fact that at the time of writing the Regimental Association membership roster contains the names of 800 ex-members of the Regiment. It has a splendid magazine, *The Eagle*, which is published every four months, and its members meet regularly at the annual dinner and many other functions arranged by its regional branches.

However, although things were beginning to move along the right lines, there was little indication in mid-1943 of the momentous part the Regiment was to play during the following few years of its country's history. No.1 Wing was not being used in an infantry role as No.2 Wing was shortly to be, but neither were its personnel getting much flying training. It was now established at Fargo Camp, from where it was necessary for the glider pilots to be taken to Netheravon by lorry for flying and lectures. On arrival they had to sign in at the guardroom before being permitted to go to the Glider Exercise Unit, and after a certain amount of flying and lectures they returned to Fargo Camp.

The Wing had managed to carry out an exercise on Salisbury Plain in September when eleven Whitleys had towed Horsas *en masse* to Shrewton, which was a rather feeble demonstration of glider tactics. Apart from the Sicily operations, (when the majority of the tug aircraft had been American), very little improvement had been made in the supply of tugs since the occasion of the first glider exercise of just over a year before, when nine Hotspurs had landed before the Prime Minister. However, as will be seen, the tug-aircraft strength was soon to be increased considerably.

One opportunity for some flying did emerge at this time. In August Eisenhower requested that twenty-five additional Horsas and ten Halifaxes be sent to the Middle East as an urgent measure, and the Chief-of-Staffs' Committee agreed at a meeting held on 9 August that this would be done. This new ferrying operation, given the codename Elaborate, was again carried out by 295 Squadron, and between 15 August and 23 September, 1943, a further fifteen Horsas were flown from Portreath to Sale and thence to Kairouan, again each carrying three pilots. Twenty-four had been despatched but eight of the tugs had been forced to cast off their gliders — five because of engine failure, two owing to adverse weather conditions, and one due to the combination being attacked by no less than twelve German JU88 aircraft. One combination had returned to Portreath after the Horsa became unserviceable.

One glider ditched in the Mediterranean forty miles from the north African coast, and all three glider pilots were picked up by a naval vessel. One glider and its tug ditched off the Spanish coast and both crews were picked up by a fishing vessel. Two gliders had landed in Portugal. One landed in the Bay of Biscay and the glider pilots were picked up by an Air Sea Rescue vessel. One glider landed in Spain. The Horsa involved in the attack by the Ju88s had been fired upon by one of them, but the pilots were eventually picked up by a naval vessel after being sighted by a Catalina aircraft. The crew of one glider were missing — the Regiment had lost three more of its members.

The crew of the Halifax embroiled with the Ju88s had immediately reported the glider's position to Portreath by radio and had then carried out a running fight with the hostile aircraft until managing to gain the protection of heavy cloud. One Ju88 was seen to have smoke coming from its port engine before it broke off the attack. The Halifax managed to get to Sale. The starboard outer oil pressure and the temperature gauges had dropped to zero, two tanks on the starboard side were leaking fuel, the rudder trim control was useless and the starboard fin and rudder, tailplane and elevator had all been damaged.

A letter sent from the Officer Commanding 38 Group (38 Wing became a Group on 19 October, 1943, after its establishment had been substantially increased by Halifaxes and Stirlings) to Major-General Browning dated 13 November, 1943, concerning the operation, contained the paragraph: 'I would like personally to add the admiration both I and all of 38 Group have for the glider pilots' courage and skill on these flights'.

One positive result of Chatterton's interview with Sir Peter Drummond was the provision of an office for him at 38 Group Headquarters, and the following entries in the Group's Operations Record Book give an indication that it was emerging as a powerful and active force:

> *11.12.43.* Authority was given by AM for staff officers of 38 Gp to visit the following airfields with a view to determining which would be suitable for use by 38 Gp sqdns — Aldermaston, Blakehill Farm, Brize Norton, Broadwell, Down Ampney, Fairford, Greenham Common, Isle Abbotts, Kingston Bagpuize, Membury, Ramsbury, Stoney Cross, Welford and Weston Zoyland.

> *30.12.43.* A conference was held at HQs, Allied Expeditionary Air Force to discuss the allocation of airfields to 38 Gp. The following was decided upon: 4 Albemarle sqdns to Aldermaston and Greenham Common; 4 Stirling sqdns to Fairford & Keevil; 1 Halifax sqdn to Tarrant Rushton. It was further decided that the following stations be allocated for Transport Command Dakota squadrons to be under the operational control of 38 Gp: Blakehill Farm; Broadwell and Down Ampney.

*1.1.44.* No.81 OTU transferred to 38 Gp.

*27.1.44.* Hampstead Norris visited and found to be suitable for use by ORTU.

*27.1.44.* Exercise Travesty carried out. Standard of glider flying was high; results suggest that area 400 x 500yds is not large enough for 24 Horsas to land in.

*6.2.44.* Exercise carried out. Navigation was poor and gliders were released in a somewhat haphazard manner. G.P.s generally made the best of the situation offered by poor towing and only one landed outside the L.Z.

*18.2.44.* Good concentration (of gliders) made. Successful parachute exercise carried out.

*10.3.44.* It was agreed at a Conference held at A.M. to discuss glider organization for 38 Gp:-

100 Horsas per airfield where 2 sqdns are based: 50 Horsas at Blakehill Farm: 50 Horsas at Tarrant: 140 Horsas at Netheravon as a reserve: 70 Hamilcars at Tarrant: 10 Hamilcars at Netheravon as a reserve.

Since the spring of 1943 the assemblage and storage of Horsa gliders had been proceeding at 24 RAF airfields throughout eastern England, and during March, 1944, these Horsas were flown by Dakota to the Group's operational squadrons. By that date these comprised No. 190 at Fairford with Stirlings; 196 at Tarrant Rushton with Stirlings; 295 at Harwell with Albemarles; 296 and 297 at Brize Norton with Albermarles; 299 at Keevil with Stirlings; 570 at Harwell with Albermarles; 620 at Fairford with Stirlings and 644 at Tarrant Rushton with Halifaxes. These nine squadrons would have a total of 180 aircraft and, in addition, the Group also had under its control the Transport Command Dakotas already mentioned which belonged to 46 Group: 48 Squadron at Down Ampney; 233 at Blakehill Farm; 271 at Down Ampney and Blakehill Farm; and 512 and 575 at Broadwell.

Chatterton had now adopted for himself the title 'Commander Glider Pilots', quite unofficially as there was no establishment for such an appointment. The minor circumstance that his office at 38 Group Headquarters formed part of a coal cellar was of no account as here he could gain access to 'authority', soon to be embodied in the person of Air Vice Marshal L.N. Hollinghurst who had just assumed command of the Group.

The 'Commander Glider Pilots' seized the first opportunity to obtain an interview with the AVM and set to work to convince him that there existed grave misconceptions as to the true status and value of glider pilots. He pointed out that until recently 100 members of No.2 Wing had been used in a variety of roles, none of which was remotely concerned with flying, under the command of 1st Airborne Division in Italy, whilst those still undergoing training in England were living on Salisbury Plain, also with little opportunity for flying.

'You know better than I,' he told the AVM, 'that your best aircrews are a team: pilots, navigators, gunners and engineers, understanding each other perfectly. Well sir, now you have two extra — the glider pilots on the end of a rope. These two must be part of the team and must live on the airfields.'

The AVM said he would give the matter thought, and the result was that the Regiment's personnel were soon living and messing with the RAF on the 38 and 46 Group stations.

Great credit should be given to the US Troop Carrier Command for arranging the despatch of the all-important telegram from North Africa following Colonel Chatterton's request for their support before leaving that Continent in August. It was due entirely to this one chance act that he was enabled to put into effect his resolve to do something about the unsatisfactory state of affairs which had befallen the Regiment and to set about laying the foundation for its future success.

Arrangements were made by Sir Peter Drummond for Chatterton to give a series of lectures to Planning Staffs of the army and RAF, and although a great deal of criticism was levelled at him by many hidebound military officers for the way in which he had bypassed the 'usual channels' his persistent refusal to modify his convictions about the way in which the Regiment should be developed eventually prevailed.

The invasion of Europe had now become an established goal and all available arms and equipment were being allocated to 6th Airborne Division for its role in that task. There was also a move afoot to place No.1 Wing under the direct command of 6th Airborne Division and No.2 Wing similarly under the direct command of 1st Airborne Division, but Chatterton was determined that the Regiment should remain an entity, independent of other command. He was now officially designated Commander Glider Pilots with the rank of full Colonel.

The Regiment soon had its own Headquarters Command structure at 38 Group Headquarters and had moved out of the coal cellar. The Commander had one staff officer, Major Peter Harding, who was responsible to a great extent for the subsequent complete reorganization of the Regiment. Chatterton also appointed an officer and two sergeants who were to be responsible for all air training and operations, and two officers for administration.

The third type of glider to be produced in large numbers in the UK was now beginning to make an appearance; this was the Hamilcar. It came from the drawing board of General Aircraft Company and was built at their Railway Carriage & Wagon Company factory at Birmingham. The design had been agreed early in 1941 and the first prototype had been flown on 27

March, 1942. It was the largest wooden aircraft built during the war, weighing 36,000lbs when fully loaded. It had a wingspan of 110 feet and a wing area of 1,657 square feet. Its length was 68 feet and the height of the cockpit from the ground was over 25 feet. The two pilots sat in tandem and were in telephone communication with their passengers and the tug crew.

The high nose door opened outwards giving access and more importantly egress for its cargo, which could weigh up to 17,500lbs — in effect a Tetrarch tank, or two Bren-gun carriers or scout cars, or a 25-pounder gun complete with motive power, or forty fully-armed troops. This was a formidable list which was continually being augmented, and special mention should be made of the works team from General Aircraft which was kept busy installing the many modifications found to be necessary to accommodate the variety of military loads which were conceived. After coming to a stop on landing, the oil pressure in the wheel-strut shock absorbers could be released, causing them to telescope and thus lowering the glider so that the load being carried could emerge without the need for ramps. If this proved to be impracticable during an opposed landing, in order to assist in the rapid deployment of the vehicle being carried, its engine was started up as the Hamilcar was coming in to land, the exhaust pipes being fitted with temporary extensions to the outside of the glider, which disengaged as the vehicle moved forward. The anchorages holding the vehicle in place were discarded by pulling on a lanyard, and the forward movement of the vehicle then operated a mechanical device which freed the nose door lock and automatically opened the door. The vehicle could therefore be in action seconds after the Hamilcar had landed.

Because of its size only the largest and most powerful aircraft could tow the Hamilcar, and the Halifax was to perform this function to perfection in the European theatre of operations. Taking into account its immensity and the remarkable fact that General Aircraft had manufactured it 'on spec' it handled well, and 412 were to be produced during the war. It was estimated that 153 Hamilcars would be required for the forthcoming invasion, to be used for the conveyance of bridging equipment and self-propelled Bofors guns. The composition of the loads was later to be revised.

As the date for the invasion of Europe approached, the role allotted to the 6th Airborne Division in that massive undertaking emerged. It was required to land on the Caen Canal and the river Orne on the left flank of 2nd British Army, which would be the extreme left flank of the entire invasion front, its task being to prevent the Germans reinforcing from the east their defending troops spread out along the Normandy coast. The Regiment's role in this task formed a vital part of it, and it was all too obvious that operational flying training would need to be stepped up drastically.

The Hamilcars, now arriving in a steady trickle, were based at Tarrant

Rushton, and the Hamilcar squadron was placed under the command of Major J.A. Dale, whose personnel consisted in the main of the glider pilots who had taken part in Beggar and Elaborate, in view of the fact that they had most flying hours. Training with the Hamilcars had begun in November, 1943, but owing to bad weather it did not really get under way until February, 1944, when during a four-week period 1,200 lifts were made, 400 of them at night. The task of flying a Halifax with a Hamilcar on tow was a daunting one; often the pilot had little more than 10 miles an hour margin of airspeed between flying and stalling, but the demanding programme was carried through assiduously.

Mass take-offs and landings were increased during April and the first air landing of tanks ever to take place in the British army also occurred during that month. The only unscheduled incident during this historic event was the too fast touch-down of one of the Hamilcars at about 110 miles per hour which caused it to bounce and crash into a group of Nissen huts, which disintegrated. As the glider came to a halt the tank continued onwards at about 80 miles an hour, and the tank driver appeared not to appreciate the fact that he was probably the fastest tank driver in history. The recommended landing speed at that time had, in fact, been set too high and it was later found that a slower one could safely be adopted. Many high-ranking officers and eminent civilians visited Tarrant Rushton to see the Hamilcars. Not the least of whom was General Eisenhower, who was suitably impressed when Captain F.C. Aston landed one at his feet.

At last the training of the Regiment began to make real progress, the army, RAF and glider pilots gaining confidence as they worked together. 1,500 British glider pilots were required to be ready to take part in the invasion of Europe, all adequately trained to land in the correct place in order that each 'load' could effectively carry out its allotted role in what was going to be a complex battle.

In order that the Regiment could meet its obligations the need was felt for a supply of second pilots. Some thirty to forty hours flying instruction were considered sufficient for them to become capable of taking over the controls of a glider under certain circumstances, and their recruitment and training proceeded apace. When the required standard had been reached the second pilot received a pair of wings (Second Glider Pilot Badge) of a different design from the first pilot's (Army Flying Badge), and he was given the rank of Sergeant compared to that of Staff Sergeant which all non-commissioned first pilots now held.

Early in 1944 some members of the Regiment were sent on detachment to the American Troop Carrier Command stationed in Nottinghamshire to convert the American glider pilots on to Horsas. The Americans also put in a request for 400 Horsas to be supplied to them.

In order to facilitate the landing of several hundred gliders at thirty-second intervals during the impending operation, as accurately as possible on to the target, a system was evolved whereby the gliders would follow each other down through a 'funnel', having first of all been manoeuvred into a long stream by the two RAF Groups. The object being to land the infantry battalions, tank squadrons, and other arms as a cohesive force, it was vitally important for the glider loads to be landed in tactical groups.

As it was impractical to make glider landings away from the training airfields because of the time and cost of retrieving them, aerial photographs of the airfields were used in this aspect of the training, various topographical features being superimposed on them. The photographs were then presented to the military commander of the particular exercise so that he could select how he wanted his forces disposed. The release height would then be agreed with the RAF and each glider pilot briefed as to the correct spot on which to land.

The loading and unloading had become a problem as the loads became more diverse. When the Horsa was first designed such loads as guns and jeeps had not been considered, as has been mentioned. Any difficulty experienced in unloading such items was overcome by placing a belt of 'Cordtex' explosive around the tail, but the consequences of activating such a device were sometimes not as intended. The tail was therefore made as a separate unit which was bolted to the main fuselage with eight bolts with quick-release nuts. A pair of powerful wire-cutters was carried to sever the control cables, and bulky loads could then be driven out of the rear of the fuselage down a ramp. This was not a method to be recommended during an opposed landing, however. The real answer lay in the Mark II Horsa which was produced later with a swing nose, but this was not to be available in time for 'D' Day.

During the period January to April, 1944, concurrently with their flying training, all the glider pilot squadrons were trained intensively on the ground in preparation for the battles which lay ahead. It was the intention that each squadron should be so equipped to be self-supporting under any conditions and able to fight as a completely independent unit or in co-operation with other forces. The pilots were also given courses in glider maintenance, and thereby became completely self-sufficient.

By 2 March the training had progressed to such an extent that it was possible to stage a large-scale mass landing at Welford airfield involving ninety-seven combinations. Only three gliders failed to arrive on the LZ, the remainder landing at ten-second intervals. This was quickly followed by a landing of 154 gliders in daylight and two flare-path landings of 135 and 150 gliders at night.

Then, on 24 April, a landing of the entire 6th Airborne Division was carried out by 38 and 46 Groups taking part in an exercise together with the American 9th Troop Carrier Command, 185 gliders being flown into Brize Norton and Harwell. Although those taking part had not realized it, this was a dress-rehearsal for D-Day — the Normandy landings. It was the first exercise in which No.2 Wing had taken part since returning from North Africa. Finally, moonlight landings of between 90 and 100 gliders were being made with complete success, one of them — exercise Dingo II — in spite of the fact that the RAF had set up the landing 'T' at 180 degrees from the direction in which the glider pilots had been briefed to land. This caused not a little consternation among the glider pilots, and no doubt to the assembled senior officers on the ground, when half the glider pilots stuck to their brief, while the other half considered it expedient to comply with the 'T'. The 100 gliders taking part were all landed without injury to anyone, albeit in diametrically opposite directions!

By the time the Regiment's intensive training was completed over 2,800 lifts had been made. Much credit for this superb effort is due to the RAF, in particular Group Captain Tom Cooper, and to Major K.J.S. Andrews the Regiment's Operations Officer stationed at 38 Group headquarters.

It was possible to carry out an impressive exercise, codenamed Exeter, in the presence of Their Majesties King George VI and Queen Elizabeth on 19 May when 100 Horsas, together with a number of Hamilcars, were towed by Halifaxes to Netheravon where they landed simultaneously with 300 paratroops dropped from Dakotas.

The extensive and protracted training which had been necessary to bring 38 and 46 Groups to their present state of efficiency made nonsense of the view which had been expressed on 22 August, 1941, that tug pilots could be trained for the role in two to three hours' flying time. How vital this training had been was to be demonstrated during the coming operations.

Everyone began to feel that at long last the Regiment had become well trained and ready for any task given it. No.2 Wing's personnel had been given refresher courses at a Heavy Glider Conversion Unit and both wings were now well organized and equipped. No.1 Wing, commanded by Lieutenant-Colonel Iain Murray, had four squadrons: 'A' at Harwell commanded by Major S.C. Griffith, 'B' at Brize Norton commanded by Major T.I.J. Toler, 'D' at Fairford commanded by Major J.F. Lyne, and 'G' at Fairford commanded by Major R.S. Croot. No.2 Wing, commanded by Lieutenant-Colonel John Place, had three squadrons: 'C' at Tarrant Rushton commanded by Major J.A. Dale, 'E' at Down Ampney commanded by Major B.H.P. Jackson, and 'F' at Broadwell and Blakehill Farm commanded by Major F.A.S. Murray.

Those eight airfields between them held fourteen operational RAF squadrons of 38 and 46 Groups, and another RAF squadron was based at the additional glider training airfields which had been set up, or were soon to be made available: Peplow and North Luffenham as HGCUs and Hampstead Norris as an Operational Refresher Training Unit. The total available airlift was 423 aircraft, and on the stations 1,040 Horsas and 80 Hamilcars, together with 1,500 glider pilots, were assembled. Much had been achieved over the past few months and the Regiment now had the full confidence of both the army and the RAF.

Three major ground exercises were carried out just before D-Day, which were designed to assist the wing commanders in taking up positions after landing in battle. One of these took place in the area bounded by the villages of Hinton, Buckland, Bampton and Aston in Oxfordshire, a location somewhat similar to the area near Ranville on the River Orne and the Caen Canal in Normandy.

As in the invasion of Sicily, the Airborne Forces were to spearhead the invasion of France. Squadron Leader Lawrence Wright, the RAF's 'Air 1 Gliders' who had been the inspiration and genius behind the military development of gliders from Ringway days, had had a lucky hunch that the Normandy coast from Caen to the Cotentin peninsula might be chosen as the invasion area. He had made a study of the terrain, which saved him at least a week's work when he eventually learnt that his guess had been correct.

The Airborne planning headquarters was situated at first in a secluded rectory at Milston near Netheravon and later at Netheravon itself and there it was that in the months before D-Day Wright plotted the glider approaches and LZs. There also the complex flight plans, embracing for each lift the assembling of aircraft from the eight airfields at rendezvous points, and their routing through flak and shipping lanes to release points, so that they arrived at the target at a rate of one every ten seconds, were worked out. The planning and reporting of all exercises and eventually the briefing material for fourteen RAF squadrons and the Regiment were also carried out there.

With the aid of a coloured film, which he took from a camera fixed to a travelling boom over a topographical model of the airborne invasion area, Lawrence Wright also simulated the run-in to the various LZs in Normandy from a pilot's point of view. It was so realistic that it was impossible to tell that it had not been taken from an aircraft, and it was shown by him at all the eight stations involved during the two days before D-Day. Wright had been an architect before the war, and was soon to become a Wing Commander, the rank he held when he eventually returned to his pre-war pursuits at the end of the war.

During the training build-up much experimental flying had been carried out at Farnborough with Beaufighter/Horsa and Spitfire/Hotspur combinations as well as a Horsa towed by two Miles Masters. Trials were also conducted in the use of 'the snatch'. This was an American technique which had been developed for the C-47/Waco combination whereby the glider could be lifted from the ground without the need for the C-47 to land. Two posts about twelve feet high were placed upright, just firmly enough in the ground to sustain the weight of the towrope which was looped between them and thence back to the nose of the glider. A shorter length of lesser diameter rope was used as a 'weak link' at the glider end as a safety device so that if the glider stuck in the ground the rope would break before undue strain was placed on the snatching aircraft. The tug aircraft carried a length of steel channel into which was slid the pick-up hook which was fitted at the end of a steel cable running back to a winch in the aircraft. This paid out the cable at a rate controlled by an adjustable brake. The aircraft flew over the parked glider at about 130 miles an hour and engaged the hook in the loop of towrope. The C-47 could snatch a weight of 8,000lbs which represented a loaded Waco or an unloaded Horsa. The Experimental Unit at Farnborough was soon snatching successively Hotspurs, Wacos, and finally Horsas with the Whitley. The experiments, which had begun in March, 1944, proved highly successful.

During this period, in the early part of May, a number of Horsas were found to have defective tail fins due to glue deterioration caused by long exposure to weather. An immediate scheme for repair was devised in co-operation with Airspeed. The production of their Oxford aircraft at Portsmouth was even suspended to release the necessary labour and 470 Horsas were restored to serviceability by 11 May.

For the marshalling and despatch of the 351 gliders which were to be sent off on D-Day all of 38 and 46 Groups' operational airfields were to be used. Much had been achieved in three and a half years; in late 1940 Haddenham's establishment had comprised a mere five Tiger Moths and five Kirby Kites. Recognition of the Regiment was specially conferred in the appointment of General Sir Alan Brooke, Chief of the Imperial General Staff, as its Colonel Commandant at this time. This was a source of special pride as it was unusual for such a young Regiment to be honoured in this way. The Regiment was paraded for the new Colonel Commandant at Brize Norton a few weeks before D-Day and the General specially remarked on the men's impressive bearing.

# VII

## OPERATION OVERLORD

THE DATE FOR THE INVASION of German-occupied Europe had been set for 5 June and the massive operation was given the codename Overlord. The Airborne Forces commitment was called Neptune and its object, as briefly stated in Chapter 6, was the seizure and defence of the ground forming the left flank of the assault bridgehead. General Gale's 6th Airborne Division had been given this task, while the 1st Airborne Division, now back from Italy, was to be held in reserve.

The Regiment's tasks were many and varied covering the period from 2220 hours on the 4th to 2100 hours on the 5th. The proper use of Airborne Forces had at last been grasped and was about to be applied by utilizing their ability to vault the formidable defences of Germany's West Wall to prepare the way for the seaborne forces.

Three waves of gliders would be needed during the night preceding the seaborne landings, the operation involving these three waves being given the

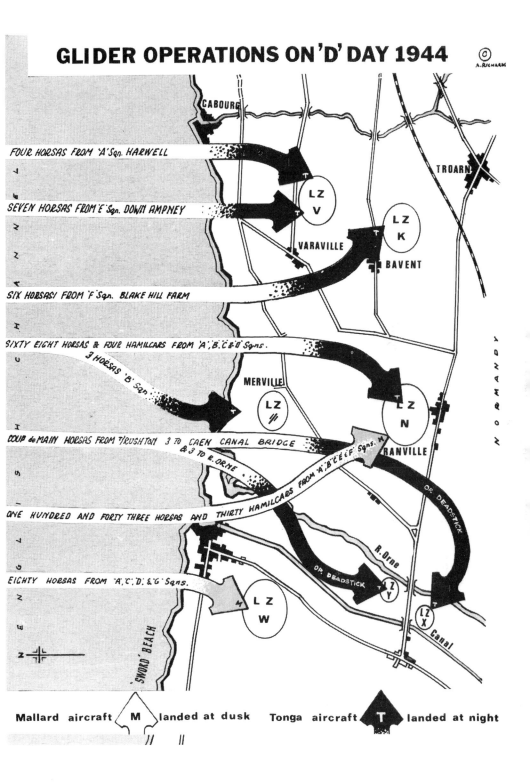

# GLIDER OPERATIONS ON 'D' DAY 1944

© A. Richards

Mallard aircraft M landed at dusk    Tonga aircraft T landed at night

codename Tonga. Another wave would be needed during the evening of D-Day for the largest airborne landings, and this was codenamed Mallard. Four main LZs were to be used: 'V' near Varaville, 'N' near Ranville, 'K' near Tonfreville, and 'W' on the west bank of the Caen Canal at Le Port.

Wave 1 of the night-time operations would involve six Horsas which were to land 138 men of 2nd Battalion, the Oxfordshire and Buckinghamshire Light Infantry, together with thirty Royal Engineers, under the command of Major R.J. Howard, as a *coupe de main* party on two other LZs, 'X' and 'Y', which were adjacent to the bridges over the River Orne and Caen Canal, six miles from the coast, at midnight. 38 Group Operational Order No. 501, covering this phase of the operation, was worded: 'Gliders are to finish their landing run as close to the bridges as is consistent with avoiding injury to the gliderborne troops'.

The bridges were to be captured and held. In order to ensure surprise the gliders would need to be released at 6,000 feet over the coast and, with only gyro-compasses and stop-watches added to the normal flying instruments to guide them, land in the darkness at the eastern end of the canal bridge and the western end of the river bridge, which was 400yds away. The Oxfordshire and Buckinghamshire Light Infantry were to be reinforced half an hour later by 7th Battalion, The Parachute Regiment which was to drop 1,000 yards from the Orne Bridge.

Wave 2, to arrive between 0026 and 0046 hours, would comprise seventeen Horsas which would be required to land on LZs 'K' and 'V' with 3rd Parachute Brigade Headquarters, elements of a Canadian parachute battalion, field ambulance units, anti-tank guns, and heavy weapons and equipment (Bangalore torpedoes and explosives, etc.) for the paratroops and sappers whose tasks would be: (i) the destruction of the Merville gun battery (see Wave 3), (ii) the seizure of ground east of the river and canal bridges, (iii) the clearing and protection of LZ 'N' for the gliders due in at 2100 hours, (iv) the destruction of four bridges over the River Dives to prevent the arrival of German reinforcements, and (v) the denial to the enemy of the use of roads leading into the Airborne area from the south and east.

Wave 3, comprising sixty-eight Horsas and four Hamilcars, would start to arrive at 0300 hours. They were to fly in Divisional Headquarters and Glider Pilot Wing Headquarters, elements of 6th Air Landing Brigade with their Brigade headquarters, and 17-pounder anti-tank guns and towing vehicles in the Hamilcars, all on to LZ 'N'. Three of the Horsas were to cast off over the coast at 5,000 feet and crash-land on to the Merville gun battery. This was sited in concrete emplacements 6 feet 6 ins thick, one and a half miles east of the River Orne estuary, and it would already be under attack by 9th Battalion, the Parachute Regiment, which had been dropped on LZ 'V' before the gliders arrived. The doors and curtains of the casemates enclosing the four guns, which were thought to be 150mm coastal guns, were of thick steel and as they had been built facing north-west towards the intended invasion area the battery was considered to constitute a real threat to the seaborne landings. The guns were defended by a 20mm dual-purpose gun which could be used to combat attacks from air or land, and six machine-guns, and it was surrounded by a cattle fence enclosing a mine field, anti-tank ditches, and thick barbed wire. The three gliders were to carry forty-seven volunteers from 9th Battalion, the Parachute Regiment, together with eight members of the Royal Engineers. Their arrival would be the culmination of the attack on the battery, which was aimed at silencing the guns well before the seaborne landings commenced. The battery was to be bombed by 100 Lancasters from 0030 hours to 0040 hours.

The daylight landings of Operation Mallard would be made on to LZs 'N' and 'W'. The gliders would land at 2100 hours and bring in the main body of 6th Air Landing Brigade. This comprised 1st Battalion, the Royal Ulster Rifles and 2nd Battalion, the Oxfordshire and Buckinghamshire Light Infantry, elements of 6th Air-Landing Brigade Headquarters, an Armoured Reconnaissance Regiment, 716 Company RASC, and Field Ambulance units on to LZ 'N' in 145 Horsas and thirty Hamilcars, and support weapons for 7th Battalion, the Parachute Regiment on to LZ 'W' in eighty-one Horsas. Production figures had not allowed the estimated requirement for 153 Hamilcars to be met, and the use to which those that were available was to be put had been altered to the conveyance of the 17-pounder guns and the Armoured Reconnaissance Regiment.

Training for the operation to be carried out at the River Orne and Caen Canal bridges started towards the end of April, eight glider crews being selected from various squadrons and posted to Brize Norton for the purpose. The training began with the Horsas, each loaded with 6,000 lbs of Bailey Bridging material, being towed by Albemarles to 6,000 feet, and descending in free flight on to marked areas. This was followed by the same exercises wearing dark glasses and landing by sodium flares. On 4 May the eight Horsas were towed to Netheravon where they carried out free flight glides of 6 miles from 6,000 feet on to a triangle marked out on the airfield with flags. The small force then moved to Tarrant Rushton where the training was continued, mostly at night, using Halifax tugs. The Albemarles would not have sufficient power to tow the fully loaded Horsas to 6,000 feet on the operation, and at Tarrant Rushton the glider pilots were teamed up with the Halifax crews who would tow them to France. The eight crews finally concentrated on night releases on to two 'fields' which had been created on the edge of Netheravon airfield to conform with those in Normandy, and the landing flares were gradually reduced in number until successful landings were being achieved with no ground lights at all.

On one of these practice flights one of the gliders hit a tree and both pilots were injured, putting them out of the operation. The last practice flight took place during the night of 30 May. A forty-five mile flight took them to a point six miles north of Netheravon where they released at 6,000 feet. Timing by stop watch and steering on a bearing of 187°, they descended in a long shallow glide to 50 feet when full flaps were applied and perfect landings made with only one flare on each field to guide them in.

For the Merville Battery attack a full-scale model of the Battery was constructed so that the paratroops could practice their attack, and the glider pilots could fly over and observe it.

It was mentioned earlier that General Browning had advocated the use of a pathfinder force in his summing-up of the Sicily invasion, and as they will be mentioned again in connection with the Regiment's activities a brief explanation may be opportune. The pathfinder concept had been developed at Netheravon and practised on exercises. The system was that specially trained paratroops would be dropped before the main bodies in order to choose LZs and DZs or to reconnoitre those already chosen, and guide the aircraft to within visual distance by means of the Rebecca/Eureka device. Lights fitted with holophane (adjustable) globes set out in the form of a 'T' would indicate landing position and direction. From this idea the 1st Independent Parachute Company had been formed, and the Regiment's Major Lander placed in command of it.

In April reconnaissance photographs had begun to show white dots covering much of the area encompassing the intended LZs in Normandy, and when subsequent photographs showed that each white dot was now accompanied by a shadow it became obvious that anti-glider poles had been erected at 35-yard intervals. Some concern was felt that the Germans had learnt where the invasion was to take place, until similar signs appeared all along the channel coast. But the appearance of the poles had caused the plans to be altered. The original intention had been to land the main glider force carrying the Air Landing Brigade in the dark during the night of the 4th/5th, but now it was obvious that sappers must be dropped to clear lanes between the poles for the use of the essential supply gliders which *had* to go in during the night, and that the main body of gliders would have to wait until 2100 hours, as has been stated, by which time the LZ would have been cleared.

Bad weather postponed the invasion for 24 hours. Conditions were very little better the following day, with thick, low cloud, but the vast assemblage was set in motion. The first element of the Airborne Force to go were the six gliders carrying the Oxfordshire and Buckinghamshire Light Infantry and Royal Engineers to the bridges, which became airborne between 2220 and 2235 hours. The entire area to be seized by the Airborne Division was on the east side of the river and canal, and the capture of the two bridges was vital in that they carried the only road linking the east side with the west, where the main assault force was to land. The Commander of 6th Airborne Division, General Sir Richard Gale, had decided that only gliders could achieve the necessary element of surprise and the concentration of troops needed to bring it off.

The operation required that the three gliders which were to attack the river bridge would have to shed their 6,000 feet as quickly as possible. They had less distance to fly than the other three, which would carry out a more orthodox approach following a longer route in order to avoid any possibility of collision between the two groups of three gliders. The 6,000-foot release for them all was necessary in order that the Germans would be deceived into thinking the aircraft were taking part in a bombing raid. In fact, once the gliders had cast off, their tugs were to go on to bomb Caen. The pilots heading for the river bridge therefore applied full flaps from the moment they were in free flight. This made navigation extremely difficult. Normally full flaps were not applied until the spot on which one had to land was in view, and then usually not until the final approach. A rapid 45° descent in darkness dropping at a rate of 2,000 feet per minute, and navigating on various courses in the process, required an immense amount of skill and nerve. The standard P.4 compass would have become unreliable at that steep angle of descent, so these three gliders had been fitted with gyro direction indicators. Staff Sergeant Roy Howard who was flying one of them, and whose glider was the last in the line-astern sequence in which they were flying, has stated that when the tug pilot's message came over the intercom, 'Good luck. Cast off when you like,' the thought struck him that whether he liked it or not was at that stage academic. However, he did so and reduced speed and applied full flaps but was unable to get his speed below 90 miles per hour even with the stick fully back. He was forced to the conclusion that the members of the Ox and Bucks he was carrying had possessed themselves of more than their quota of grenades and ammunition; the weight certainly appeared to be greater than had been allowed for. He shouted to the Officer in Charge of his passengers to send two men from the front to the back of the glider which was promptly done, correcting the glider's trim.

Nothing had yet been seen of the ground and they continued on a course of 212° for 90 seconds which covered the first two miles, and 268° for 2 minutes 30 seconds which covered a further 3.3 miles, followed by the final run-in at 212°. Howard's second pilot, Staff Sergeant Fred Baacke, had a light strapped to his hand in order to read the altimeter, map and stop-watch without interfering with his first pilot's night vision which, in the next few minutes, was going to be of vital importance for all of them. Suddenly, at a height of 1,200 feet, the canal and river were seen shining like silver, with the two bridges instantly recognizable from the elaborate sand-table model of the area which they had studied during training.

Howard raised the flaps for a moment to slow their headlong descent and to ensure he would be left with sufficient height. There was no margin for error now; if he overshot they would all be crushed by the weight as the glider hit the embankment at the end of his landing run. If he undershot he would hit the line of trees over which he had to scrape in order to get into his small field. He deployed the arrester parachute and rumbled to a stop a few minutes after midnight in exactly the correct spot.

One of the other gliders bound for the river bridge, flown by Staff Sergeant Stan Pearson with Staff Sergeant Len Guthrie acting as second pilot, landed in the field just behind Howard's glider. Pearson had also realized his glider was overloaded as soon as he was in free flight, which prevented him adopting the correct air speed. A long stream of orange flak came slowly up at them and then died away. At 4,000 feet it was obvious that, overloaded as they were, they would not reach the bridge by keeping to their planned compass courses, so they headed straight for the target area. At 3,000 feet flashes were to be seen on the ground from the direction of the canal bridge, and at 1,000 feet an inrush of air from the Horsa's doors which had been opened for a quick exit caused the glider to swing badly. They were now at tree-top height and Guthrie applied half and then full flaps, while Pearson touched down and, with the help of the parachute arrester gear, brought the glider to a stop after a run of only a few yards.

The third river bridge glider, flown by Staff Sergeants Lawrence and Shorter, had landed at a bridge over the River Dives seven miles away. It had been towed to the wrong cast-off point which the tug crew had incorrectly identified, but by a remarkable piece of airmanship the glider was landed safely in the dark. Having captured the Dives bridge the glider party fought their way back to the correct one and rejoined the defenders there.

All three gliders bound for the canal bridge finished their landing runs within yards of the target. Staff Sergeant Jimmy Wallwork and his second pilot, Staff Sergeant Ainsworth, were both thrown through the perspex nose of the leading glider as it was brought to a sudden stop by the nose burying itself in the barbed wire defences around the bridge. They could not have got much nearer to the target than that! Close behind them were the other two gliders which had also delivered their occupants in exactly the correct position. They had been flown by Staff Sergeants Hobbs and Boland and Staff Sergeants Barkway and Boyle.

All six gliders had been flown in such a masterly fashion during these unprecedented landings, resulting in all the assault troops and their equipment being landed intact, that it was possible for both bridges to be captured quickly, despite fierce resistance from the German defenders and for them to be held until the arrival of Lord Lovat and his Commandos at 1300 hours. The glider pilots' accomplishment was later described by Air Chief Marshal Sir Trafford Leigh-Mallory as 'one of the most outstanding flying achievements of the war'. The two bridges now bear the proud names of 'Pegasus Bridge' and 'Horsa Bridge'.

About ten minutes after the six gliders carrying the bridge parties became airborne, six Albemarles took off from Harwell with the Pathfinders who were to mark the LZs and DZs. Two sticks were to drop on each of 'K', 'N', and 'V'. All the aircraft reached the target area, but one of the two bound for 'K' dropped its Pathfinders on to 'N' where the wrongly-coded Eureka was set up, whilst both radio beacons for 'V' were damaged in the drop and were inoperative. Most of the remaining equipment was damaged in the drop, lost in the boggy ground, or dropped wide of the target.

The seventeen gliders of Wave 2 took off at approximately 2250 hours. Seven from 'E' Squadron and four from 'A' Squadron which were scheduled to land on 'V' (five of which were carrying the heavy equipment and explosives for the raid on the Merville Battery) were mostly unsuccessful. The weather was unfavourable with low cloud and bumpy conditions; as has been mentioned the Eureka beacons had not been set up, and a heavy bombing raid which had just taken place on the Battery had obscured the LZ in dust and smoke. Even so four of the gliders landed correctly, three others had been compelled to cast off over the French coast because of the cloud and two of them landed in the sea, two others landed on the wrong LZ, and the other two crashed, all the occupants being killed or badly injured. Of the other six gliders, which were from 'F' Squadron and bound for 'K' with heavy weapons for the 8th Parachute Battalion, only two reached the target, the others being misled by the wrongly-placed beacons. However, much of the equipment they carried was used in the fighting which followed. That *any* gliders landed successfully was remarkable under the circumstances, as the LZs had to be located without benefit of markers (the Pathfinders had been scheduled to set up the beacons and 'T' lights only some six minutes before the first of the gliders were due to arrive, which was somewhat marginal). The choice of LZ 'V' had been fraught with difficulties from the start. Because it was seen to have been completely covered with obstructions, Chatterton wanted it changed for a larger field 1,000 yards away, but his suggestion had not been accepted because of its distance from the Battery; there had been changes in orders at the 'E' Squadron briefings because of this.

LZ 'N' had also been prepared with anti-glider poles; however, most of these had been removed and landing flares put in position by the paratroops of 12th and 13th Parachute Battalions by the time the Horsas and Hamilcars of Wave 3 started to arrive at 0300 hours for the main glider landings that night. Two of the seventeen 'B' Squadron Horsas, eight of the thirty 'D' Squadron Horsas, and two of the 'C' Squadron Hamilcars did not arrive at the LZ because of broken tow-ropes and other difficulties, but the remainder were able to land along flare-paths laid out in strips 1,000 yards by 60 yards (with one strip 1,000 yards by 90 yards for the Hamilcars). These landings were also made difficult by the strong wind, and a few crashes occurred when some of the gliders were unable to find room for themselves through those poles which had not been dealt with, but all their loads were safely delivered. Major S.C. Griffith, the Sussex and Test cricketer, had flown the glider in which the Divisional Commander was conveyed, and he and other glider pilots formed a defensive position around General Gale's Headquarters, in which capacity they were soon engaged with enemy patrols and snipers. Not one of the glider pilots failed to take some part in the subsequent fighting. General Gale quickly established contact with 3rd and 5th Parachute Brigades and prepared for the battle ahead.

Two of the three gliders from 'B' Squadron which were to crash-land on the Merville Battery also arrived over the French coast at 0300 hours. Prior to the operation the three crews had been promised that they would have the best gliders available, fitted with parachute arrester gear and Rebecca/Eureka equipment. A few days before D Day they arrived – three gliders with parachute arrester gear and another three gliders with Rebecca/Eureka. Someone had blundered. Hectic efforts were made to obtain replacement gliders fitted with both devices, but these did not arrive until late on the day before take-off, and the crews had no time to test fly them. Two of the gliders appeared to be brand new, but the third was an old one and the pilots decided to draw lots to determine who should fly it. Staff Sergeant Baldwin drew the short straw. When he took off with the grossly overloaded glider, which was carrying thirty men and a flame-thrower, the tug only just managed to scrape over the airfield boundary.

Baldwin immediately discovered that it was only possible to control his charge by applying full right rudder, a circumstance which he was unable to convey to the tug pilot as the intercom was not working. Then the inevitable happened – they flew into cloud and the glider was so unstable that it was impossible for him to go into the low tow position and use the blind flying instrument. The glider soon became completely unmanageable and when they emerged from the cloud the tow rope broke, with the result that the glider was forced to land at Odiham, before they had even crossed the Channel. One can imagine the feelings (and language) of the pilots and passengers after the training and 'build-up' for the operation.

One of the other two gliders, flown by Staff Sergeant Kerr and Sergeant Walker, encountered more heavy cloud over the French coast, and the combination was forced down to 1,000 feet. This made the planned remote release an impossibility and the tug took the glider on to the Battery position. It was impossible to locate the target visually in the darkness and the tug pilot switched on his landing lights and, with great courage, made six runs across the area, both tug and glider receiving hits repeatedly during the process. Four of the troops in the glider were injured by the flak, and the glider eventually landed fifty yards from the Battery after the arrester parachute had caught in a tree.

The turbulent passage over the Channel had caused the third glider's arrester parachute to stream out, almost stalling the combination before the glider crew, Staff Sergeant Bone and Sergeant Dean, managed to release it. The tug pilot of this combination was also forced to descend to 1,000 feet over France, and he circled the Battery position four times with his landing lights on, as a result of which both tug and glider were hit by flak many times. The glider eventually landed 200 yards from the Battery and, although unable to take part in the assault, the paratroops and glider pilots were immediately met with machine-gun fire and engaged a German patrol hurrying to reinforce those defending it, preventing them from getting through.

As a result of the Pathfinders' equipment not being set up, the paratroops' aircraft bound for the Battery were unable accurately to fix the exact DZ so that the parachutists were widely scattered. This situation was worsened by the strong wind, and by 0300 hours only 150 of the 600 men dropped had reached the rendezvous. The dispersed drop also affected the two gliders in that much of the paratroops' equipment had gone astray, thus preventing the illumination of the Battery for the glider pilots by means of flares fired from mortars as intended.

The assault was carried out with outstanding bravery by the small body of men available for the task, and the garrison was quickly subdued, but because of the complete absence of the necessary explosives it was not possible to destroy the guns. However, as a result of the attack they were not brought into action until the afternoon of D-Day when their ineffective activities brought down onto them a backlash of fire from Allied warships. The casemates actually contained, not 150 mm coastal guns as reported by Intelligence, but Czech 37 or 40 mm guns of First World War vintage.

The stormy conditions which had caused such difficulties had also lulled the Germans into the conviction that no enemy activity could be expected in such bad weather, and their response was slow in coming. Not until 0600 hours were all German coastal units in Normandy placed on full alert, by which time the Allied seaborne forces were heading in towards them. By 0530 hours the Commander of 21st Panzer Division in Caen, growing tired of waiting for orders, had decided to move his Division against the airborne troops on the River Orne, but as he was about to move he did at last receive orders, which, luckily for the airborne troops, were contrary to his own intentions, and which resulted in the only Panzer Force in Normandy spending the remainder of D-Day redeploying. The Panzer reserves held near Paris were not told to start moving to Normandy until 1600 hours, and their movement was then made difficult by the actions of allied aircraft.

At 2100 hours 248 gliders from all squadrons of the Regiment engaged on Operation Mallard were flown into LZs 'N' and 'W'. 139 Horsas for 'N' were carrying 1st Battalion, the Royal Ulster Rifles, 2nd Battalion, the Oxfordshire and Buckinghamshire Light Infantry (less Major Howard's *coup de main* party), 716 Company RASC, elements of 6th Air-Landing Brigade Headquarters, and field ambulance units; a total of 3,200 troops together with their equipment and artillery. Twenty-nine Hamilcars for 'N' were carrying an armoured reconnaissance regiment. Eighty Horsas for 'W' were carrying heavy support weapons for 7th Parachute Battalion at the bridges. Thirty Hamilcars and 226 Horsas had taken off, but one of the Hamilcars ditched after being hit by flak, two of the Horsas had been shot down by flak and five forced to land prematurely owing to broken tow ropes.

Operation Mallard made history in that it was the first time an armoured formation had been flown a distance of 200 miles directly into battle.

By now the weather had improved, only a light wind was blowing and the clouds were well over 2,500 feet as this huge armada arrived.

As further airborne operations had been planned, it was intended that all the glider pilots taking part in the invasion should immediately be withdrawn to England and this was carried out the following day. Thirty-four members of the Regiment had lost their lives and many more had been injured, but the Regiment had successfully carried out 95% of its tasks.

By the end of D+2 6th Airborne Division was firmly established on the eastern bank of the River Orne, and it held that most important sector of the Allied front for several months against repeated German attacks aimed at threatening the left flank of the invasion forces.

# VIII

## AIR ARMADA INTO HOLLAND

DURING THE FOLLOWING three months sixteen major airborne operations were planned, only to be postponed and finally cancelled at the last minute owing to the rapid advance made by the Allies once they broke out from the invasion bridgehead. As a result members of the Regiment standing by for the next operation were continually on tenterhooks, but the circumstances were unavoidable as it was extremely difficult to time an airborne operation in conjunction with the fluid state of the battle.

These airborne operations included another landing into the D-Day perimeter to reinforce the American airborne troops who were being hard-pressed in the Cotentin Peninsula; a landing by 1st Airborne Division around an airfield south of Caen; 1st Air Landing Brigade to glide in by night and capture St Malo; a landing at Lannion; the blowing-up of a viaduct at Morlaix; landings at Vannes airfield, Chartres, on to the V-1 sites, the Seine bridges, astride the French/Belgian border, and in the island of Walcheren. Perhaps the most optimistic was Operation Comet. This presented 1st Airborne Division with the task of capturing, on its own, the bridges which, one week later, were attacked by three Airborne divisions. It would have involved a main glider landing at Nijmegen and *coup de main* glider landings on the bridges similar to those carried out on the River Orne and Caen Canal. In anticipation of the operation the Albemarle/Horsa combinations at Brize Norton were moved to Manston because of their limited range. 'Comet' was cancelled only four hours before take-off.

One minor operation did take place, however. Operation Dingson 35A involved ten Hadrians which were towed by Halifaxes of 644 and 298 Squadrons from Tarrant Rushton to Brittany. At the end of May eleven glider pilot crews had been taken off their D-Day training, formed into a Flight which was given the designation 'X' and placed under the command of Captain 'Peggy' Clarke. They were instructed to collect the required number of Waco/Hadrian gliders from American bases and fly them to Netheravon. The first pilots of the crews which had been chosen had all taken part in the Sicily invasion and were therefore familiar with the Wacos. They were told very little except that they would be taking part in a special operation, and an intensive flying programme was begun at Netheravon designed to enhance their knowledge of the American gliders.

On 7 June the Flight moved to Tarrant Rushton and continued their training with Halifax tugs. And then on the morning of 4 August Colonel Chatterton arrived at the airfield accompanied by ten jeeps crewed by thirty-five French SAS men. Each jeep had twin Vickers K machine guns mounted fore and aft, and the loads included a plentiful supply of sten guns, explosives, and a PIAT anti-tank weapon. The glider pilots were then briefed. They were to carry the French SAS troops 170 miles behind the German lines to Vannes in southern Brittany. The SAS were part of a force of 150 men from the 4th French Parachute Battalion which had already been dropped in the Vannes area with a vast amount of weapons and supplies from Stirlings of 299 and 196 Squadrons based at Keevil. The SAS were to join forces with 3,000 French resistance fighters of the Maquis.

The ten combinations took off from Tarrant Rushton at 2000 hours on 5 August for the LZ, which was a small field surrounded by orchards at St Helena about 10 miles from the town of Aurai. They were provided with an escort of thirty-two Spitfires which, shortly before reaching Brittany, would fly off to Brest to engage a squadron of German Focke-Wulf fighters stationed there.

The escort soon joined them and positioned themselves in four groups of eight to port, starboard, above and ahead of the combinations. The gliders and tugs flew across to France at 800 feet, and as they approached the North

Brittany coast they descended to 200 feet to avoid the German radar, and their fighter escort left them. No enemy opposition was encountered from any source as they crossed the Brittany peninsula, where the French population were to be seen waving flags and towels at them. Dusk was descending as they touched down and were greeted by members of the Maquis.

At about 2300 hours the glider pilots and their party of thirty-five SAS men set off in convoy with an escort provided by the Maquis. They travelled along dusty lanes avoiding main roads, with many stops at junctions where other members of the Maquis were stationed, and arrived at an inlet near the coast in the early hours of the morning. The SAS troops drove off into the night and the glider pilots were plied with red wine and strong French cigarettes.

With the arrival of dawn they were rowed across the water to some isolated farm buildings which turned out to be the headquarters of the local Maquis. This was their home for the remainder of their stay, and while there they had ample leisure to observe the SAS and Maquis at work. Whilst actively engaged cutting all rail, telephone and other links being utilized by the Germans, they were disposing of many of the enemy at the same time. The glider pilots were kept informed of the latest war news by a Special Operations Executive officer who was camped in a nearby wood with his radio.

The SAS took great pleasure in informing the glider pilots that the Germans had circulated posters offering 20,000 francs for their capture, dead or alive, and they were not too heartbroken eventually to be passed through the advancing American lines to Vannes and on to the Hotel de Paris at Rennes, which was the headquarters of British Intelligence. They arrived back at Netheravon by Dakota eleven days after leaving England. 'X' Flight was to do one more operation as such — Market — after which the survivors would be posted to 'C' Squadron to fly Hamilcars on the Rhine crossing.

During this period the notion that glider pilots should be provided from RAF sources was again in vogue at the Air Ministry. On 28 June, 1944, the Director of Operations ended a report to the Acting Chief of Air Staff with the recommendation that the policy should once again be changed in favour of RAF pilots on the grounds that 'the reintroduction of RAF glider pilots will undoubtedly make for more efficiency'.

On 22 July the Air Ministry was pointing out that the training of army glider pilots was absorbing 1,500 RAF personnel at a time when the RAF had a large surplus of trained pilots from which source they could guarantee to meet army requirements for glider pilots for the next two years. They considered that it was logical for replacement glider pilots to come from these surplus pilots, thus releasing the 1,500 men for other duties, provided the

RAF glider pilots were absorbed into the establishment of RAF airborne squadrons and not seconded to the Regiment.

Again on 28 August at an Air Ministry meeting called 'to discuss future policy regarding the provision of glider pilots and the somewhat anomalous position which had arisen between the army and the RAF', the unanimous view was that 'the primary role of a glider pilot was to fly a glider and that his participation in the land battle was secondary. It is therefore felt that *the higher efficiency of RAF glider-pilots combined with the great advantage of having an RAF glider-pilot/tug-pilot team* (authors italics) outweighed the known objection of the War Office to the disbandment of the Glider Pilot Regiment.' (It is not known who had been responsible for such a suggestion which caused the War Office to make known its objection.) The meeting affirmed: 'We are now in a position to recommend that the Air Ministry should assume responsibility for the future provision of glider-pilots.'

It was agreed, however, at yet another meeting, at which the Director Air, War Office, was present, that the question should be postponed for two months. It is interesting to speculate on the outcome of all this had not the Regiment, by force of circumstances, been required to ask for a proportion of the surplus RAF pilots before the expiration of the two months. It is to be understood from the Air Ministry's statement to the effect that they wished to assume responsibility for the future provision of glider pilots, that they intended to take command of the future organization. However, the RAF was, in fact, setting up its own glider pilot units in South-East Asia Command at this time, since they also had surplus pilots in that theatre readily available when the urgent need arose.

By September, 1944, forty-eight Allied divisions were advancing on a broad front from the west towards the Rhine, while the Russians were approaching Germany's eastern border. The success of the airborne operations in Normandy had encouraged Eisenhower to create a new Combined Headquarters to command all British and American Airborne Divisions. Lieutenant-General Lewis H. Brereton was placed in command of this 1st Allied Airborne Army, with Lieutenant-General 'Boy' Browning as his Deputy.

General Montgomery had been urging that the time was ripe for a rapid thrust to be made through Belgium and Holland and around the right flank of the Siegfried Line into Germany, and he decided to make use of this massive airborne force to pave the way for him. His intention was that it should secure a corridor fifty-five miles in extent in front of his ground forces along which they could race and cross the River Rhine. It was hoped the European war could then be finished that year.

The British 1st Airborne Division was now commanded by Major-General R.E. Urquhart, General Hopkinson having been killed in Italy by

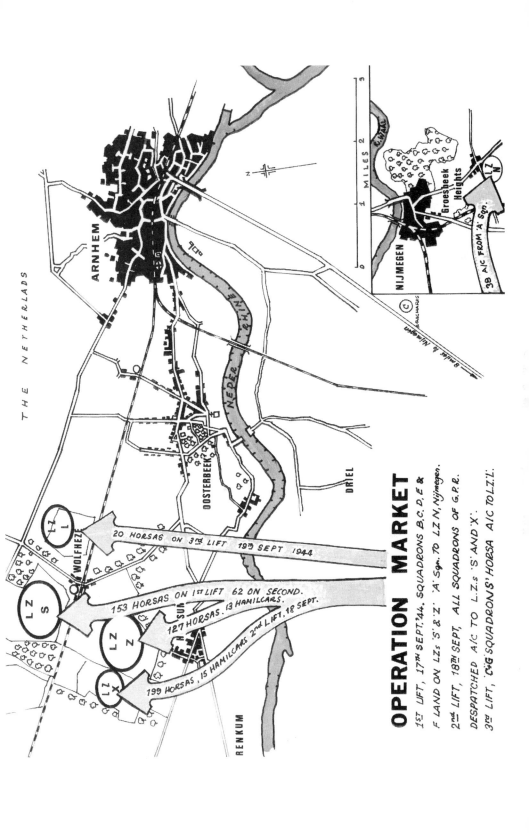

THE NETHERLADS

ARNHEM

OOSTERBEEK

DRIEL

WOLFHEZE

RENKUM

LZ
L

LZ
S

LZ
Z

LZ
X

20 HORSAS ON 3RD LIFT 19TH SEPT. 1944.

153 HORSAS ON 1ST LIFT 62 ON SECOND.

127 HORSAS, 13 HAMILCARS.

199 HORSAS, 15 HAMILCARS 2ND LIFT, 18 SEPT.

NEDER & RHINE

# OPERATION MARKET

1ST LIFT, 17TH SEPT. '44. SQUADRONS B. C. D. E &
F LAND ON LZs 'S' & 'Z'. 'A' Sqn. TO LZ N, Nijmegen.

2ND LIFT, 18TH SEPT, ALL SQUADRONS OF G.P.R.
DESPATCHED A/C TO L.Z.s 'S' AND 'X'.

3RD LIFT, 'C' & 'G' SQUADRONS' HORSA A/C TO L.Z.'L'.

N

NIJMEGEN

Groesbeek
Heights

LZ
N

38 A/C FROM 'A' Sqn.

R. WAAL

0    1    2    3
  MILES

8 miles to Nijmegen.

machine-gun fire while watching an engagement between 10th Parachute Battalion and German parachutists.

The Division was growing impatient with so many cancelled operations and it eagerly anticipated this one, which was given the codename Market Garden; 'Market' being the airborne involvement and 'Garden' the ground phase. It would involve three Airborne Divisions and a Polish Parachute Brigade: the American 101st was to seize a canal bridge at Son, and the route between Eindhoven and Grave; the American 82nd was to take the bridges over the Maas north of Grave and the Waal at Nijmegen; and the British 1st with the Polish Parachute Brigade would secure the bridge over the Lower Rhine at Arnhem. The plan also included the air-lifting of the British 52nd Division into the Arnhem area and the provision by the RAF of forward fighter support into the battle area in the form of Mosquito and Typhoon aircraft, once an airstrip had been prepared by D+8 and D+9.

It was decided that the operation would take place during daylight to obviate any possibility of a recurrence of the confusion caused by darkness in Sicily and Normandy. Because insufficient aircraft were available to carry the entire force involved in one lift it would be necessary for three lifts to be made over three consecutive days. The risks inherent in this were well known, primarily that the second and third lifts would not have the benefit of surprise, and the troops could not be concentrated at once for maximum effectiveness.

It was known that the enemy forces at Arnhem were formidable. The apparatus needed to read messages relayed on Germany's Cipher Machine 'E', or Enigma, which could produce messages in 'unbreakable' cipher, had been in the hands of British Secret Intelligence since August, 1939. This enabled them to decipher much of Germany's wireless signals traffic throughout the war, the information obtained being passed only to a very few. The most important information obtained in this way was given the codename 'Ultra', and the fact that we had access to this invaluable source of intelligence was kept secret throughout the war, and indeed until 1974.

One of the few occasions when 'Ultra' information was ignored now cropped up. It provided the information that 2nd SS Panzer Corps of two armoured divisions was refitting in the Arnhem area, and that the Commander of German Army Group 'B', Field-Marshal Model, had his headquarters at Oosterbeek on the outskirts of Arnhem. However, it would appear that it was decided nothing was going to interfere with the mounting of this operation. The Regiment's role was to take place primarily at Arnhem, and this narrative will therefore confine itself with that part of the operation.

The aircraft to tow the gliders were once again to be provided by the RAF squadrons which had been involved in 'Tonga' and 'Mallard', with the addition of 437(RCAF) Squadron which had recently been formed at

Blakehill Farm with Dakotas to augment the other airborne squadrons of 46 Group. 1,378 members of the Regiment would be needed to carry out the operation, and it was considered to be essential that they be used only in defensive roles once on the ground and withdrawn as soon as possible as this number represented 90% of the entire regimental strength. Heavy casualties were therefore to be avoided; quite apart from the fact that further airborne operations might be carried out in Europe, South-East Asia Command was in need of glider pilots.

At 1025 hours on 17 September, 186 pathfinders of 21st Independent Parachute Company took off from England in twelve Stirlings to mark the DZs and LZs. Between 0940 hours and 1140 hours, 304 Horsas, thirteen Hamilcars and four Hadrians were lifted from the operational glider airfields. The combinations were bound for LZs 'S' and 'Z', and the gliders were carrying Divisional Headquarters; 1st Air-Landing Brigade Headquarters; elements of 1st Battalion, the Border Regiment, 2nd Battalion, the South Staffordshire Regiment, and 7th Battalion, the King's Own Scottish Borderers; 1st Air-Landing Anti-tank Battery; 1st Air-Landing Light Regiment RA; 9th Field Company RE; 17-pounder anti-tank guns; heavy American radio equipment in the Hadrians; and Field Ambulance units.

Between 1120 hours and 1210 hours another thirty-two Horsas and six Hadrians took off from Harwell and Manston carrying 1st Airborne Corps Headquarters to Nijmegen, together with the Regiment's advanced Headquarters which included Colonel Chatterton, Major K.J.S. Andrews GSO2(ops), and Captain G. Rostworowski GSO3(int).

The weather over England was far from ideal with the cloud base ranged from 500 feet to 2,000 feet, and before the English coast was reached twenty-three gliders had parted from their tugs. All the occupants of one of these were killed when it crashed in a field near the village of Paulton in Somerset. The troops it carried were twenty-one members of 9th Field Company RE, the unit which had provided the men for the ill-fated Freshman operation. The loads of twenty-one of the other gliders were delivered to Arnhem on the second lift. Four other gliders ditched, two with broken tow ropes and two as a result of tug engine trouble, and two landed near Drunen in Holland, again because of tug engine failure.

Unfortunately the Horsas which broke loose over England included some of those carrying the Reconnaissance Squadron which was to have reconnoitred the route from the LZs into Arnhem. This was a serious loss; it was thought, when the operation was being planned, that heavy concentrations of anti-aircraft guns were sited at Arnhem itself and at Deelen airfield, and the DZs and LZs which had been selected were six to eight miles from the bridge, near Wolfheze, west of Oosterbeek.

Little anti-aircraft fire was encountered at the LZs, and the hostile fire met with on landing was fairly light. There were a few crashes, including two of the Hamilcars which overturned when their wheels dug into the soft earth resulting in all on board being killed.

The role of part of the force which arrived in this first lift was to seize and hold the DZs and LZs so that the subsequent lifts could land in safety, and despite the heavy mortaring and counter-attacks which soon developed, this was carried out. But the necessity for these men to be tied down in this way at the very beginning of the operation, when it was vital that maximum force should have been devoted to the assault on the bridge, undoubtedly helped the situation to become critical almost from the start. Only one unit managed to get through to the objective, 2nd Battalion, the Parachute Regiment, together with supporting arms and glider pilots, under the command of Lieutenant-Colonel Frost. This Battalion captured the bridge and held it with great gallantry for four days until its ammunition was exhausted and most of its members had been killed or wounded.

The exact number of glider pilots who arrived at the bridge to fight with the paratroops is not known, but one of the survivors, Sergeant Arthur Rigby, remembers twenty-one, all from 19 Flight of 'B' Squadron, and there could well have been more. Rigby acted as loader of the 6-pounder anti-tank gun which he had carried in his glider, while the official gun crew commander pumped shells into a pillbox strong-point on the northern end of the bridge, which was finally finished off with a flame-thrower. He then spent the remainder of that first night manning a Bren gun with his first pilot Staff Sergeant Healey, helping to repulse determined German attacks from the southern end and eastern side of the bridge. The glider pilots' numbers were mercilessly eroded during the defence of the bridge over the next few days.

330 gliders had been landed on or very near to the correct LZs on that first lift. The second lift was due to arrive at 1000 hours on the 18th, but all the airfields in England were fogbound and the aircraft were grounded for five hours. This delay also had an adverse effect on the early stages of the battle. 4th Parachute Brigade eventually dropped, followed by 275 Horsas, fifteen Hamilcars and four Hadrians which had taken off from the same airfields used the previous day. The combinations had managed to get airborne between 1043 hours and 1207 hours bound for LZs 'S' and 'X', and in the case of four of the Horsas, Nijmegen.

The loads consisted of more elements of the Air Landing Brigade and, in addition, 2nd Air Landing Anti-tank Battery, elements of 1st and 4th Parachute Brigades and 1st Polish Parachute Brigade. Eighteen Horsas and one Hamilcar failed to arrive because of broken tow-ropes, tug engine failure, and in two cases having been shot down by flak. Those that did get to the LZs encountered much congestion caused by the previous day's landings on

'S', and considerable damage was caused to gliders and loads as they manoeuvred to find a landing space. They had to contend also with a much heavier concentration of flak and small-arms fire, which caused many casualties.

It is worth recording the movements of one of the Horsas which landed successfully on this day: its first take-off had been from Tarrant Rushton at 1020 hours the previous day but the tug developed engine trouble which caused it to return to base. A second attempt behind a different tug at 1205 hours that day met with the same result, but they finally made it at the third attempt.

One of the gliders which had failed to reach Arnhem on this second lift had landed near s'Hertogenbosch, and the courage and resourcefulness of the Dutch people following this forced landing, and the two forced landings at Drunen on the previous day, typify the manner in which Allied soldiers and airmen escapers were looked after by the gallant Dutch people during the war. Within minutes of the two gliders landing near Drunen on the 17th local Dutch Resistance members had taken charge of the situation, and the crews and passengers, totalling thirty-four, were in hiding. For the next thirty-four days the Resistance played a 'cat and mouse' game with the German army, risking not only their own lives, but those of their families in concealing their British 'guests'. Circumstances forced the Dutch to move the Airborne officers and men frequently. Eventually the party was found shelter in part of a lunatic asylum, being joined by the occupants of a United States Army glider, making the total now forty-seven. As if this was not risky enough, German soldiers then occupied the ground floor of the asylum while their enemies were upstairs. This situation obtained for two days until the Resistance found safer quarters. Eventually the allied troops made their way to the village of Boxtel and safety.

Two of the passengers of the glider which landed in a field south-east of s'Hertogenbosch on the 18th were wounded and captured by the Germans. The other two passengers and the glider pilots separated and remained in hiding for several days. One of the glider pilots, Sergeant Dan Griffiths, eventually contacted a local farmer, and within minutes he was fitted out with civilian clothes and given a good meal. After nine days spent in the company of the farmer and his family a German gun battery moved into the farmyard and Griffiths was moved by the Dutch underground to the nearby town of Den-Dungen. There, to his great surprise, he was reunited with his first pilot, Staff Sergeant 'Skip' Evans, together with the two passengers from their glider and two Americans, one of whom was a Waco pilot, who were being looked after by the Dutch. As Den-Dungen was receiving a lot of attention from British guns the six of them were moved to safety into a sewer. When British forces eventually overran Den-Dungen the six men had been hidden by the Dutch, at very great risk to themselves, for the best part of six weeks. Den-Dungen served as a 'Safe Station' for evaders and escapers from 1941 to 1944 and, in addition, the townspeople hid many Jews. Drunen and Den-Dungen are just two of the unknown number of Dutch towns whose occupants, without thought for their own safety, assisted hundreds of Allied soldiers and airmen during the war.

The third lift to Arnhem comprised thirty-six Horsas which became airborne just after 1200 hours on the 19th bound for LZ 'L' with elements of the Polish Parachute Brigade, and seven Horsas and one Hamilcar which had not completed their journeys on the previous two days for various reasons and were now bound for LZ 'X'. The take-off had again been delayed, this time because of low cloud in England, and en route two of the Horsas were shot down by flak, eleven had broken tow-ropes, and two returned to base due to the tugs developing engine trouble. Those that did arrive found that the LZs were now in enemy hands, and heavy opposition was encountered. The gliders were subjected to ground fire before they were fully unloaded and many were burned out in groups by mortar fire.

The Polish Brigade's parachute drop, due to take place on the south bank of the river that day, was also postponed because of the weather and did not, in fact, take place until the 21st, when part of the Brigade managed to link up with the advancing 2nd Army tanks at Driel, Arnhem bridge by then being back in German hands. When the paratroops and glider pilots at the bridge had finally been eliminated the Division formed a perimeter with its base spreading for half a mile along the river and its sides extending northwards for a mile and a half encompassing the Arnhem suburb of Oosterbeek.

The original plan was that the glider pilots should initially remain with the loads they had carried and be responsible for the defence of both Divisional and Brigade Headquarters. As soon as the situation had stabilized they were to go into reserve until such time as they could be withdrawn completely from the action. It was realized, however, by the afternoon of the 19th, that this was an impossibility as they were all heavily engaged with the enemy. Some were holding various sectors of the perimeter while others were still with the gun crews they had carried. In that perimeter the glider pilots fought alongside the rest of the Division for the remainder of the action; one of them, Lieutenant M.D.K. Dauncey, with such outstanding gallantry that he was subsequently recommended for the Victoria Cross. The recommendation, submitted by Lieutenant-Colonel Iain Murray, was worded:

> During the action at Arnhem from Sept 20th to Sept 25th, 1944, Lieut
> Dauncey was in command of a party of men defending the guns of the
> Air/landing Light Regiment RA at Oosterbeek. The position was

16. Halifax tugs with Horsas and Hamilcars lined up for 'D'-Day at Tarrant Rushton.

17. Hamilcars and their Halifax tugs approaching the Normandy coast 'D'-Day, 6 June, 1944.

18. The three gliders at Pegasus Bridge, Orne canal, Normandy, taken on 'D'-Day after the midnight landing.

19. Colonel Chatterton welcoming back the 'D'-Day glider pilots, 9 June, 1944. *Left to right:* S/Sgts Lawrence, Howard, Guthrie, Shooter, Boyle and Pearson.

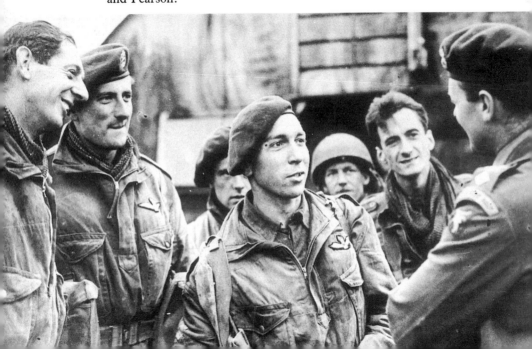

20. Glider pilots decorated at the Palace, 1944. S/Sgts Bruce Hobbs, Stan Pearson, Wally Herbert, Jim Wallwork (all DFMs) and Tommy Moore, MM.

21. Arnhem LZ — Horsas and Hamilcars, showing one just right of centre with tracks of its load clearly seen leading off towards the road and wood at top of picture.

22. After the Battle of Arnhem, POWs, including a glider pilot with arm in sling.

23. Major-General Roy Urquhart talking to glider pilots on their return from Arnhem. *Left to right:* S/Sgt J. Bonome, Sgts. D. Hartley and J. Woodward and S/Sgt Cawnter with S/Sgt Bowman at rear.

continually attacked by superior forces of enemy tanks and infantry. On three occasions the enemy over-ran the sector necessitating a counter-attack. Lieut Dauncey, on his own initiative, organized and led each sortie with such determination that the positions were regained with heavy loss to the enemy. In face of heavy small arms and mortar fire he personally attacked machine-gun posts, showing remarkable coolness and complete disregard for his own personal safety. During these attacks he was wounded on three occasions but refused to be evacuated from the area.

On Sept 24th a more determined attack was made by the enemy using tanks and S.P. guns. Lieut Dauncey, whilst leading his men in a further counter-attack, was wounded again — losing the sight of one eye. In spite of pain, and handicap of defective vision, he continued to lead his men in a fearless manner thus recapturing the lost ground and inflicting heavy loss to the enemy.

On Sept 25th the position was subjected to intense fire from an enemy S.P. gun. The houses were set on fire and an order was received to withdraw. By now no anti-tank weapons were available and there was an imminent danger of the enemy S.P. gun penetrating the gun positions. Realizing this fact, Lieut Dauncey, who had remained alone, assaulted the enemy vehicle single-handed with gammon bombs. By his action the critical situation was averted, but Lieut Dauncey received further injuries which resulted in his capture by the enemy.

The high morale of the men, who had been drawn from many units, was undoubtedly due to the fine example of this officer. Had the enemy broken through this sector, the gun positions would have become untenable and thus unable to support the Airborne Division.

Lieut Dauncey's indomitable courage, initiative, coolness, and selfless devotion to duty, in spite of his wounds, was in keeping with the highest traditions of the service.

The recommendation was supported by Colonel Chatterton and Generals Urquhart and Gale, but it finally resulted in the award of the Distinguished Service Order. Lieutenant Dauncey escaped from a prison hospital in December, 1944, and made his way to the British lines.

'Mike' Dauncey (now Brigadier M.D.K. Dauncey DSO Retd.) has recently supplied the following account of his activities, given in a characteristically restrained style:

'G' Squadron was based at RAF Fairford at the time of the operation. It was an exhilarating flight; we carried a group from The Light Regiment, RA and I was encouraged to see that an MC and an MM were worn by two of our passengers. Apart from seeing one Horsa down in the sea there were no mishaps on the flight. Alan Murdoch

[Staff Sergeant Murdoch − 'Mike' Dauncey's first pilot] made an excellent landing in the fields not far from the lunatic asylum. The gliders poured into the area without opposition, but it was sad to see a Hamilcar turn completely over on to its back, having burrowed into the soft earth on landing. The Gunners' vehicle and trailer were soon taken from the tail of our Horsa, which came off more easily than I had expected. Shortly afterwards we watched 1st Parachute Brigade drop − a marvellous sight.

On landing, our role was to act as close protection for The Light Regiment and I did this throughout the whole week of the battle. The Gunner Battery Commander decided that the Battery should stay near the landing zone for the night and the Glider Pilots dug in around them as a screen. That night I learnt two lessons, firstly that a Sten gun could be unreliable. I could not get mine to fire a shot during our first brush with the enemy. Secondly, how easy it is to be fooled, especially at night. The Germans pretended to be local Dutch people and when within range, dropped a grenade into one of our slit-trenches, wounding a Glider Pilot.

**Monday 18th September, 1944.** The Light Regiment and Glider Pilots set off for Oosterbeek church, approaching it from the west. The Dutch people were particularly welcoming and generous as regards gifts of fruit etc, and there was a carnival mood. Oosterbeek was a charming place, with well-kept houses, some old, some new, and a church which was built in about 1000 AD. The gardens were all immaculate with their flowers and fruit trees. Its destruction within the following week was something I will never forget.

We formed a line as local protection for the Gunners; not far away we could see the railway bridge over the river.

Three of us were sent off to pick up a German soldier, who was hiding in a house some two miles away; he proved to be a source of information.

In the early evening Staff Sergeant Cowthray arrived in great form; he had had to land south of the river, but had got his party with jeep and trailer over on the ferry.

We were in buoyant mood; the real battle had yet to start for us. However, the night was not so good, as we spent it lining the river bank in expectation of a night attack, which did not take place. It was not easy to keep awake all night.

**Tuesday 19th September 1944.** The Dutch underground made touch with Major Bob Croot, as a result of which the houses of the known German sympathizers were checked. They had all fled, leaving their framed photographs of Hitler behind.

In the afternoon disorganized groups of soldiers started appearing on the road from Arnhem. On arrival, they were formed into a defence line between the river and the road and soon got their form back. In fact, this was really the start of the perimeter where the final stages of the battle were fought. This was the first time that we realized that things were not going as well as we had expected.

In the early evening, a group of us, including 2 Lt Frank Derbyshire, Staff Sergeant Bill Mack and Sergeant Wild, were sent to seize the Oosterbeek Telephone Exchange, which was still being used by the enemy. It took quite a bit of finding, being about a mile from our positions. The building was unoccupied and locked so we had to shoot off the locks. It was rather eerie, as the place was full of rooms with telephone machinery all clicking away. Luckily, we found the main fuses, which stopped most of the exchange from working. At this stage, new orders came instructing us to destroy the Exchange, no easy task, and then to return to the Light Regiment.

About this time the Royal Air Force came in and were met with heavy flak. Major Croot told us to take over a small house overlooking the river meadows. It had been a German soldiers' billet and they had left much of their equipment behind.

**Wednesday 20th September, 1944.** The battle was beginning to come closer to us. We had been lucky to have had such an easy start and to gain experience by stages. There was some shelling that morning in the water meadows, the unfortunate cattle being the only casualties. I went down the road to Arnhem to find out the form. About ¼ mile from our house was part of a Para. Battalion, in very good order. They were in positions overlooking the railway bridge. The enemy launched an attack over the railway embankment across the water meadows. I had never seen a Vickers machine gun in action before, although I had been trained as an MMG Officer. It was devastating; the attack crumpled and those left were harried mercilessly as they tried to get back to safety behind the embankment.

That afternoon the Paratroops were withdrawn to our houses for a rest. We took over some houses in the northern part of our area, still with the task of protecting the Light Regiment. We were astride the Weversstraat road. On the right of the road were groups led by CSM Smith of the Paras, Lt Max Downing, Capt Mike Corrie and 2 Lt Frank Derbyshire. We were a mixed bag, but all got on well. I was on the left of the road. In my group were Staff Sergeant Halliday, Sergeant Wyatt, a South Staffords soldier and Paratroopers from different Battalions. The soldiers looked to the Glider Pilots to lead, which was a compliment to us. The Paras quickly named Major Croot the 'mad major'. It must have been he who organized this deployment which proved itself during the final days of the battle. Had it not held, the Division could have been cut off from the river. Later that day we patrolled forward until meeting a group of the enemy, complete with a self-propelled gun. There was a short sharp contact, then both sides withdrew.

That evening we dug in, in the garden of our house. Being on a slight bend in the road there was a good view covering the crossroads to our north, as well as being able to link up across the road with CSM Smith. Incidentally, that night we found a delicious cake in our house, which we ate with much relish.

**Thursday 21st September, 1944.** Somehow I kept awake during the night and in the morning liaised with CSM Smith. We were in the two most northerly houses. Then occurred my first piece of good luck, which did not desert me throughout the week. The CSM was in his slit-trench and had warned me of enemy marksmen. The latter put a neat shot through my red beret, just enough to cut the scalp. Blood came over my face. 'This must be it.' I thought. I lay very still for about 10 seconds, warned the CSM that I was coming to his slit-trench and just managed to beat the enemy's second shot. I had now learnt another lesson. The Germans were on the higher ground, so it was better to be in the upper floors in houses against their infantry. However, the slit-trenches were useful against their tanks and SP guns, so we had both.

The battle had now begun for us and later that morning two soldiers were hit. During the afternoon there was shelling followed by their first proper attack on our position. It was seen off, but two more of our chaps were hit. A spent bullet hit one soldier, lodging in his forearm. We all tended to laugh, but quite rightly he was annoyed with us — it must have been painful. I was lucky again, a bullet hit the fleshy part of my nose.

To the right of our positions we heard that an SP had been knocked out by a PIAT anti-tank weapon. Unfortunately our PIAT was withdrawn (for Div HQ I was told). It left us vulnerable to enemy armour as the anti-tank gunners were behind us further down the road which led to Oosterbeek church.

**Friday 22nd September, 1944.** This morning we patrolled to our left to link up with another group of Glider Pilots. Unfortunately, we were too far apart and too few to maintain a constant link.

There were two enemy attacks on our position on this day. The first one was seen off, but on the second occasion an SP gun scored a direct hit on us at probably no more than 50 - 80 yards range. The effect was devastating. Sergeant Wyatt was killed instantly and about eight men were hit, either slightly or badly, one having a terrible wound at the top of his arm and shoulder. Major Bob Croot was with us at the time. Again we were lucky, both of us having only very slight cuts on the hand.

The remaining three or four soldiers in my group were sent to the Gunners for the night to enjoy a rest, another group of Glider Pilots taking on our task. Major Croot and I went to the Gunners' HQ. I suddenly realized how tired and hungry I was; we were each given a tin of cold baked beans which we ate in great spoonfuls – delicious. I think that we had had only some three or four properly prepared meals since our arrival. By now it was late, 11pm, and we enjoyed a proper sleep until 4am, which was marvellous.

**Saturday 23rd September, 1944.** Lt Max Downing had been killed in action going forward to engage the enemy, and 2nd Lt Frank Derbyshire was missing from a patrol, so we reformed and with some reinforcements (who had had a rest in the church, or the school hall) took up new positions on the Arnhem side of the Weversstraat road. Mike Corrie's group and mine were next to each other. We occupied the upper floors of adjacent houses, the one I was in having a distinctive brick design.

During the day enemy mortars and SP guns engaged our lines. When they were too close to us we went downstairs and behind the houses. However, the German infantry did not follow up their advantage.

By the early evening a group of the enemy had been pin-pointed in a house about 30 - 40 yards in front of our lines. So, supported by a little Bren-gun fire, two Paratroopers and I went out to get them. After throwing a grenade into their house and threatening them as to what would happen if they did not come out at once, eight sheepish Germans appeared, three of them wounded. We were so pleased with ourselves that the whole party marched straight across the open ground to our lines. This was too much for the enemy mortars. One bomb brought down the branches of a leafy tree 5 yds from us and we were all covered in leaves. Miraculously no one was seriously hurt except one German, but most of us had scratches. We also brought back a German machine gun and some Luger pistols. We were delighted with our unexpected success at this stage; it certainly boosted morale. The prisoners were handed over to Major Croot; sadly we never met again as, after Arnhem, he was killed in an aircraft accident en route to the war in the Far East. He was a wonderful commander, a fine shot and an able pilot.

**Sunday 24th September, 1944.** It had been a noisy night, with lots of shooting, and shouting of orders by the enemy, but nothing materialized.

In the morning the SPs, mortars and small arms continued their pressure on us and I had some little bits of a mortar bomb in my shoulder, but nothing to worry about. To get a better angle to spot an enemy marksman a South Stafford and I went a little way down the street near to the school. We went upstairs but after half an hour smoke started to fill the room so that we couldn't see. On investigating downstairs we found some chaps round a huge smoking fire in the school hall, on which was a large tin bath full of dead chickens being cooked!

In the afternoon, we were still looking for the enemy marksman. To get a different view I went to the top of the house to a little dormer window. Unfortunately, he spotted me first. The bullet hit a stove-pipe by my head and a splinter from the pipe struck me in the left eye, over which a dark red film spread, blinding me at once. A paratrooper tried to get the metal out of my eye with a couple of matches, but without success, so it had to be left. Things were fairly sticky that evening, in that the Germans put a proper attack down the Weversstraat road. At one time two tanks were level with us firing indiscriminately at everything. Fortunately, Captain Mike Corrie frightened them off by throwing two grenades at them, after which they withdrew. It was lucky for us that the enemy infantry had not kept closer to the tanks. However, later we found a dead German officer outside the house. He had been killed by a grenade so perhaps they were nearer than we had realized.

This was the day that a Paratrooper paid the Glider Pilot Regiment a real compliment, when he said how glad he was to be fighting with us. It was so simple – yet so sincere. For my part, the Airborne soldiers and Paratroops with me were outstanding; it was a real privilege and honour to fight with them. They never wavered nor complained and always put their friends first.

That night when things were quiet a Paratrooper helped me down to the Regimental Aid Post, which was the house of Mrs Kate ter Horst and her husband. The MO could not be found and the Medical Corporal did not have the equipment to get the metal out of my eye, so we returned to our house. As I was feeling tired I did not stay awake but had a good sleep, to try to get myself right for the following day. **Monday 25th September, 1944.** Things started up pretty early on the Monday morning, with the tanks coming down the road yet again. I felt that if they did not meet some opposition they would go right through. So a soldier and I, armed with our only gammon bomb (an anti-tank bomb, which I had never seen before) set off through the back gardens up the road, and settled down to wait for the tanks at the side of a house. We could hear them all too clearly. Eventually the first tank crept cautiously into view. I waited until it was level with me, then ran forward and let fly with the gammon bomb. The result was disappointing. The fuse must have been a long one as there was such a lengthy pause and I thought it was not going to work. Eventually there was a loud explosion and lots of dust, then silence. When the dust had settled, the tank looked very much as before. The gammon bomb had landed slightly short of the tank-tracks, but I think that the shock of the explosion had startled them.

As I only had a Luger pistol there was not much future in staying put so I made my way back to my house; my companion had disappeared. My house had been evacuated in my absence, but further down the road I joined four Airborne soldiers in a group of outbuildings. We quickly arranged a little ambush position and there was an exchange of hand grenades, but the enemy did not rush us. On the other side of the Weversstraat road the enemy infantry had broken through and were running down the road towards the church. We opened up with our Luger pistols and a Bren gun. I was then shot through the thigh and fell down. Two of the Airborne soldiers were very good. One dressed my leg while the other, though wounded in the face, kept a lookout. We found an empty slit-trench and got in. Almost immediately something came over the corner of the outhouse and landed about 3 feet to my left. I turned to see what it was and the stick grenade, which it turned out to be, exploded in my face.

The two paratroopers were excellent and put a shell-dressing over my mouth. I could think clearly, but felt very weak. They helped me to Mrs Kate ter Horst's house which was so full that I could not get inside. They left me near to the house, next to a dead soldier, and I went to sleep. The rain awakened me later and I pulled part of my neighbour's blanket over me. I couldn't get to the house so stayed where I was, until someone came outside and I was able to attract his attention.

Inside, the house was completely full of wounded, including the MO. However, a blanket on the floor was a luxury. My jaw had been broken in two places and it was difficult to speak. Any liquid I took resulted in some coming out through the hole in my chin, an amazing sight according to those who saw it.

The Padre and orderlies were extremely brave. Some of them went out to stop the enemy tanks from firing at the RAP; this no doubt saved many lives.

**Tuesday 26th September, 1944.** When I woke up I discovered that I had lost my own beret, so got a paratrooper's one instead. There was shouting. I realized that the enemy were with us. We were made to go outside. The first thing that happened to me was that a German soldier took my wristwatch. I tried to walk but could not keep up so finished our first journey on a stretcher. My mouth was beginning to swell and the medics gave me something to stop the infection.

After a couple of days I arrived at Appledorn Barracks. About 20 - 30 of us were put in an empty room and slept on the floor. The following day a German interpreter asked us to tell him the whereabouts of various senior Airborne officers; there was a deathly silence from us all. I found myself next to an English officer who had come all the way from Argentina to fight for us. I was sad not to have seen Lt Mike Bewley while in the barracks as, sadly, he died of his wounds.

Two days later Padre Pare came across me and as a result I was seen by a doctor, who had me transferred to a Dutch hospital in Appledorn, where the treatment was splendid. Later, six of us were put in an ambulance, and we discovered that we only had four good eyes between us. In fact we were being taken to the famous Eye Hospital in Utrecht, where we were treated marvellously. Later, I escaped with a major in the Black Watch and, with the help of the Dutch underground and friends, we got back to our own lines in early April, 1945.'

Other examples of the flexibility of members of the Regiment which were made evident during that time were the distinctive manner in which Lieutenant-Colonel Murray took command of 4th Parachute Brigade when Brigadier Hackett was seriously wounded, Major T.I.J. Toler taking over command of No.1 Wing and Staff Sergeant Tilley took command of 7th Battalion, the King's Own Scottish Borderers after all its officers had been killed or wounded.

The nine days during which the battle raged are summed up in the following extracts from the War Diary of the Regiment's No.2 Wing:

**17.9.44.** Flak very light and landing successful.

**18.9.44.** Landings were good. Flak much heavier and number of aircraft shot down.

**19.9.44.** 0930. Several Messerschmitt 109s carried out a 30 min strafe.

1600. 3rd lift carrying elements of 1 Polish Para Bde Gp arrive. Intense flak. The LZ too was under fire.

2030. The situation for the first time appeared a little difficult, and orders were issued for a fairly small perimeter to be held by the Div. (Then followed particulars of various positions around the perimeter which were to be held by glider pilots.)

**20.9.44.** 1000. A day during which enemy pressure greatly increased. During the morning 'F' Squadron were forced out of their wood by a much superior force of SS tps supported by S.P. guns. They retired with considerable losses to Div H.Q. Heavy pressure also forced us to relinquish our hold on the high ground at 689789.

**21.9.44.** 0330. The Div perimeter was contracted ... a day of continual attack in our sector. The enemy brought down an S.P. gun into the wood at approx 690788. In the afternoon 'F' Sqdn counter-attacked the infiltrating Germans in the wood and drove them back. Mortaring was severe and we had considerable casualties.

**22.9.44.** A message from the Brigadier: 'We're up agin it'. Heavy mortaring and shelling throughout the day but our posns. were held intact. Continued casualties caused our line to become dangerously thin.

**23.9.44.** Intense shelling and mortaring. Stocks of food and water very low. Many casualties.

**24.9.44.** In the afternoon a combination of shelling, mortaring, S.P. guns and a flame-throwing tank forced us to abandon the wood. The survivors took up posns. in the houses across the rd. covering the exits from the wood. No reinforcements could be obtained.

**25.9.44.** 1400. Bde O Gp Orders for the evacuation of the remnants of 1 Airborne Div across the river to the south bank were issued. 2100. 2 Wing vacated its positions in the houses and moved in small parties to the river bank, suffering considerable losses through shelling on the Common at 693786. The crossing was made under fire in assault boats.

As an example of the fundamental difference in the British and German characters, it is interesting to contrast the rather understated summing-up of the situation on the 22nd by one of the Brigadiers, with a German War Diary entry made on the same day. Sturmbannführer Sepp Krafft, SS Panzer Grenadiers, had apparently been criticized by, he wrote, 'people of importance', for keeping his forces at Oosterbeek between the British LZ/DZs and Arnhem, immediately after the first days landings instead of taking them back to defend Arnhem bridge when it had become apparent that this was the British objective. (In retrospect, of course, Krafft had made the right decision, and was probably instrumental in preventing reinforcements getting through to Frost.) However, *his* entry on the 22nd was worded:

There are occasions occurring every day when only a virile offensive spirit can lead to success. That is the opinion, often repeated, of our highest War Lord − the Führer − who calls to account any officer who shuns an enemy far superior to himself. Any commander who had led a Battalion of first-class tps. back to Arnhem, even if it had been intended to occupy the town and hold the bridge, should have been summarily court-martialled.

Later entries made by Krafft are worth noting:

**22.9.44.** The mortar platoon continues to have success in the heavy fighting. They are able to fire off fifty bombs a day due to a well-organized munition supply.

**25.9.44.** The concentrated British forces fight desperately and ferociously for every house and every position. Our attack has little success.

Repeated attempts to drop supplies to the beleaguered 1st Airborne Division had been made by Dakotas of 46 Group and Stirlings of 38 Group but owing to the complete failure of the divisional wireless from the outset the Division had been completely cut off. That the DZ for these supplies was in enemy hands was unknown to anyone not actually involved in the fighting. The much-needed ammunition and other stores, brought over with such gallantry in the unarmed, unarmoured Dakotas, therefore finished up in German hands.

Two instances which occurred on the 19th, the day when 'the situation for the first time appeared a little difficult', both insignificant in themselves relative to all that was happening during the nine days of the battle, obstinately refuse to join all the others mercifully long forgotten by the author. The first concerns a colleague from 'C' Squadron who was seen amongst a file of other glider pilots who were moving off to another part of the perimeter. He was accompanied by his inseparable Alsatian dog which had come across in his glider, but he had also possessed himself of a bicycle which was bearing his rifle and equipment. When asked why he had burdened himself with such a seemingly unnecessary item he replied, 'All this aggression is bad enough without the additional irritation of having to carry one's equipment on one's back.' Neither he nor his dog were seen by the author again. The second involves another member of 'C' Squadron with whom the author was conversing while standing on the 'safe' side of a tree. 'Lofty' was explaining that 2nd Army was sure to arrive that day because it was his 21st birthday. The very instant he had finished making this hopeful prophesy he was shot clean through the head.

The heavy fighting in which the two American Airborne Divisions were involved, and the failure of the Guards Armoured Division in the van of 2nd Army to break through to Arnhem has been detailed elsewhere. It has also been pointed out in other places that the members of the Regiment had proved beyond doubt once again that they were also 'total' soldiers. It is noted that General Gavin, the Commander of the 82nd American Airborne Division, was to say that because of their lack of military training *his* glider pilots were a liability to him once on the ground in spite of being eager to do the right thing.

While the remnants of the British 1st Airborne Division were withdrawing across the river members of the Regiment were chosen to act as guides, pointing the way, and such was their discipline that they remained throughout the night showing others the way to freedom. The Regiment had flown 4,500 men, 95 guns, 544 jeeps, and other vehicles, trailers and handcarts, across 200 miles of sea and enemy-occupied country, and delivered them sixty miles behind enemy lines, and although the operation has been referred to as a tragic but heroic disaster, the planning and execution of its initial stages was remarkable.

As we have seen above, the Regiment's Padre stayed behind with the wounded after the battle and many benefited from his kindness. He later escaped and went into hiding with a Dutch family, working with the Dutch Resistance, and eventually managed to return to England after cycling across half of Holland. Captain the Reverend G.A.F. Pare had also taken part in the Normandy landings and the Regiment was justly proud of him.

Many others also remained in hiding in the woods and farms, being cared for by the Dutch at great risk to themselves. These included the wounded Brigadier Lathbury and the more seriously wounded Brigadier Hackett who was hidden by the local population for four months and eventually managed to get to the British lines during the following winter. One mass escape across the river by those in hiding was made, but a second attempt at a mass escape was unsuccessful. Other escapes were achieved in piecemeal fashion during the weeks and months following.

The Division's Chief Medical Officer, Colonel Graeme Warrack, together with most of his medical staff, also stayed behind to care for the wounded. On 26 October the Germans decided to close down the emergency hospital which he had been running, and transfer the wounded to prisoner-of-war camps in Germany, so the good doctor decided that his task had been completed and hid for three days before making his escape. He eventually reached the British lines with Brigadier Hackett.

Many others who had been captured were taken initially to the Krone Wilhelm Barracks at Apeldoorn before being conveyed in grossly overloaded cattle trucks to Germany and Poland and several months of German 'hospitality'. Several escapes were made from this building, including one of brief duration by Staff Sergeants Clarke, Blanthorn and Eason, who got away with one collar-stud compass as their only navigational equipment. They managed to evade the considerable German presence in the area and slept that night in a woodman's hut. The following day they decided that it would be inadvisable to press on during daylight, but towards late afternoon their impatience got the better of them and they vacated the hut and took up position behind a brushwood screen designed as a deer-stalker's hide. Unfortunately this happened also to be the immediate destination of a German officer and NCO, complete with sporting guns, against which one collar-stud compass was not of much use.

Staff Sergeant Blanthorn's glider had been hit by flak during the third day's landings on to LZ 'L' and he was immediately embroiled in close fighting on landing and received a bullet in the leg. His subsequent incarceration was at Stalag VIIIC at Sagan in Poland where, in common with all the other glider pilot prisoners-of-war spread throughout eastern Europe, he spent the winter thinking of loved ones at home who, it often seemed, would never be seen again – and of food. (The writer speaks with feeling, since he was one of them.)

The Dutch Resistance movement had provided invaluable help during the fighting, for which fifty of them were to be executed, and a great deal of succour had been given to the wounded by Dutch civilians throughout the battle. These civilians had suffered several hundred casualties while the action had raged in and around their homes, only 150 of which remained undamaged. Worst of all, the entire 94,000 inhabitants of Arnhem were subjected to forcible evacuation by the Germans after the British had withdrawn.

In a letter to Colonel Chatterton dated 27 September, Major General Urquhart wrote: 'The glider-borne elements of the Division made possibly the best landing that has ever been achieved to date. The skill of the pilots was quite first-class, and all ranks appreciated the benefit of the good start given by the pilots to the operation. Very early on in the nine days of the battle it became more and more apparent that we had to call upon the glider pilots to the full. They played all kinds of parts but everything they were asked to do they did whole-heartedly. I'm afraid your losses were rather heavy.'

At the subsequent Regimental rollcall it was found that 229 members had been killed and 469 wounded or made prisoners-of-war. This appeared to be a death blow to the Regiment for the recruiting and necessary flying training of so many replacements looked like being an impossibility.

It must be asked, too, remarkable as Operation Market had been, and however much gallantry had been displayed during the action, what would have happened if Arnhem Bridge had been held and the entire Market Garden operation had ended in success. Would the Allies' entry into Germany along the narrow corridor opened up have been possible? The supply bases were 300 miles away in Normandy, so that circumstance alone would have prevented the vast ground forces from going far against any sort of opposition. As it was, Bomber Command was being called upon to fly motor-transport fuel to Brussels to supply the army's requirements (450,000 gallons had been flown in during one week). Would it have been better to have employed smaller forces in far more useful ways? An airborne brigade group, for example, to capture the terrain and islands around the Scheldt estuary and so free the approaches to Antwerp so urgently needed as a main supply base. This port was not opened to allied shipping until 28 November, at a cost of 40,000 casualties. Or to fly petrol and ammunition by glider to 2nd Army to keep it's armoured thrust going towards Antwerp? Had the thinking been too ambitious?

Three vital lessons in the employment of Airborne Forces had been learnt, however: the absolute necessity for a lightly-armed Airborne Division to be able to join up with conventional forces, with their heavy guns and tanks, before the enemy has been given time to muster his strength after the initial surprise; (the fact that this lesson had been learnt was given ample proof in the planning for the next operation); the need for the DZs and LZs to be as near as possible to the objective without the requirement to fight through miles of enemy-held country to get to it, and a theme which has been running throughout the pages of this book from the beginning, the absolute necessity for sufficient tug-aircraft to be made available to obviate the necessity for a large airborne force to arrive in battle piecemeal.

# IX

## OPERATION VARSITY

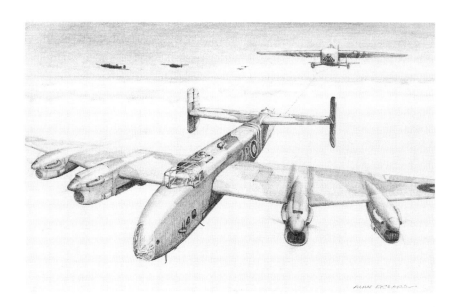

IT WAS NOT LONG before Chatterton was directed to attend a conference at the War Office. In the Chair was General Brereton, whose Airborne Army comprised 1st and 6th British and 82nd and 17th United States Airborne Divisions. This was an imposing force of 40,000 paratroops and Air-Landing troops with access to a fleet of aircraft belonging to the two RAF Groups and one United States Air Force Wing. (When the German General Student, first mentioned in the Introduction, had watched the arrival of part of the 'Market' forces from his headquarters in Holland where he was serving as Commander of the German 1st Parachute Army, he had remarked, 'What might I have accomplished if only I had such a force at my disposal!' Had he been aware of the forces now under the command of General Brereton he would have had even more cause for such thoughts.)

At the Conference the Commander Glider Pilots was told of the projected crossing of the Rhine. Two complete Airborne Divisions were to drop simultaneously on the east bank of the river at Hamminkeln, five or six miles

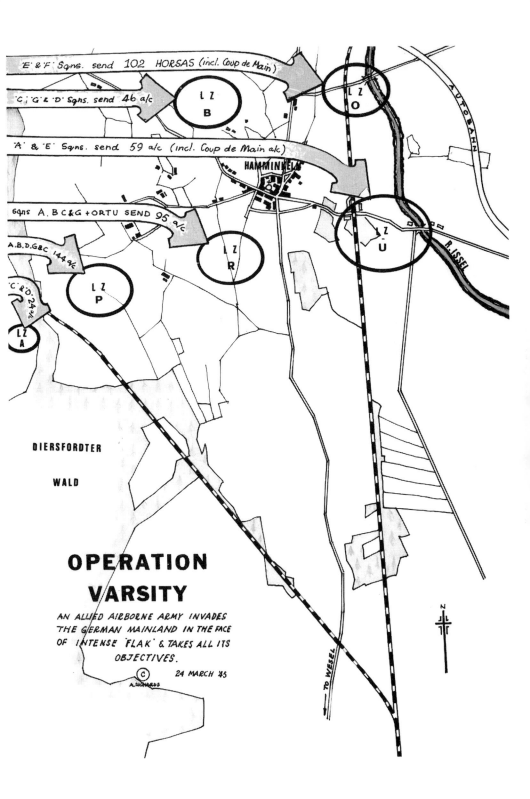

'E' & 'F' Sqns. send 102 HORSAS (incl. Coup de Main)

'C', 'G' & 'D' Sqns. send 46 a/c

L Z
B

L Z
O

'A' & 'E' Sqns. send 59 a/c (incl. Coup de Main a/c)

HAMMINKELN

Sqns A, B, C & G + ORTU SEND 95 a/c

L Z
U

L Z
R

A, B, D, G & C 144 a/c

L Z
P

R. ISSEL

AUTOBAHN

'C' & O. 24 a/c

L Z
A

DIERSFORDTER

WALD

# OPERATION
# VARSITY

AN ALLIED AIRBORNE ARMY INVADES
THE GERMAN MAINLAND IN THE FACE
OF INTENSE 'FLAK' & TAKES ALL ITS
OBJECTIVES.

© 24 MARCH '45
A.RICHARDS

TO WESEL

N

north of Wesel, whilst 21st Army Group were to assault across the river which at that point is over a quarter of a mile wide. The ground operation was given the codename 'Plunder', and the intention was to seize a bridgehead on the east bank five to ten miles wide and five miles deep so that 21st Army Group's bridging operations could be undertaken relatively unhindered by artillery fire.

The plan called for the largest single airborne lift ever made, and the Regiment was required to provide the pilots to fly 440 gliders. This was less than the total number flown for 'Market' on successive days, but the largest single lift then comprised 359 gliders out of the total of 697, and the Regimental strength had then been sufficient to meet that requirement. Clearly rapid improvisation was called for.

In view of the high losses suffered at Arnhem, and faced with insufficient time in which to replace them from army sources, the obvious and only course was to obtain the necessary pilots from the RAF reserve pool which the Air Ministry had been so anxious should be used for such a purpose. 1,500 of them were placed on the strength of the Regiment and were to remain so until 8 December, 1945.

The RAF pilots were given a fourteen-day course on small arms at Fargo Camp, and a week of assault courses and field training at Bridgnorth, followed by conversion courses on the Hotspur, Horsa and Hamilcar. Chatterton decided to match rank with rank; the Wings remained under the command of their army commanders, with Squadron Leaders as Seconds-in-Command, but the command of the Squadrons was divided equally between Majors and Squadron Leaders, and Flights between Captains and Flight Lieutenants. Individual crews were made up as far as possible of one army and one ex-RAF pilot. All this was necessary so that the RAF personnel should become versed in army methods. The vast armada of RAF and American aircraft required for the airborne operation, codenamed 'Varsity', was made ready; 546 for the paratroops and 1,346 for glider towing. As the Continental battlefield had by now moved 300 miles eastwards since D-Day the British airborne bases also moved the same way into East Anglia on to airfields occupied by the United States 9th Air Force until their departure to North-west Europe in late 1944. For this, which was to be the last airborne operation of the European war, 38 and 46 Groups were to be stretched to the full, and in order to provide the 440 aircraft needed, the strength of each squadron was increased by keeping tour-expired crews on duty. The fleet would comprise:-

| RAF Squadrons | Aircraft | Flying from |
|---|---|---|
| 295 and 570 | Stirlings | Rivenhall |
| 196 and 299 | Stirlings | Shepherds Grove |
| 190 and 620 | Stirlings | Great Dunmow |

| | | |
|---|---|---|
| 296 and 297 | Halifaxes | Earls Colne |
| 298 and 644 | Halifaxes | Woodbridge |
| 512, 575 and 271 | Dakotas | Gosfield |
| 233, 437 and 48 | Dakotas | Birch |
| ORTU | Stirlings | Matching |

These squadrons would be towing a total of 392 Horsas and 48 Hamilcars.

The airborne assault across the Rhine was to be made by 14,000 men of the British 6th and the American 17th Airborne Divisions, which together formed XVIII Airborne Corps. The American Corps Commander, General Matthew Ridgway, was making certain that, unlike Market, the entire force could be conveyed in one lift; they would at all times be within range of 21st Army Group's artillery; every essential unit would be landed before the enemy had time to assess the intention; and there would be no need to rely on resupply aircraft. The plan had also to ensure a rapid join-up with 21st Army Group. The planning had been considerably influenced by a German appreciation of the mistakes made at Arnhem. This document fell into Allied hands in December, 1944, and had been carefully studied.

The GOC 6th Airborne Division was now Major-General Eric Bols and he had decided that the gliders were to make tactical landings as opposed to mass landings. This concept had earlier been suggested by Chatterton, and entailed descending directly on top of the enemy at the spot required by the Commander concerned, from company level upwards, whilst fitting in with the overall plan. The new Mark II Horsas were a distinct advantage in the execution of this concept as the loads could roll straight out of the nose into action.

The airborne troops were required to capture the high ground forming the western edge of the Diersfordter Wald in order to neutralize the enemy troops and artillery positioned there, who would otherwise be able to cause havoc among the four divisions forming the assault forces on the ground. They were also to capture two road bridges and one rail bridge over the River Issel across which the main break-through into Germany would be made. The Regiment's task would be to land 6th Air Landing Brigade at Hamminkeln. This comprised 2nd Battalion, the Oxfordshire and Buckinghamshire Light Infantry; 1st Battalion, the Royal Ulster Rifles; 12th Battalion, the Devonshire Regiment; 53rd Light Regiment RA; 3rd and 4th Air Landing Anti-tank Batteries RA; the Airborne Armoured Reconnaissance Regiment; Royal Engineers and Field Ambulance Units. It was also required to land elements of 3rd and 5th Parachute Brigades within their DZs, and Divisional Headquarters east of the Diersfordter Wald.

One of the tasks given to the Air Landing Brigade was the capture of the Issel bridges, and their preparation for demolition in case their recapture by the enemy appeared certain. For this purpose fifteen gliders were to land with *coup de main* parties supplied from the Oxfordshire and Buckinghamshire Light Infantry and the Royal Ulster Rifles. Three of the Horsas making up this party, and 196 of the others, would be the new Mark II version.

Intelligence sources provided the information that none of the LZs contained anti-glider poles and that the ground was firm and level, but that within a twenty-mile radius of the assault area were ten German divisions, whose combined strength amounted to about 50,000 men together with 100 tanks and self-propelled guns. Defending the area around Wesel itself was the 1st Parachute Army reinforced by two infantry divisions – a force which included 7th Airborne Division which had captured Crete in 1941 – and 8,000 Volkssturm.

One week before the operation it was considered necessary for a rehearsal flight to be made in order to test navigational aids. On 17 March six Stirling/Horsa and Halifax/Horsa combinations from Great Dunmow and Earls Colne, and one Halifax/Hamilcar combination from Woodbridge, took off from Earls Colne ballasted with concrete, and made their way via Cap Gris Nez to the Rhine in the neighbourhood of Xanten. They were provided with a high-altitude escort of fighter aircraft, and the glider pilots were required to carry side-arms and fifty rounds of ammunition, parachutes and 'Mae Wests'. The combinations returned to the UK without incident, no flak or enemy fighter being encountered. How vital it was for this exercise to take place will never be revealed. It was codenamed 'Token' and one result of it was undoubtedly that the Germans were given fair warning that a large airborne operation was to be expected at any time, although this had obviously been guessed for some time in view of the massive build-up of forces on the west side of the river.

However, undaunted by what may be perceived with hindsight to have been a High-Command indiscretion, (but in the knowledge that Token is defined as a 'sign or symbol, evidence or indication'), 439 Horsas and Hamilcars of No. 1 Wing, led by Lieutenant-Colonel Iain Murray, took off in perfect flying conditions between 0600 hours and 0750 hours on 24 March, 1945, bound for the target. One tug had failed to take off because its undercarriage collapsed. At the same time 906 Waco gliders carrying the Americans were taking off from airfields in France. The British paratroops of 3rd and 5th Parachute Brigades flying from England in 243 aircraft, together with the American paratroops who were lifted from their French airfields in 303 aircraft, were conveyed by the American Troop Carrier Command.

General Brereton had made it plain that he required the German anti-aircraft defences in the area to be suppressed before his forces arrived, and the town of Wesel to be subjected to heavy bombardment. It was to be found that the anti-aircraft defences were very far from crushed, and that the residual dust caused by the bombing of Wesel, together with the smoke-screen put up by the ground assault forces to cover their river crossing, had resulted in a dense smoke haze. Many recognizable landmarks, and much of the target area, were obliterated when the air armada arrived.

Thirty-five gliders aborted during the flight for various reasons. The release height had been fixed at 2,500 feet but some arrived over the target at 3,500 feet and the subsequent descent from such a height made them more vulnerable.

At 1021 hours eight Horsas with the Ox and Bucks were timed to land on LZ 'O' to capture one of the two road bridges and the rail bridge, followed by fifty-eight Horsas with elements of the Air-Landing Brigade at 1023 hours. At 1022 hours seven Horsas were to arrive on LZ 'U' with elements of the Royal Ulster Rifles to capture the other road bridge, followed at 1028 hours by fifty-nine Horsas with further elements of the Brigade. At 1034 hours eighty-eight Horsas and six Hamilcars with Brigade Headquarters among their passengers were to release on to LZ 'R'. At 1035 hours one hundred and sixteen Horsas and twenty-eight Hamilcars were to arrive at LZ 'P', and their loads would include 6th Airborne Division Headquarters. 1057 hours would see the arrival on to DZ 'A' of twenty Horsas and three Hamilcars. Also at 1057 hours thirty-five Horsas and eleven Hamilcars would descend on to DZ 'B'. This was the intention and it was carried out to a remarkable degree, although such concentrated numbers making virtually blind landings resulted in few reaching the six British LZ/DZs unscathed. Seventy-five per cent of the gliders were hit by flak or small-arms fire. Some disintegrated in midair while others went up in flames as the flak hit them.

Surmising that the mass landings carried out at Arnhem would again be used, the Germans had selected a disused airfield north-west of Hamminkeln as the one which would possibly be used for the main glider landings, and had concentrated large numbers of 88mm anti-aircraft guns there, but they were also entrenched all around the LZs and DZs in strength. One possible redeeming factor of the extremely hazy conditions over the target area was that it probably affected the accuracy of the German anti-aircraft gunners and in that respect prevented even higher casualties being inflicted on tugs and gliders.

The Hamilcars were also taking part in the tactical landings whilst carrying loads of eight tons, including much petrol and, because of their size, they presented easy targets. (In view of his remarks concerning the inadvisability of using gliders in direct assaults on the enemy, Colonel Rock would not have approved; in a report dated 9 December, 1940, he had affirmed that because of its landing speed the projected Hamilcar should only be landed on an airfield which would first of all have to be captured.)

Staff Sergeant 'Andy' Andrews, who was flying a Horsa, has stated:
If Arnhem had been one of my best landings, then this was one of my worst. With some difficulty due to a faulty tug engine we struggled across the North Sea and got over the target as number 100. The element of surprise was completely gone and there was very active German ack ack fire to greet us. Smoke obliterated the LZ and I had to pull off blind. Eventually I saw the canal running North to South and turned in approximately in the right direction. We had lost valuable height in free flight and the ack ack had damaged something. In any case the descent and the gliding speed were too fast. Until we got to 500 feet I couldn't see the ground and, when we did, there was no place to land. Flying straight ahead, I made for a small field but knew that at 250 feet I would have to go through some tall trees to get in. I got through the trees but the undercarriage was half off. The next thing I knew was that the Horsa II was disintegrating around me, and the tail detached itself to fly over the nose and land facing me. All seemed OK except for Colonel Carson, C.O. of the Royal Ulster Rifles, who was injured. We organized a successful defensive position astride the railway line.

Andrews was one of only six members of the Regiment who took part in, and survived, all four of the major airborne operations of the war; Squadron Sergeant-Major Lawrence Turnbull and Staff Sergeants Nigel Brown, Jimmy Wallwork, Bert Holt and Brian Taylor being the others. The Rhine crossing landing made by Lawrence 'Buck' Turnbull is also worth recording. He had cast off for his approach run when a Dakota flew across his front and the tow-rope, which was still attached to the tail of the aircraft, struck the glider's starboard aileron, ripping it off. The rope then wrapped itself around the underside of the Horsa's cockpit, smashing the perspex and ripping out the air-bottles, thereby making both brakes and flaps inoperative, and at the same time carrying away half of the control column. The Horsa was turned almost on to its back by the rope, but, displaying remarkable coolness, Turnbull managed to regain control by using what was left of the control column, and landed safely in his allotted place, going into action with the troops he had carried. For this outstanding feat he was awarded the Conspicuous Gallantry Medal, the only such decoration given to a soldier in World War II.

Altogether 4,844 troops, 342 jeeps, 348 trailers, 3 gun-trailers, 7 Locust tanks, 14 lorries, 2 bulldozers, 11 carriers, 19 x 5cwt cars, 59 light motorcycles, 127 heavy motorcycles, 68 bicycles, 20 field cycles, 378 panniers, 53 handcarts, 10 x 4.2″ mortars, 2 x 75mm guns, 50 x 6-pounder anti-tank guns, 12 x 17-pounder guns, and 2 x 25-pounder guns were delivered to the battlefield by the British gliders. Undoubtedly many lives had been saved in the fiercely opposed landings due to the use of the nose-swinging Mark II Horsa which speeded unloading.

The entire force involved in Varsity was landed in a space of sixty-three minutes, and although the planning had ensured that there would be no reliance on resupply drops, 239 Liberator aircraft dropped essential supplies within an hour of the landings taking place. Over 200 aircraft of RAF Fighter Command had accompanied the UK aircraft to the Rhine and 1,227 Thunderbolts and Mustangs of VIII USAAF carried out support sweeps over the battle area. No enemy fighter aircraft had put in an appearance during the course of the operation. Four of the tug aircraft had been shot down by anti-aircraft fire, three were missing, thirty-two had been damaged by flak and two had ditched in the Channel. Ninety-eight members of the Regiment had lost their lives, fifty-eight of whom were ex-RAF pilots. Many others had been wounded.

Further supply drops had been organized but were not required, for such was the complete success of the airborne operation that by 1300 hours on the 24th all objectives had been captured, and by 1000 hours on the day following the landings the link-up between the airborne forces and 21st Army Group was achieved in strength. Another innovation had been the employment by the Royal Air Force of two Forward Visual Control Posts which were flown in with the Division. As a result of their actions directing fighter support sixteen enemy tanks were knocked out by aircraft under their control.

The Regiment was withdrawn from the fighting as soon as circumstances permitted, and returned to the UK; it was never again to be used in its true role. The war in Europe was rapidly drawing to a close and the régime which had brought such immeasurable suffering to almost the entire world was reaping the whirlwind with a vengeance. Varsity had been a brilliant achievement and crowned the years of hard endeavour with a success which Colonel Rock and the other indefatigable pioneers of Ringway, Netheravon and the early GTSs of such a short time ago could never have imagined. All the hard lessons had been learned and the techniques perfected. The Regiment had been in the forefront of a victorious army, and had performed a vital part in its accomplishments.

A message from the GOC 6th Airborne Division to General Sir Alan Brooke dated 29 March, 1945, was worded, 'Feel sure you would like to know G.P.R. has done magnificent work for 6 Airborne Div. Their skill and bravery are spoken of by all'. To which the CIGS replied, 'Very grateful for your message. Please convey to G.P.R. my heartiest congratulations on their wonderful performance in operations connected with the crossing of the Rhine. The skill and bravery displayed by them in this magnificent action of airborne forces will pass down to history as one of the highlights amongst the deeds of valour of this war'.

Two further airborne operations were planned before the end of hostilities in Europe. One of them, codenamed 'Arena', was the largest ever projected and was cancelled at the last moment because of the rapid advance of the allied Land Forces. The plan was to drop 1st Allied Airborne Army in the Cassel – Fritzier – Hofgeismar area. The other was the seizure of airheads in front of Seventh US Army by 13th US Airborne Division in the vicinity of Bisingen and in the Cassel area.

In addition various situations were catered for in the event of a German surrender: 'Eclipse' covered the seizure of Berlin by 82nd and 101st U.S. Airborne Divisions; 'Jubilant' was aimed at the protection of Allied prisoners-of-war should the Germans get tough; 'Talisman' would have resulted in the capture of important areas generally. Provision was also made for the capture of the port of Kiel by airborne troops.

# X

## INDIA

THE RAISING OF 44th Indian Airborne Division which, it was stipulated, was to be ready for operations by November, 1944, had been decided during a visit to India by General Browning in September/October, 1943, and General E.E. Down from 1st Airborne Division had been placed in command with headquarters at Secunderabad. The Division was to comprise not only 150th Indian Parachute Brigade, the formation of which had been decided in 1941, but also 2nd Parachute Brigade from the Mediterranean, and an Air Landing Brigade to be formed in India. An Airborne Forces Depot was formed at Rawalpindi, and Hadrian gliders soon started to arrive at Chaklala where they were assembled by RAF personnel.

In January, 1944, the War Office was asked to supply eighty glider pilot crews for the Hadrians, but as the entire strength of the Regiment was fully committed in the planning for the Normandy invasion it was only possible at that time to send the thirty pilots already mentioned in Chapter 5. Headquarters, South-East Asia Command, (hereinafter referred to as SEAC) therefore asked Middle East Command for forty NCOs from the army who would be trained in India as second pilots. The Regiment's thirty members went to Ambala in East Punjab for a three-week refresher course on light powered aircraft, and the required forty NCOs from Middle East Command were soon on their way to India to start their training.

In August, 1944, the Glider Pilot detachment was designated 10 Independent Glider Pilot Squadron with an establishment of ten officers and one hundred and thirty-three NCOs, the extra manpower to be obtained from army units in India.

Vice Admiral Lord Louis Mountbatten, the Supreme Allied Commander, SEAC, was quick to foresee the requirement for a much greater glider pilot strength. He let it be known that 517 would be needed for forthcoming operations, reporting, 'Provision of glider-pilots is now a matter of real urgency and failure to provide may severely handicap our ability to exploit present favourable situation in Burma'. He was shortly to put it in writing that he would need two British/Indian Airborne Divisions in 1944/45 and three in 1945/46, and that 600 Horsas and 2,000 Hadrians were to reach India by the end of 1944 for operations being planned in SEAC.

In August, 1942, as we have already seen, the British Ministry of Aircraft Production had ordered Wacos from America, and all the operations already undertaken in the Far East in connection with Wingate's long-range patrols in Burma had been with those Wacos, flown by American glider pilots.

It was decided that the only way in which Mountbatten's demands could be met was by the conversion of RAF pilots as an interim measure until a sufficient number of army glider pilots was available. A conference was convened at Headquarters, Air Command, SEA, on 19 September to discuss gliders and glider pilot organization in that theatre of operations, and it was decided that two RAF Wings, numbers 343 and 344, would be formed comprising six squadrons, each with eighty Hadrians, later to be supplemented with Horsas and Hamilcars, and with Halifax and Dakota tugs. Four-fifths of the glider pilots would be RAF pilots who were surplus to requirements and the remaining one-fifth would be provided from the Regiment. Plans for the conversion of their pilots on to Hadrians were put in hand by the RAF immediately and on 22 September the Air Ministry informed Air Command, SEA, that two squadrons of Halifax Mark IIIs from 38 Group and six squadrons of Dakotas from 46 Group would shortly be on their way for the forthcoming planned operations.

The War Office made a tentative suggestion that the glider pilot organization in India should be an army one and that all senior posts should be filled by the Regiment, but the Air Council countered that the circumstances made this quite impossible because of the large commitment the RAF would have to make. They were also quick to point out that in any case their pilots had been given an assurance that after conversion on to gliders, they would remain in the RAF. They (the Air Council) stipulated that it was the intention that both Wings would be commanded by RAF Wing Commanders with Army Majors as seconds-in-command. Three of the six squadrons, which were to be numbered 668 to 673, would be commanded by RAF Squadron Leaders and three by Army Majors so that 'there will be a chain of RAF command which is essential in order to implement the promise we have given to RAF glider pilots that they will serve under their own officers'. It was the intention that the Army glider pilots would be evenly distributed throughout the six squadrons so that, as Headquarters, Air Command, SEA, put it, 'their considerable practical experience of glider operations is made available to us, and because of the fundamental necessity of providing RAF crews with trained leadership in the ground phase'.

The legal aspect re-emerged in a message on 26 November from Headquarters, Air Command, SEA, which affirmed, 'Army personnel in the Glider organization will be attached, not seconded, to the RAF and will be subject to RAF Act by virtue of Section 179 (a) of the Act.'

It was with difficulty that reinforcements from the Regiment were eventually moved to India. During the period when preparations were being made for 'Varsity' a tragic loss of life occurred on 5 December, 1944, when a Dakota from Northolt en route to India crashed near Usson in the Massif Central. Of the twenty members of the Regiment who were passengers in the aircraft only five survived. The second part of this particular draft arrived safely, but as their documents were in the aircraft which had crashed, it was some time before anyone in India took any notice of them.

Several Staff Sergeants from the original North African contingent had received commissions, and they manned selection boards set up to interview the volunteer glider pilots from the Army in India. Those selected were sent to RAF EFTSs at Ambala, Jodhpur and Begumpet, and on completing their initial training they were promoted to Sergeant and awarded the Second Glider Pilot Badge. On 9 November Chatterton was authorized to form the Regiment's number 3 Wing for service in India, so that it now had thirteen squadrons on its strength.

By 1 January, 1945, 343 Wing Headquarters was established at Fatehjang and 344 at Bikram, and it was decided that a group organization on the lines of 38 Group in the UK was necessary; 238 Group was therefore formed for airborne purposes and started preparing for the airborne participation in the recapture of Malaya.

668 Squadron had been formed at Calcutta, 669 at Basal, 670 at Fatehjang, and 671, 672 and 673 at Bikram. The squadrons were later to extend to Dhamial, Upper Topa, Chaklala, Belgaum, Kargi Road, Tilda and Lalaghat, and 470 RAF and army glider pilots were eventually converted onto Hadrians. 10 Independent Squadron was disbanded in March and all the Regiment's personnel from it transferred to 670 Squadron.

During the build-up it was realized that in the event of casualties occurring among the officers of the Divisional Air-Landing Brigade, it would be necessary for the glider pilots to take command of Indian troops, and they were therefore given a special six-week Platoon Commanders' course at Belgaum, one squadron at a time being posted there for that purpose. The Jungle Survival School at Marbleshwar and the RAF Mountain Centre near Srinagar in Kashmir taught other necessary skills.

Back in England the second Indian draft comprising two officers and twenty-two NCO's from the Army element of 'E' and 'F' Squadrons had begun to move out to India in January, 1945. At this time the strength of the Regiment in the UK was 1,906 1st and 2nd pilots, of which 949 were ex-RAF personnel. Five of the squadrons, based on 38 Group stations, and two based on 46 Group stations, formed the First Line under command of Headquarters 2 Wing; the remaining six squadrons formed the Second Line under Headquarters 1 Wing, and were based on the RAF Groups' Training stations and the Regimental Depot.

A meeting was held at the Air Ministry on 6 April, 1945, to consider the operational requirements of Airborne Forces for the remainder of the war with Germany and for all theatres thereafter. Without the knowledge that the European war would be over in one month's time it was decided that it was necessary to retain sufficient glider pilots in the UK to fly 700 Horsas and fifty Hamilcars; any surplus could be sent to SEAC to maintain the glider pilot strength there, as all the RAF glider crews in 343 and 344 Wings would be time-expired by September, 1946. SEAC's requirements for gliders were given as 4,000 Wacos and 540 Horsas, for which a sufficient number of tug-aircraft would be available once Rangoon had been captured, when the demand for air transport would be reduced. Operational requirements for gliders in SEAC were given as 800 Wacos and 100 Horsas for the regaining of Singapore by December, 1945; 1,100 Wacos and 150 Horsas for Bangkok by March, 1946; 600 Wacos and ninety Horsas for Sumatra by June, 1946, and 200 Wacos and thirty Horsas per month for opportunity targets.

On 6 May, 1945, an additional squadron, 'N', was formed as part of the Regiment's No. 1 Wing. The one hundred and one members of the 1st Independent Squadron were about to rejoin the Regiment's UK strength and one thousand crews would then be available in England.

After Varsity had taken place the CO of No. 2 Wing had told his Squadron Commanders that the likely requirements for SEAC made it necessary for members of the Wing immediately to start training on Hadrians at Keevil and Fairford. A syllabus was drawn up designed to give each crew twelve lifts (five hours' flying time) between 6 May and 1 July. In July all personnel for SEAC were concentrated into four squadrons, at Blakehill Farm and Fairford under Majors H.J. Bartlett, B. Murdoch, M.W.D. Priest, and

B.H.P. Jackson, and shortly after that the Regiment sent to SEAC 231 army glider pilots and 740 of their ex-RAF pilots.

44 Division had moved to Bilaspur in Central Provinces by then, which was then one of the worst malarial areas in India. However, five of its airfields were in the vicinity, including Chaklala where the advanced training of glider crews was to take place. The RAF glider pilots were also becoming proficient in military matters; to such an extent that Air Command, SEAC, reported to the Air Ministry: 'There is a danger that the army will retain them as Company and Section Leaders as was done with RAF liaison officers working with the Chindits' (Wingate's special forces in Burma). 'This will mean that instead of collecting glider pilots after having carried out their operation and returning them to base, they will be retained in the jungle, leading bodies of army personnel into the attack.'

However, the army was now in a position to satisfy the requirements for glider pilots from the Regiment and despatched the following cypher telegram to C-in-C India, 'RAF provides G.P.s as emergency measure only; this was necessary after Arnhem and G.P. organization in SEAC thus became an RAF organization with a small number Army G.P.s attached. Army crews now available and Army must concede A.M. request that their crews should gradually be released on phased programme. SEAC G.P. organization must therefore gradually become completely Army.'

A great deal of reporting and discussion had been in progress for some time concerning suitable gliders for the tropics to supplement the Waco/Hadrian. It had been decided at the end of 1943 to send out both Horsas and Hamilcars for trials, although doubt existed as to whether or not the tugs in current use were capable of towing these gliders under tropical conditions. Two Hamilcars and four Horsas were shipped out in early March, 1944, for trials to begin, and on 30 June Air Command SEAC, reported to the Air Ministry, 'Tests show neither Lancaster/Hamilcar nor Dakota/Horsa combinations suitable for this theatre. Lancaster/Horsa and Dakota/Hadrian suitable, but use of Dakota/Hadrian only recommended.'

The War Office asked for trials to be continued, as Horsas and Hamilcars were so much more suitable from a military point of view, and Halifax IIIs and Lancaster IIIs were provided from the UK. In January, 1945, it was reported that during these further trials the Halifax III/Horsa and Lancaster III/Horsa combinations had met all reasonable requirements, but both had put up a poor performance towing a Hamilcar.

It was agreed that work should be pressed forward to experiment with the fitting of two Mercury engines to the Hamilcar to assist the tug on take-off, and by March, 1945, a powered Hamilcar had flown unloaded and untowed, and trials were proceeding to see whether or not Halifax/loaded powered Hamilcar combinations were feasible. The tests resulted in the Mark 10

Hamilcar Air Freighter being developed, and at the time of the Japanese surrender the prototype powered Hamilcar was undergoing exhaustive tests in the hands of the Airborne Forces Experimental Establishment. Quantity production began and twenty-two of them were to be produced.

Horsa Mark II's soon began to arrive in India and were assembled at Kanchrapara near Calcutta, and the ferrying of these to the bases in Central Provinces began in August, 1945. The Command possessed 866 Hadrians by this time, that is until a cyclone which struck the area destroyed some sixty of them which were assembled on the airfields.

Then came the surrender of the Japanese in August, 1945. This resulted in 44th Indian Airborne Division being disbanded on 23 October, and between 24 October and 1 July, 1946, all six RAF squadrons suffered the same fate. It had been the intention that 6th Airborne Division would be sent to India as soon as possible, but this was now unnecessary; other duties would soon be found for it to fulfil.

All the glider pilots were concentrated at Rawalpindi and, when all the RAF glider pilots had been disposed of, two squadrons of army glider pilots were formed within 238 Wing at Chaklala. The members of the Regiment soon found themselves dispersed all over India — and grounded, to become involved in the task of repatriating ex-prisoner-of-war and tour-expired servicemen.

It did not take matters fiscal long to replace the supportive goodwill which had prevailed between USA and Great Britain throughout the hard years of war, and it was being pointed out on 19 September that, as a result of the end of the American Lend-Lease Scheme, the Wacos held in the UK and SEAC should be returned to America, or they might have to be paid for in dollars!

# XI

## THE RUN-DOWN OF THE REGIMENT

THE TWO REMAINING squadrons in India were soon themselves disbanded and a proportion of the pilots were posted to Palestine, soon to become embroiled in the unhappy situation which prevailed there.

Great Britain had been able to maintain a strategic presence in Palestine since the end of the First World War when the Ottoman Empire had been dismembered by the Allies and a Mandate to govern that particular part of it was presented to her. During that war Britain had promised the independence of all Arab-populated areas of the Ottoman Empire, which of course included Palestine, in return for Arab help against Turkey. In 1917 the Balfour Declaration viewed with favour the establishment in Palestine of a national home for the Jewish people, providing nothing should be done to prejudice the civil and religious rights of the existing non-Jewish communities living there.

These irreconcilable promises had been the cause of much bitterness as the

Jewish population in the Mandated Territory increased during the years between the wars. This situation rapidly approached flash-point as soon as hostilities in Europe ended in 1945, when the Jews who had managed to survive the Nazi holocaust were clamouring to be allowed to settle in what they had come to claim as their own country.

The British 6th Airborne Division was sent to Palestine early in 1946 in a strategic peace-keeping role in connection with Russia and the 'cold war', but following one particularly active day of Jewish violence directed against the British there, it found itself embroiled concurrently in a very different role. During a widespread and co-ordinated expression of hate against the British, and wearers of the Red Beret in particular, several hundred devices were exploded throughout the Mandated Territory with the intention of furthering the cause of Zionism.

The Regiment's 'A' and 'D' Squadrons, together with 1 Wing Headquarters and a detachment from 'G' Squadron, under the command of Lieutenant-Colonel J.F. Lyne, were sent to join 6th Airborne Division. The advance party left Rivenhall on 25 January, 1946, and established Headquarters at Qastina, 20 miles from Tel Aviv, and the main party sailed from Tilbury on RMS *Strathnaver* on 1 March, 1946, and disembarked at Port Said, going into transit camp at Tel-el-kebir, 50 miles north-east of Cairo. There they were joined by the pilots from India.

One Flight from 'G' Squadron moved to RAF Kabrit, half way between Suez and Ismailia, where they took charge of Horsas which had been shipped from the UK. These were assembled by the RAF before being flight tested and flown to Palestine. 'A' Squadron and the remainder of the 'G' Squadron detachment, commanded by Major F.C. Aston, went to RAF Qastina, and 'D' Squadron, commanded by Major A. Murdock, to RAF Aqir nearby. From these two bases the new duties for the Regiment were performed with self-discipline and patience under much provocation.

Qastina was one of three RAF Stations which were attacked by Jewish terrorist gangs on 25 February, 1946, when twenty-two aircraft were destroyed or severely damaged. Three further examples of the activities which were a continual part of everyday life for the Palestine garrison at this time will suffice to show just how difficult was their task. On 25 April that year seven members of the Parachute Regiment were shot dead by the Jewish Stern gang in Tel Aviv; on 22 July part of the King David Hotel in Jerusalem was blown up, killing ninety-one people, including twenty-eight British; and two off-duty Sergeants of the Parachute Regiment, Paice and Martin, were hanged in a eucalyptus grove near Nathana.

Lieutenant-Colonel R. Gaitley assumed command of the detachment later in 1956 and during October, the 'G' Squadron Flight previously stationed in the Canal Zone at Kabrit rejoined the other members of the Squadron at Qastina and the 'G' Squadron personnel were absorbed into 'A' Squadron.

During October and November a certain amount of flying was carried out with the Horsas, flying from Aqir behind Halifaxes and Dakotas, including three exercises with members of the Air Landing Brigade. A different role was undertaken during December and January, 1947, when members of the Regiment supported the Palestine Police who were conducting house to house searches at Tel Aviv and Petah Tiqva for Stern Gang terrorists. During January, 1947, there was another change of command, Lieutenant-Colonel F.A.S. Murray taking over.

Further flying from Aqir with the Horsas took place during May, June and July, 1947, ending with exercise 'Gilt' which was carried out on 23 July. This took the form of a demonstration provided for senior officers. Some members of the Regiment even managed to do some unofficial Auster flying from Aqir.

On 29 November, 1947, the United Nations voted in favour of the partition of Palestine into separate Jewish and Arab States, and Britain declared a policy of non-participation in this decision, having opposed such action throughout her Mandate. She therefore declared her intention to withdraw from Palestine by 1 August, 1948.

The Regiment's detachment had already started to return to England, Headquarters and 'D' Squadron arriving back in June, 1947. 'A' Squadron remained at Qastina as an independent unit under the command of Major Aston until it, too, returned to the UK at the end of December, 1947. But before 'A' Squadron left it was necessary for arrangements to be made for nine Horsas, still at Aqir, to be flown back to Kabrit in Egypt, and three Staff Sergeants were left behind to accomplish this task. The ferrying was completed on 31 December, only for the three glider pilots to learn that the Horsas were to be destroyed, possible by burning. They made their own individual ways back to the UK the following month and joined 'D' Squadron at Oakington.

Back in England the run-down of the Regiment had started to take effect. The first series of releases were effected from Finmere in Buckinghamshire in 1945-46, and it was from the newsletter *Age and Service* published there, which supplied details concerning the method whereby the order of release was assessed, that the magazine of the Regimental Association, *The Eagle*, was formed.

1946 also saw the closure of Tarrant Rushton as a glider station on 30 August (the gliders and crews being moved to Brize Norton), and the closure of the Regimental Depot at Fargo Camp in November. 'N' Squadron Headquarters had moved there in May to supervise the shut-down. A small

Headquarters, comprising three officers, twelve NCOs and six other ranks designated the Glider Pilot Depot Squadron, moved from Fargo to Aldershot to become part of the Airborne Forces Depot. The Depot Squadron continued to perform the normal Depot role formerly carried out at Fargo: volunteers for the Regiment were received there and trained for 6 weeks to the standard of Infantry Corporals, after which they were posted to EFTS. Also in 1946 the Regiment provided a squad to take part in the Victory Parade in London.

During June, 1947, 1 Wing Headquarters arrived at Aldershot from Palestine, and 'N' Squadron moved to Netheravon. By the end of 1947 the Regiment's strength had so diminished that it was down to two operational squadrons, 'D' at Oakington and Waterbeach and 'N' at Netheravon and Fairford, with Regimental Headquarters and Depot Squadron at Aldershot. Chatterton had been appointed Acting Brigadier on 17 April, 1945, and soon after retired from the army with the rank of Honorary Brigadier, and the Regiment was now commanded by Lieutenant-Colonel C.J. Deedes, MC. Many of the RAF Elementary Flying Training Schools had also been closed and all courses for potential glider pilots were confined to RAF Booker. In connection with future developments it is interesting to note that in addition to the Tiger Moths this airfield was now equipped with Auster light aircraft for training Air Observation Post pilots destined for the Air O.P. School at Middle Wallop. From EFTS at Booker the glider pilots were converted straight on to Horsa IIs at the Heavy Glider Conversion Unit, originally at Brize Norton but later at North Luffenham and Upper Heyford, and finally at Abingdon. In 1948 'D' and 'N' Squadrons were retitled 'A' and 'B'.

During this time two glider pilots were stationed at the Transport Command Development Unit at Brize Norton, later Abingdon. Since 1944 that unit had been perfecting the snatching technique referred to in Chapter 6, and regularly demonstrated it at displays, using a Dakota and a silver Hadrian. The glider pilots were often assisted in this by two Air OP pilots based there, and sometimes flew in the AOP Sikorsky Hoverfly helicopters.

This was not the first time the Regiment had been involved in experimental work, for two pilots had been working at Aero Airborne Flight of the Royal Aircraft Establishment from a very early date. They had assisted in a wide variety of trials, including multiple tows, rocket-assisted takeoff, and the introduction of the powered Hamilcar 10.

The Regiment's peacetime establishment was now reorganized to one of sixty crews, both pilots being first pilots. In April, 1948, 85 Flight from 'B' Squadron was moved to RAF Schleswigland in North Germany with six Horsas as part of an Airborne Brigade Group. Its task was to show the flag by generating such a level of activity as to give credence to the cover story that the formation was an Airborne Division. Two squadrons of Dakotas and

24. Hamilcars and Halifax tugs at R.A.F. Woodbridge for Operation 'Varsity' 24 March, 1945.

25. Crashed Horsa at Hamminkeln showing congested LZ behind.

26. Colonel G.J.S. Chatterton, DSO.   27. Lieutenant-Colonel J.F. Rock.

28. Brigadier M. Dauncey, DSO.   29. Lieutenant-Colonel Iain Murray, DS

30. S.S.M. L.W. Turnbull, CGM.

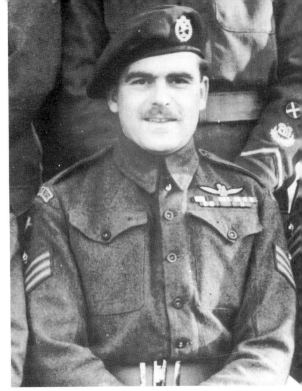

31. At the launching of the Glider Pilot Regimental Association, Savoy Hotel, 21 November, 1945. On the left is Staff Sergeant Alan Richards, DFM, whose drawings appear at each chapter opening in this book. He is talking to actor Michael Wilding. In the centre is Brigadier Chatterton; on the right actresses Sally Grey and Valerie Hobson.

32. The Face of Arnhem.

one squadron of Halifaxes were part of the Force, which was designed to show the Warsaw Pact that their pressure to annex Berlin would be resisted. 85 flight eventually became part of an Airborne Practice Camp based in Schleswig Holstein. When the Russians subsequently blockaded Berlin and the NATO allies replied with the Airlift, a temporary end to glider flying resulted, as every available tug aircraft was needed to maintain the Airlift.

Colonel Deedes then persuaded the RAF that the Regiment's personnel, left with very little to do, would be a valuable source of assistance to Transport Command while they were engaged in the Airlift. Consequently one Flight, made up of pilots from both operational squadrons, attended an Air-quartermasters' course at RAF Hartford, and on New Year's Day, 1949, they reported at RAF Wunstorf in Germany to take up their new duties. In the event they were never required as the RAF had the situation well under control, but, never at a loss for showing ingenuity, they soon found employment for themselves as second pilots on the York aircraft being flown in a continual procession into and out of Berlin. This detachment was controlled by 'A' Squadron and its personnel were rotated through the Squadron to give everyone a tour and a rest.

85 Flight, which was renumbered 5 in June, also took part in the Airlift, acting as second pilots on the Hastings aircraft flying from RAF Schleswigland. Many of the Hastings pilots had previously put in many hours towing gliders with Halifaxes, so the glider pilots were among old friends. In this capacity much instrument flying practice was obtained, and the glider pilots were warmly accepted by the aircraft captains. One member of the Regiment, Sergeant Joseph Toal, was killed during this operation in a Hastings crash at Tegel airfield when an engine cut on take-off.

Both detachments finally closed in November, 1949, and everyone returned to England. It might be thought that the Hamilcar gliders would have made good load carriers, but by this time there was only one flight left and even that was closed down during 1949. In any case the slow speed and weight of this combination was probably deemed not worth the slight gain in loading capacity. During 1947-48 a powered Hamilcar 10 had had a short spell under RAF operation at the Telecommunications Research Unit at Defford near Worcester: there it had been fitted with a large glass nose and an airborne radar installation.

It was possible to resume glider training eventually, once the Airlift finished, and the members of the Regiment who had been waiting for their Horsa training were able to attend the last two courses in 1949-50. The second of these courses was moved from Upper Heyford to Abingdon half way through its training, and would have been stopped completely but for the pressure applied by Deedes.

In March, 1950, 21 EFTS at Booker closed, and in September of that year the Regiment's strength was further diminished. 'B' Squadron was closed and 'A' Squadron was amalgamated with Depot Squadron at Aldershot, which had now been redesignated 'Training Squadron'. The Squadron was commanded by Major R. King-Clark, MC, and comprised thirty pilots and a few administrative personnel. The title '1st Independent Squadron' was resurrected for the combined unit.

After the reduction of the Regiment to this single squadron, based at Aldershot but keeping its gliders at Netheravon, no new recruits were taken into the Regiment. It appears that a decision had been made that the concept of the slow-moving tug glider combination was no longer tenable in view of the relative speeds and armament of jet fighters. The advent of the Hastings in an airborne support role was an additional indication that the glider's days as a troop carrier had ended.

Even so, some towing behind the Hastings was tried, though it was not entirely successful: and for some time each of the three battalions of 16th Parachute Brigade Group had a flight of glider pilots attached to it for field training. In addition, during this period several members of the Regiment volunteered to do parachute courses.

Two alterations to the insignia worn by members of the Regiment now appeared. Army Order 66/1950, dated 13.5.50, announced that the Regiment would in future form part of the Infantry Arm and that the Parachute Regiment would cease to be a separate Corps, both Regiments becoming component parts of a Corps of Infantry designated 'The Glider Pilot and Parachute Corps' (a name which had been suggested by Colonel Deedes) with effect from 22 May, 1950. The Army Air Corps would be disbanded as from that date. This resulted in a newly-designed cap badge; the laurel wreath and the initials 'A.A.C.' which had formed part of it since the formation of the Regiment being replaced by a scroll bearing the Regiment's name. Since the inception of Airborne Forces in February, 1942, the Record Office nomenclature 'Army Air Corps' had embraced firstly the Glider Pilot Regiment on its own, and then the Parachute Regiment when it was formed some four months later, and lastly the Special Air Service Regiment from 1944. The two latter had eventually adopted their own badges but the Regiment had kept the 'A.A.C' one. The SAS had by now been disbanded but was later to be re-formed as a Corps in its own right.

The other alteration was the adoption of special arm badges in common with the Border Regiment and the South Staffordshire Regiment. These took the form of a Horsa glider in flight, and were worn incorporated into the battledress shoulder titles, or alone on No.1 dress, and were authorized in Army Order 35/1950 to commemorate the part the three regiments had played in the first main operational landing of troops by glider in Sicily. Modern versions of these are still worn by the successor Regiments after their amalgamations.

The final flights of the troop-carrying glider in 1950 were: the end of the second course in July; three Valetta/Horsa 'snatch' pickups; a demonstration of the snatch technique by a Dakota and Hadrian of the Transport Command Development Unit at an RAF Display at Farnborough (this formed part of a battle scene based upon the bombing raid which had been carried out on Amiens prison, and was responsible for a legend which grew up that gliders had been involved in that raid); another 'snatch' and general flying at Boscombe Down with a Valetta and a Horsa to test winches; and, finally, the return of all the remaining gliders to Hawarden in November for disposal.

On 9 December, 1950, a splendid memorial window designed by Mr Stammers of York was unveiled in Salisbury Cathedral by Field Marshal Lord Alanbrooke KG GCB OM GCVO DSO, the Colonel Commandant, to the honour and glory of God, and to those 553 members of the Regiment who had given their lives during 1942-45; the Roll of Honour rests nearby in the Chapel of St Michael. The Regiment had lost over one third of its strength killed, and had collected 123 awards for gallantry and sixty-four Mentions in Despatches.

An Army Council meeting held on 20 March, 1951, confirmed that it was now accepted that in future gliders would not take a major part in airborne operations as such loads as had been carried by glider could now successfully be dropped by parachute. This meeting decided to disband No.1 Independent Squadron (the purpose of which was now learnt to have been to maintain available a nucleus of glider pilots), and to set up six regular and twelve TA 'light aircraft liaison flights', each with six Auster aircraft (later to be replaced by helicopters). All ranks forming these flights were to be seconded to the Regiment.

The reasoning behind the decision to form these 'Light Liaison Flights', as they became known, is to be seen as a consequence of the increasing demands which had been made for some time on the pilots of the Air Observation Post squadrons to perform communications flights and other non-AOP duties with their Austers. During the Second World War these AOP squadrons had been formed with officers of the Royal Artillery trained to fly and accurately to access the effects of artillery fire, and it was considered that forming these flights would relieve them of the many extraneous duties which were interfering with their primary duties.

The decision to start the training of the Regiment's personnel on Austers must, in fact, have been taken before the Army Council meeting, as six courses were run at the AOP School between June, 1950, and September, 1951, for the remaining forty-two glider pilots. Thirty-one of these successfully completed the courses and were joined by nine others who had previously served with the Regiment and who now returned to flying duties.

The intention was that one Light Liaison Flight would be attached to each Air OP squadron, and once the Regiment's personnel had been absorbed recruitment into the Flights would be opened to all Arms of the army. Everyone accepted into them would wear the regimental badge and red beret. All commanders were made aware of the existence and possible uses of the new Flights and it was not long before their services were being sought.

From the output of the first two of the six courses, sufficient Auster pilots were trained to convert one flight of 656 AOP Squadron stationed in Malaya to a Light Liaison role. The members of the Regiment selected arrived in Malaya in August, 1950, and were, at first, allocated out throughout the Squadron until February, 1951, when they were all concentrated into 1911 Flight under Captain R.J. Royle. The Air OP pilots of that Flight were posted to others, and the Flight became 1911 Light Liaison Flight from 14 February.

Their duties included searching for terrorists in their jungle hideouts, and marking their presence for attack by Lincolns, Canberras, Vampires and Venoms; air observation for naval bombardments, and supporting the ground forces against communist activities. Two members of the Regiment were killed during these operations, and two others survived jungle crashes and with great determination and the will to survive managed to find their way out of the almost impenetrable jungle to safety.

The emergence of this new role coincided with yet another break with the recent hectic war years. In a letter from the War Office to Field-Marshal Lord Alanbrooke dated 19 July, 1951, he was informed that his appointment as Colonel Commandant of the Regiment would expire on the 23rd of that month as he would then reach the age limit for the post. It suggested that Major-General W.J. Eldridge be asked if he was willing to accept the appointment. Lord Alanbrooke suggested that the honour be offered to Brigadier Chatterton but it was pointed out that he was barred as he had not been a Regular Army officer, and officers appointed to such a post must have reached the rank of Lieutenant-Colonel in the Regular Army. An invitation was therefore sent to Major-General Eldridge and he accepted on 16 August. The appointment was approved by HM The King and published in the London Gazette supplement with effect from 23 July.

It soon became apparent that it would not be possible to form the twelve TA Light Liaison flights for some time, and only five regular flights were, in fact, created. As we have seen, 1911 Flight was converted within 656 Squadron, and in the last quarter of 1952 another Air OP flight based in Malaya was re-styled 1907 Light Liaison Flight. The other three flights were created from scratch as follows:

1912 Flight was created in June, 1951, at Middle Wallop, as part of 657 Air OP Squadron, under Major G.H. Wotton. For the remainder of that year and part of 1952 it was used as a continuation training flight, and moved to Buckeburg in Germany on 14 July, 1952, becoming 1912 Independent Liaison Flight. It has remained in Germany under various titles ever since and at the time of writing is based at Wildenrath as 12 Flight AAC.

1913 Flight was formed on 1 April, 1952, at Middle Wallop, as part of 657 Squadron, and it was not long before Major-General Cassells, GOC of the new Commonwealth Division being formed in Korea, was asking for two flights of light aircraft to perform tasks other than in an Air OP role, having seen the value of these light aircraft within the American Divisions. One flight, 1903 Air OP Flight, was immediately available from RAF sources in Hong Kong, and 1913 was ordered out to join it.

1913 was commanded by Captain P.A. Downward, later to command the Regiment and eventually to become Major-General Downward, CB DSO DFC. It immediately went into training in North Wales, flying its Austers among the mountains which bore some resemblance to the Korean terrain. It eventually arrived at Iwakuni, Japan, in September, its aircraft having been despatched by sea. The Flight moved to Seoul in Korea the next month, and then on to the battle area where it joined 1903 Flight on an airstrip known as 'Fort George' on the edge of the Imjin River. The Royal Artillery pilots of 1903 passed on much valuable experience which they had gained during the few weeks they had already served in the theatre, and the members of the Regiment set to with a will, gradually developing a reconnaissance role for themselves. They were quickly 'adopted' by various front-line units who made much use of their services. Unusually 1913 Flight operated a Cessna 'Bird Dog' aircraft in addition to its Austers.

Knowledge gained during the performance of the tasks which were undertaken by 1913 over the following four and a half years in Korea were to form the basis for the training syllabus given at Middle Wallop. It included Pilot Reconnaissance – the reporting of enemy movements and field works, ground conditions, damage caused by our own aircraft and artillery, etc; Passenger Reconnaissance — the carrying of an officer who was to lead a patrol into enemy territory, or an engineer officer wishing to assess the strength of enemy field-works; Rear Area Reconnaissance — for engineers wanting to survey roads and tracks in our own area; Air OP shoots when opportunity targets presented themselves; VIP communication flights, mainly undertaken in the Cessna; the carrying of urgent classified documents; leaflet drops; and searching for our own pilots who had been shot down. One of the members of the Regiment, Sergeant Cameron, was in fact shot down on 7 May, 1954, and taken prisoner: he returned safely after the armistice.

When the British contribution in Korea was cut down, 1913 Flight returned to 657 Squadron in February, 1955, leaving behind three aircraft as the 1st Commonwealth Division Light Liaison Section until mid-1956. The Flight moved to Cyprus in November, 1956, as part of the preparations for the occupation of the Canal Zone, and three of its aircraft were sent to El Gamil after the actual landings. However, they returned soon afterwards and the Flight returned to England. In March, 1957, it moved to Aldergrove in Northern Ireland, where a presence has been maintained ever since.

1915 Flight formed under Captain J.F. Tippen in April, 1956, at Middle Wallop and immediately moved to Cyprus as an Independent Light Liaison Flight.

Meanwhile, after the March, 1951, decision to disband it referred to earlier, 1st Independent Squadron closed down its offices in Corunna Barracks, Aldershot, and prepared to move to Middle Wallop. A final parade to commemorate Sicily was held in July, 1951, under Major King-Clark, at which Brigadier Chatterton took the salute and inspected the unit, and then the Squadron closed and the headquarters element moved to become 'Regimental Headquarters' and also act as the staff of the Commanding Officer in his capacity as 'Chief Instructor Light Liaison, Light Aircraft School', the Air OP School changing its name on 1 April, 1952, to reflect its additional commitment.

This small headquarters, apart from the instruction to the courses, also controlled the Regimental Association and the publication of *The Eagle*. The Chief Instructor Light Liaison also attended the aircrew selection boards to watch for suitable candidates, and where necessary assisted the School and the Air OP Squadron commanders in Light Liaison pilot and groundcrew manning matters.

All Light Liaison pilots became members of the Glider Pilot Regiment on completion of their courses. This was not, however, enforced rigidly after 1956.

The main reason for this was the formation of the Joint Experimental Helicopter Unit in 1955. JEHU was a separate entity from the Air OP Squadrons and the Light Liaison Flights. It was manned by Army and RAF personnel and equipped with Sycamore and Whirlwind helicopters, numbering several members of the Regiment among its pilots. Charged with investigating the uses to which helicopters could be put in both the RAF and the army, it carried out a programme of experimental helicopter projects.

As already mentioned, when the Suez Canal was annexed by Egypt in 1956, an operation to repossess it was mounted. JEHU was part of the force involved, and on 6 November, 1956, it carried out a helicopter assault on Suez from the deck of an aircraft carrier. This was the first such operation carried out by the British Forces, and pilots of the Regiment took part, alongside those of the RAF. For a while the wartime spirit of Army/RAF joint operations was rekindled, but sadly JEHU was disbanded in 1957.

As it had been found that the Light Liaison pilots were well able to carry out Air OP duties when required, the two types of courses at Middle Wallop were, in fact, amalgamated with both Air OP and Light Liaison students attending the same course. Regimental Headquarters had become, more by default than by intention, the 'Army' office there, Middle Wallop being at this time entirely RAF. The instructors of the Light Aircraft School were army personnel, but those of the Basic Flight were RAF.

Apart from those who served in the Light Liaison Flights, some pilots were posted to 651 Air OP Squadron in the Middle East, and some attended flying instructor courses and served in Air OP units and at the School as such. In addition, some were given helicopter courses and served either in JEHU or with 1906 Helicopter Flight in 657 AOP Squadron. The proposed TA element was never formed, and the nearest the Regiment got to it was service by some pilots as flying instructors in the five Auxiliary Air OP squadrons, which were themselves disbanded in March, 1957.

From the time of their inception the Light Liaison Flights were seen by the Air Ministry as yet another way in which the army was setting itself up in an air role. Air Chief Marshal the Hon Sir Ralph A. Cochrane had urged that the pilots for the Flights should be from the RAF as there were ample men available in that Service who were resting from operations, or had medical categories which prevented them from flying the modern high-speed aircraft. He advocated that the army pilots who had already received their initial light aircraft training should be replaced by RAF pilots when they had completed their tours.

The War Office countered that as the Light Liaison pilots would at all times need to have a good understanding of army organization and requirements Army pilots were the obvious choice for the job. It was pointed out that the RAF 1903 Air OP Flight had been switched to Light Liaison duties in Korea to meet a special requirement at the time. In the end the War Office view prevailed and the Flights remained with Army pilots. This drawn-out inter-service rivalry would finally be resolved to a great extent on 1 April, 1964, by the creation of a unified Ministry of Defence which would absorb the Air Ministry and War Office, and be responsible for the formulation of defence policy and the control and administration of the entire armed forces.

The fateful day on which the Regiment was to be disbanded eventually arrived, and was announced by Royal Warrant given by HM The Queen on 12 July, 1957, which also announced the formation of a new 'Army Air Corps', both to take effect on 1 September. This was promulgated in Army Order 82 dated 19 July, and Army Council Instruction 358 of 1957 published the details. The ACI explained that with effect from 1 September the Army would assume responsibility for all existing Air OP squadrons as well as the Light Liaison Flights and the Light Aircraft School, all of which would form part of the new Corps.

For three weeks after the official disbandment date, Captain R.W.G. Nicholls (Adjutant) and Staff Sergeant E.J. Willard (chief Clerk), remained at Regimental Headquarters to administer the close-down of the Regiment. Regimental property, silver and paintings were handed over variously to the Officers' and Sergeants' Messes. Thus Nicholls and Willard were the last two members of the Regiment.

Could the decision to revive the 'Army Air Corps' title have been made so that a link with the Regiment being disbanded was thereby perpetuated? Whether or not this was so the remaining eleven members of the Regiment were absorbed into the new Corps, and some of them continued their flying on helicopters.

The numbers of the Light Liaison Flights were retained, although the new Corps obtained its squadron numbers, infrastructure and much else from the Air OP organization. The new Corps adopted the Glider Pilot Regimental light and dark blue colours, and the 'eagle-style' of cap badge suitably modified. It had been hoped to continue the wearing of the maroon beret, but although this was not approved, the principle of a beret and badge and arm flash common to all ranks and Arms was continued (apart from REME and RAOC) until 1964, when the demise of battledress and the provision of groundcrew by other Arms than Royal Artillery led to the wearing of parent Arm cap badges and no arm flash. However, the flash, an eagle on a black square, which had replaced the Pegasus badge, did survive as a flying-suit badge for Army Aviation.

In April, 1955, a strange discovery was made which was associated with the Regiment's recent past. An aerial photographer of KLM-Aerocarto had noticed certain phenomena in the form of bare patches in the fields surrounding Wolfheze over which he was flying, and he took some photographs with the intention of having them studied later. A first investigation of the photographic evidence took place in 1957 and it was at once clearly discernible that the bare patches were the distinct forms of aircraft. A comparison of the KLM photographs with an Allied photograph of the same area taken on 17 September, 1944, a few hours after the arrival at Wolfheze of the first lift of operation Market, revealed that the bare patches were the spots where Horsa gliders had stood in 1944. An inspection carried out on the ground following this discovery showed that the bare patches lay thick with burnt wood, melted aluminium and melted perspex, indicating that the gliders had been burned. Aerial photographs taken on 19 September, 1944, had shown some gliders already burnt out, and a German newsreel taken soon after that had shown German soldiers systematically setting fire to all the gliders shortly after they had reoccupied the LZs. During the immediate post-war years hardly anything had grown on the spots where the gliders had been burned, and despite annual ploughing and fertilizing these spots would still be recognizable twenty years after the war from the lighter colour and shorter growth of the crops, and the fields have never recovered completely.

On the day of the disbandment of the Regiment, now commanded by Major M.W. Sutcliffe, a parade was held at Middle Wallop in appropriately dismal weather to mark the occasion. A distinctive and very special family of officers and NCO's had proved that it had been deserving of its motto that 'Nothing is Impossible'. Army Order 20/1957 announced that it had been awarded the following Battle Honours: 'Landings in Sicily', 'Sicily 1943', 'Normandy Landings', 'Pegasus Bridge', 'Merville Battery', 'Southern France', 'Arnhem 1944', 'North West Europe 1944-45', 'Rhine'.

Many books have been written about the Regiment's wartime activities which contain dramatic accounts of momentous deeds, and the commentaries of those engaged in them. This book gives but brief mention of only a few such personal accounts. Countless situations involving valour and devotion to duty shown by members of the Glider Pilot Regiment are, and will probably remain, unrecorded. It is hoped that the preceding pages give a balanced account.

The men of the Glider Pilot Regiment had been succeeded by the equally highly professional army helicopter and light aircraft pilots of the new Army Air Corps whose role includes armed action against armour, observation, reconnaissance, and the controlling of artillery and mortar fire and close-support aircraft with their Lynx and Gazelle helicopters. The deployment of the modern army's Airmobile troops with their complex and devastating weapons, who are the successors of the Air-Landing troops of World War II, is now undertaken by the RAF's Support Helicopter squadrons with their Chinook and Puma helicopters.

No history of the Glider Pilot Regiment would be complete without a tribute to the headquarters staffs, air crews and ground crews of the RAF's 38 and 46 Groups who performed prodigious feats during the war years, gaining much honour in the process. A close and happy relationship existed between all the RAF personnel concerned and the glider pilots. In all, by the end of the war, nineteen operational airfields (six of which were also used for advanced glider training) and forty-nine airfields used exclusively for training, had been used for the Regiment's activities.

The Glider Pilot Regiment was possibly the smallest and most short-lived of the Regiments of the British Army, but its unique role ensured that it possessed a comradeship and *esprit de corps* second to none, and had secured for itself a place high in the proud annals of the British Army.

# APPENDIX I

## ROLL OF HONOUR

### Operation FRESHMAN

| Name | Rank | Age | Date of Death | Place Buried/ Commemorated |
|---|---|---|---|---|
| STRATHDEE, Malcolm F.C. | SSgt | | 20.11.42 | Eiganes Z 11 |
| DOIG, Peter | Sgt | 25 | 20.11.42 | Eiganes Z 12 |

### Operation BEGGAR or TURKEY BUZZARD

| | | | | |
|---|---|---|---|---|
| HALL, E.W. | Sgt | | 12.6.43 | |
| WHEALE, F. | SSgt | | 12.6.43 | |

*Flying accident Thiersville

| | | | | |
|---|---|---|---|---|
| CASSELDEN, Daniel Stephen | SSgt | 23 | 27.6.43 | Brookwood Memorial |
| CHANDLER, Mark Albert Charles | Sgt | 27 | 27.6.43 | Brookwood Memorial |
| NORRIS, Harold | Sgt | 25 | 27.6.43 | Brookwood Memorial |

*Missing UK to Sale.

| | | | | |
|---|---|---|---|---|
| HIGGINS, A. | Sgt | | 27.6.43 | |
| HARRISON, J.E. | Sgt | | 27.6.43 | |

*Tail fell off on move to Sousse.

### Operations LADBROKE and FUSTIAN

| Name | Rank | Age | Date of Death | Place Buried/ Commemorated |
|---|---|---|---|---|
| AYLOTT, Henry James | Sgt | 23 | 9.7.43 | Cassino Memorial |
| BARKER, Ernest | Sgt | 23 | 10.7.43 | Cassino Memorial |
| BEDDOWS, Ralph | Sgt | 22 | 14.7.43 | Cassino Memorial |
| BENNETT, Douglas James Vincent | Sgt | 22 | 9.7.43 | Cassino Memorial |
| BENNETT, James Albert Arthur | Sgt | 26 | 9.7.43 | Cassino Memorial |
| BOORMAN, John Arthur | SSgt | 26 | 10.7.43 | Cassino Memorial |
| BROADHEAD, John Matthew | Sgt | 26 | 14.7.43 | Catania 3.J.36 |
| BROWN, Ronald Victor | Sgt | 23 | 10.7.43 | Cassino Memorial |
| BURTON, Robert Ridsdale | Sgt | 22 | 9.7.43 | Cassino Memorial |
| CARR, James Cyril | SSgt | 27 | 10.7.43 | Syracuse 2.F.7 |
| CHURCH, John | Sgt | 23 | 10.7.43 | Cassino Memorial |
| CONNELL, Michael Bourke | Lt | | 10.7.43 | Cassino Memorial |
| COOPER, Astley John, AFC | T/Maj | 31 | 14.7.43 | Catania 2.J.22 |
| CRASKE, Duncan | Sgt | 26 | 14.7.43 | Salerno 5.C.30 |
| DENHOLM, John Neil Campbell | Capt | 28 | 10.7.43 | Syracuse 2.D.12 |
| GOODALL, Alexander | Sgt | 23 | 14.7.43 | Catania 3.G.16 |
| GREGG, Dereck Pease | Lt | | 13.7.43 | Cassino Memorial |

| | | | | |
|---|---|---|---|---|
| HALL, Robert Brown | Sgt | 29 | 9.7.43 | Cassino Memorial |
| HAMPSHIRE, Peter Lawrence Gray | SSgt | 22 | 10.7.43 | Cassino Memorial |
| HANSON, Richard M | Capt | | 9.7.43 | Cassino Memorial |
| HARMER, Jack | Sgt | 23 | 9.7.43 | Cassino Memorial |
| HILL, George Albert Victor | Sgt | 29 | 10.7.43 | Syracuse 5.A.10 |
| HILL, Herbert Dennis John | Sgt | 23 | 10.7.43 | Cassino Memorial |
| HOLLAND, William Roy | Sgt | 25 | 9.7.43 | Cassino Memorial |
| IMPEY, Gordon Charles (Peter) | Lt | 23 | 10.7.43 | Syracuse 2.A.17 |
| IRON, Hedley James | SSgt | 26 | 9.7.43 | Cassino Memorial |
| JONES, David Goode | Sgt | 24 | 9.7.43 | Cassino Memorial |
| KENT, Douglas Edward | SSgt | 24 | 10.7.43 | Syracuse 2.F.11 |
| KITCHING, Alfred Harold | Capt | 23 | 14.7.43 | Catania 4.C.31 |
| KNOTT, Ronald Albert | Sgt | 21 | 10.7.43 | Cassino Memorial |
| LAIDLAW, T.G. | SSgt | | | |
| MATHIAS, Owain Ernest | Lt | 23 | 9.7.43 | Cassino Memorial |
| MAYNARD, Sidney Alfred | Sgt | 24 | 10.7.43 | Syracuse 2.E.12 |
| MILLER, Brendon McLennon | Sgt | 25 | 9.7.43 | Cassino Memorial |
| MONTAGUE, Terence | SSgt | 21 | 14.7.43 | Catania 3.G.34 |
| MOREL, William John | Sgt | 20 | 9.7.43 | Cassino Memorial |
| MORGAN, Cyril Paget | Sgt | 24 | 14.7.43 | Catania 2.J.20 |
| NELSON, Geoffrey Edward | Sgt | 25 | 9.7.43 | Cassino Memorial |
| PERCY, William John | Sgt | 23 | 9.7.43 | Cassino Memorial |
| PRESTON, John Allen | WO2 | 27 | 14.7.43 | Catania 3.J.37 |
| PURCELL, Phillip Stephen | Sgt | 23 | 10.7.43 | Syracuse 2.F.9 |
| RANDALL, John Elliott | Sgt | 22 | 10.7.43 | Cassino Memorial |
| REEVES, George Arthur Leonard | SSgt | 29 | 9.7.43 | Cassino Memorial |
| RICHARDS, David William John | Sgt | | 12.7.43 | Syracuse 3.G.10 |
| RYAN, Lawrence Nicholas | Sgt | 28 | 9.7.43 | Cassino Memorial |
| SHEPHERD, Alec George | Sgt | 30 | 9.7.43 | Cassino Memorial |
| SMITH, Donald Herbert | SSgt | 31 | 9.7.43 | Cassino Memorial |
| STREET, Frederick Highfield | Sgt | 24 | 14.7.43 | Cassino Memorial |
| SURRY, Stanley Albert | Sgt | 24 | 9.7.43 | Cassino Memorial |
| WHEATLEY, John Russell | SSgt | 22 | 19.7.43 | Cassino Memorial |
| WHITTINGTON-STEINER, Victor | Lt | | 9.7.43 | Cassino Memorial |
| WIKNER, Eric Brian | SSgt | 23 | 10.7.43 | Syracuse 2.B.11 |
| WILLIS, Dennis Norman | Sgt | 21 | 9.7.43 | Cassino Memorial |
| WITHAM, Donald Edwin | Sgt | 22 | 9.7.43 | Cassino Memorial |
| WOOD, Donald Stuart | Sgt | 24 | 9.7.43 | Cassino Memorial |
| WOOD, James Fortune | Sgt | 24 | 9.7.43 | Catania 4.L.41 |
| WOODLAND, Herbert James | Sgt | 27 | 9.7.43 | Cassino Memorial |

## Operation ELABORATE

| | | | | |
|---|---|---|---|---|
| BAKER, Laurence James | Sgt | 22 | 23.9.43 | Brookwood Memorial |
| BARON, John Kenneth | Sgt | | 23.9.43 | Brookwood Memorial |
| SARGENT, Hugh Wilfred | Sgt | 23 | 23.9.43 | Brookwood Memorial |

*Glider prematurely released by Halifax off coast of Portugal and force-landed in Bay of Biscay.

## Operations TONGA and MALLARD

| | | | | |
|---|---|---|---|---|
| BEVERIDGE, Henry | Sgt | 25 | 6.6.44 | Ranville 1A.C.1 |
| BRABHAM, J.P. | SSgt. | | 6.6.44 | St Desir 6.B.14 |
| BROMLEY, John Lee, MA | Lt. | 25 | 6.6.44 | Ranville 4A.G.20 |
| CHADWICK, Richard | Sgt | | 6.6.44 | St Desir 3.A.2 |

| | | | | |
|---|---|---|---|---|
| CODDINGTON, James Frederick | SSgt | 23 | 6.6.44 | Ranville 3A.E.8 |
| FOSTER, P. | Sgt | | 18.6.44 | La Deliverance, Douvres |
| FUELL, J.H. | Sgt | | 6.6.44 | St Desir 3.A.7 |
| GIBBONS, J.R.M. | Sgt | | | |
| GOODCHILD, Ernest John | Sgt | 28 | 6.6.44 | Ranville 3A.H.8 |
| HAINES, V. | Sgt | | | Abbeville Communal Ext (Somme) |
| HOPGOOD, C.H. | SSgt | | | St Vaast-en-Auge, Calvados |
| HOWE, William Richard | SSgt | 28 | 6.6.44 | Ranville 2A.J.5 |
| LIGHTOWLER, Eric | Sgt | 24 | 6.6.44 | Ranville 5A.E.6 |
| LUFF, Roy Samuel | SSgt | 23 | 6.6.44 | Ranville 4A.M.20 |
| MARFLEET, W.K. | SSgt | | | Bayeux 10.J.17 |
| MARTIN, Eric | Lt | 25 | 6.6.44 | Ranville 3A.F.8 |
| NASH, J.H. | Sgt | | | |
| NEW, R.G. | SSgt | | | Ste Marie, Le Havre |
| OCKWELL, H.V. | SSgt | | | Ste Marie, Le Havre |
| PERRY, Stanley Wood | Sgt | 22 | 6.6.44 | Ranville 5A.H.4 |
| PHILLIPS, D.F. | Sgt | | | St Vaaste-en-Auge, Calvados |
| PHILPOTT, G.E. | SSgt | | | |
| POWELL, Barry | Sgt | 22 | 6.6.44 | Ranville 4A.J.20 |
| RIDINGS, Leslie | SSgt | | | St Vaast-en-Auge, Calvados |
| RIGG, A | Sgt | | | |
| ROBINSON, C.B. | SSgt | | | |
| SAUNDERS, V.C. | SSgt | | 6.6.44 | St Desir 3.A.6 |
| SEPHTON, Alec Hugh (Sam) | Sgt | | | Hermannsville |
| STANLEY, E. | Sgt | | | |
| STEAR, A.T. | SSgt | | | |
| STONEBANKS, W.H. | Sgt | | | Brucourt |
| TAYLOR, E.M. | Sgt | | | |
| TURVEY, P.P. | SSgt | | | |
| WRIGHT, Duncan Frank | SSgt | 25 | 6.6.44 | Ranville 3A.B.2 |

### Operation ANVIL/DRAGOON

| | | | | |
|---|---|---|---|---|
| JENNER, W. Roy | Sgt | | 15.8.44 | Mazargues Ext 4.C.18 |

### Operation MARKET

| | | | | |
|---|---|---|---|---|
| ADAMS, Norman Vere Maxwell | Lt | 27 | 18.9.44 | Groesbeek Memorial |
| ADAMS, Richard Allen | Sgt | 19 | 18.9.44 | Oosterbeek 6.D.12 |
| ALLISON, Gordon Stanley | Sgt | 23 | 24.9.44 | Groesbeek Memorial |
| ANDERSON, Dermod Green | Lt | 29 | 25.9.44 | Groesbeek Memorial |
| ANDREWS, Dennis | Sgt | 22 | 21.9.44 | Oosterbeek 31.A.10 |
| BAKER, Ernest John, DFM | SSgt | 28 | 24.9.44 | Oosterbeek 21.C.14 |
| BANKS, Richard, DFM | SSgt | 25 | 19.9.44 | Oosterbeek 3.D.6 |
| BARRIE, William Nicholson, DFC | Capt | 25 | 2.10.44 | Oosterbeek 3.B.5 |
| BASHFORTH, Arthur Lionel | SSgt | 26 | 18.9.44 | Groesbeek Memorial |
| BAXTER, George Seymour | SSgt | 22 | 17.9.44 | Oosterbeek 32.B.4 |
| BELL, Alfred | SSgt | 32 | | Tull en t'Waal (Utrecht) Jt Gr 16 |
| BEWLEY, John Michael Died of wounds while PoW Apeldoorn | Lt | 24 | 7.1244 | Oosterbeek 18.C.15 |
| BINNINGTON, Geoffrey Lewis | SSgt | 27 | 25.9.44 | Oosterbeek 3.B.3 |

| | | | | |
|---|---|---|---|---|
| BONHAM, James F. | Sgt | 24 | 19.9.44 | Oosterbeek 3.D.20 |
| BONSEY, Robert Albert | Sgt | 25 | 24.9.44 | Oosterbeek 23.A.10 |
| BOORMAN, Norman John | Sgt | 29 | 18.9.44 | Oosterbeek 5.A.1 |
| BOSLEY, Jesse | Sgt | 24 | 18.9.44 | Oosterbeek 27.C.3 |
| BOYD, James Frederick | SSgt | 22 | 23.9.44 | Oosterbeek 3.D.11 |
| BRACKSTONE, Charles Thomas | Sgt | 23 | 17.9.44 | Oosterbeek 3.C.12 |
| BRALEE, Stanley | Sgt | 20 | 18.9.44 | Groesbeek Memorial |
| BRAZIER, Peter John | Lt | 22 | 23.9.44 | Oosterbeek 21.A.18 |
| BRIGGS, Geoffrey Alan | Sgt | 22 | 22.9.44 | Oosterbeek 30.B.8 |
| BRIGGS, Geoffrey Rennie | SSgt | 21 | 23.9.44 | Oosterbeek 3.D.10 |
| BRISCOE, Richard William (Dick) | Lt | 27 | 10.4.45 | Overloon 4.A.13 |
| Escaped from hospital, Oflag 9A | | | | |
| BROWN, George W | SSgt | 29 | 14.3.45 | Hanover 7.B.7 |
| PoW | | | | |
| BROWN, Harry Vickers | SSgt | 23 | 24.9.44 | Oosterbeek 3.D.2 |
| BROWN, John W. | Sgt | 23 | 25.9.44 | Heteren General 2.A.23 |
| BRUCE, Reginald Charles | Sgt | 23 | 25.9.44 | Groesbeek Memorial |
| BURGE, John Gilbert | Sgt | 25 | 25.9.44 | Groesbeek Memorial |
| BURRIDGE, George H. | Sgt | 25 | 25.9.44 | Oosterbeek 5.B.3 |
| CARTLIDGE, Dennis | SSgt | 26 | 18.9.44 | Oosterbeek 3.C.17 |
| CASTLE, Vernon Edward | SSgt | 23 | 25.9.44 | Oosterbeek 22.C.19 |
| CAVES, John James | Sgt | 22 | 31.3.45 | Berlin 1939-45 10.A.14 |
| PoW | | | | |
| CHANDLER, Francis James | Sgt | 18 | 18.9.44 | Oosterbeek 3.B.18 |
| CHITTLEBURGH, Kenneth Trevor | Lt | 23 | 20.9.44 | Oosterbeek 3.B.6 |
| CLARK, Alfred Anthony | SSgt | 24 | 18.9.44 | Groesbeek Memorial |
| CLARKE, Ernest Eric | SSgt | 26 | 22.9.44 | Oosterbeek 24.B.2 |
| COLE, Henry Charles Livesey | Lt | 29 | 21.9.44 | Oosterbeek 30.A.3 |
| COOK, Laurence A.L. | Sgt | 23 | 17.9.44 | Bergen-op-Zoom 13.C.1 |
| COWAN, Eric Alfred | Sgt | 19 | 26.9.44 | Oosterbeek 18.C.3 |
| CROFT, Roger Malcolm | Sgt | 20 | 18.9.44 | Oosterbeek 3.A.16 |
| CULVERWELL, Stanley Martin | Lt | 23 | 22.9.44 | Oosterbeek 20.B.1 |
| CUMMINS, Bernard Arthur | SSgt | 22 | 22.9.44 | Oosterbeek 3.D.7 |
| CURLEY, James | SSgt | 27 | 25.9.44 | Oosterbeek 23.C.3 |
| DALLIMORE, Albert John | Sgt | 28 | 21.9.44 | Groesbeek Memorial |
| DANIELS, Dennis Deane | SSgt | 25 | 19.9.44 | Oosterbeek 3.D.3 |
| DAVEY, Trevor Edward | Sgt | 23 | 25.9.44 | Oosterbeek 3.A.11 |
| DAVIES, David Garfield | Sgt | 25 | 25.9.44 | Groesbeek Memorial |
| DERBYSHIRE, Francis Alexander | Lt | 25 | 19.9.44 | Oosterbeek 6.A.15 |
| DITCH, Ronald R | SSgt | 30 | 26.9.44 | Wijk bij Durstede 4.18 |
| DOBBINGS, William David | Sgt | 23 | 25.9.44 | Oosterbeek 18.A.19 |
| DODD, William | SSgt | 20 | 19.9.44 | Oosterbeek 22.A.16 |
| DOWNING, Maxwell William | Lt | | 22.9.44 | Oosterbeek 27.B.4 |
| DRUREY, Bernard | SSgt | 21 | 25.9.44 | Oosterbeek 26.A.14 |
| DUNN, Henry | SSgt | 29 | 18.9.44 | Oosterbeek 3.B.14 |
| ELLIN, James B.C. | SSgt | 21 | 25.9.44 | Blankenberge-zur-See, Belgium A.12 |
| EVANS, John | SSgt | 26 | 18.9.44 | Groesbeek Memorial |
| EVANS, William Edward | SSgt | 28 | 22.9.44 | Oosterbeek 3.B.17 |
| FAIRWEATHER, John Strang | SSgt | 25 | 4.4.45 | Durnbach (Bad Tolz) 3.D.6 |
| PoW | | | | |

| | | | | | |
|---|---|---|---|---|---|
| FENDICK, Harry | SSgt | 26 | 4.10.44 | Deptford (Grove Park) Lewisham JG.6 | |
| Died of Wounds | | | | | |
| FERGUSON, William Skene (Jock) | Sgt | 29 | 31.3.45 | Durnbach (Bad Tolz)3.D.23 | |
| Died after march from PoW Camp. Aschaffenburg | | | | | |
| FIRTH, Everett Hildred | SSgt | 26 | 22.9.44 | Oosterbeek 3.D.16 | |
| FISHER, Cyril | SSgt | 34 | 20.9.44 | Groesbeek Memorial | |
| FOLLINGTON, Douglas Charles | Sgt | 26 | 23.9.44 | Oosterbeek 32.B.1 | |
| FORRESTER, Robert | Sgt | 20 | 24.9.44 | Groesbeek Memorial | |
| FOWKES, Thomas | Sgt | 23 | 23.9.44 | Oosterbeek 3.C.7 | |
| FRANKS, Ronald | Sgt | 25 | 22.9.44 | Oosterbeek 3.C.3 | |
| FRASER, Robert A | Sgt | 25 | 17.9.44 | Weston-super-Mare Y.294 | |
| Combination crashed near Paulton | | | | | |
| FREW, Ernest | SSgt | 24 | | Oosterbeek 17.C.1 | |
| GARDNER, Leonard J | SSgt | 27 | 17.9.44 | Weston-super-Mare Y.294 | |
| Combination crashed near Paulton | | | | | |
| GAULT, Basil Thomas (Jimmy) | Sgt | 19 | 20.9.44 | Oosterbeek 3.D.17 | |
| GELL, Cyril | Sgt | 29 | 18.9.44 | Oosterbeek 30.B.4 | |
| GITTINGS, John Harrison | Sgt | 23 | 25.9.44 | Groesbeek Memorial | |
| GOODWIN, William | SSgt | 25 | 24.9.44 | Oosterbeek 3.A.7 | |
| GOOLD, Douglas Stanley | SSgt | 24 | 25.9.44 | Oosterbeek 27.B.10 | |
| GOULD, Raymond Percy | SSgt | 23 | 23-25.9.44 | Oosterbeek 27.B.9 | |
| GRAHAM, John Frederick | Sgt | 22 | 20.9.44 | Groesbeek Memorial | |
| GREEN, Kenneth William | Sgt | 22 | 19.9.44 | Groesbeek Memorial | |
| GREENE, John Christopher | Sgt | 27 | 20-22.9.44 | Oosterbeek 29.A.10 | |
| GREENHILL, Frederick William | Sgt | 28 | 25.9.44 | Oosterbeek 22.B.1 | |
| GWINN, Malcolm Alan | Sgt | 22 | 4.10.44 | Oosterbeek 24.B.5 | |
| Died of Wounds, Apeldoorn | | | | | |
| HANNAM, Ian Charles | Sgt | 25 | 19.9.44 | Oosterbeek 29.B.1 | |
| HARDIE, J. Norman George | Capt | | 20.9.44 | Oosterbeek 8.B.19 | |
| HARRIS, Archy Aneurin | SSgt | 23 | 16.11.44 | Oosterbeek 18.C.19 | |
| Died of wounds, Apeldoorn | | | | | |
| HARRIS, Howard Stephen | SSgt | 24 | 25.9.44 | Groesbeek Memorial | |
| HARRIS, John William Robert | SSgt | 28 | 18.9.44 | Oosterbeek 4.C.10 | |
| HEBBLETHWAITE, Bryan | Sgt | 21 | 19.9.44 | Oosterbeek 3.B.16 | |
| HIGHAM, Ralph Bernard | Sgt | 26 | 25.9.44 | Oosterbeek 3.A.14 | |
| HILL, Peter B. | SSgt | 22 | 25.9.44 | Mauril RC | |
| HODGES, Kenneth Stanley | SSgt | 24 | 11.3.45 | Durbach (Bad Tolz) 3.D.9 | |
| Died after march from PoW Camp, Aschaffenburg | | | | | |
| HOGG, George Henry | Sgt | 29 | 21.9.44 | Oosterbeek 3.D.15 | |
| HOLDREN, Charles Robert | SSgt | 29 | 25.9.44 | Oosterbeek 17.C.3 | |
| HOLLINGSWORTH, Thomas | Sgt | 21 | 6.10.44 | Becklingen 4.E.13 | |
| Killed during air raid on Stalag 9B | | | | | |
| HOLLOWAY, Eric John, MM | SSgt | 24 | 18.9.44 | Oosterbeek 3.A.15 | |
| HOWELL, Horace Gordon | SSgt | 24 | 20.9.44 | Oosterbeek 6.B.6 | |
| HOWES, Lawrence Herbert | Sgt | 30 | 20.9.44 | Oosterbeek 18.A.20 | |
| HUARD, Jean F | Sgt | 26 | 4.10.44 | Enschede East 194 | |
| Died of wounds | | | | | |
| HUMPHREYS, Charles Henry | SSgt | 29 | 18.9.44 | Oosterbeek 23.B.15 | |

| | | | | |
|---|---|---|---|---|
| HUNTER, John Sinclair | Sgt | 28 | 25.9.44 | Oosterbeek 3.A.20 |
| HUXLEY, Benjamin | Sgt | 26 | 18.9.44 | Oosterbeek 6.C.17 |
| IRVINE, Robert | Lt | 29 | 22.9.44 | Oosterbeek 3.D.13 |
| JEAVONS, Wilfred Thomas | Sgt | 26 | 25.9.44 | Groesbeek Memorial |
| JOHNSON, Dennis Alfred | Sgt | 25 | 30.3.45 | Durbach (Bad Tolz) 3.D.21 |
| Died after march from PoW Camp, Aschaffenburg | | | | |
| JOHNSON, Peter David | Sgt | 19 | 19.9.44 | Groesbeek Memorial |
| JOHNSTONE, Joseph | Sgt | 27 | 25.9.44 | Oosterbeek 3.B.8 |
| JONES, Arthur L | Sgt | 25 | 22.9.44 | Bergen-op-Zoom 13.C.2 |
| JONES, Lawrence Vincent | Sgt | 28 | 18.9.44 | Oosterbeek 29.B.3 |
| JONES, Peter Reginald | SSgt | 23 | 18.9.44 | Oosterbeek 3.C.11 |
| JOYCE, Thomas A | Sgt | 25 | 17.9.44 | Liverpool (West Derby) 6.RC.519 |
| KERR, David Fisher, DFM | SSgt | 24 | 22.9.44 | Groesbeek Memorial |
| KIFF, Leonard Thomas | Sgt | 21 | 24.9.44 | Oosterbeek 15.C.5 |
| LAWRENCE, Arthur Cyril | SSgt | 32 | 18.9.44 | Oosterbeek 3.D.12 |
| LAWSON, Ernest | Sgt | 28 | 17.9.44 | Oosterbeek 32.A.9 |
| LAWSON, Geoffrey | Sgt | 24 | 18.9.44 | Oosterbeek 3.D.18 |
| LEE, Joseph Bernard | WO2 | 27 | 18.9.44 | Oosterbeek 3.C.14 |
| LEVISON, John Oliver | SSgt | 23 | 19.9.44 | Oosterbeek 17.A.12 |
| LEYSHON, Leslie | Sgt | 24 | 20.9.44 | Oosterbeek 3.C.19 |
| LIVINGSTON, Duncan Mathieson | Sgt | 26 | 19.9.44 | Groesbeek Memorial |
| LYON, Matthew | Sgt | 26 | 18.9.44 | Groesbeek Memorial |
| MACKENZIE, Bruce William | Sgt | 21 | 20.9.44 | Groesbeek Memorial |
| MALTBY, Ralph Alexander | Lt | 26 | 17.9.44 | Oosterbeek 3.C.18 |
| MANBY, Hendry Middleton | SSgt | 24 | 25-26.9.44 | Oosterbeek 3.A.9 |
| MANN, John Robert | Sgt | 22 | 23.9.44 | Oosterbeek 2.A.15 |
| MARKWICK, Eric John | Lt | 26 | 22.9.44 | Oosterbeek 3.C.4 |
| MARRIOTT, Claude | Sgt | 27 | 21.9.44 | Oosterbeek 3.C.8 |
| MATHEWS, Sidney Frederick (Tim) | SSgt | 30 | 25.9.44 | Oosterbeek 22.C.11 |
| MAYES, Thomas William | SSgt | 24 | 18.9.44 | Oosterbeek 3.A.8 |
| McCARTHY, Albert Francis | Sgt | 19 | 18.9.44 | Groesbeek Memorial |
| McGOWAN, Denis | Sgt | 23 | 20.9.44 | Oosterbeek 3.B.11 |
| McLAREN, William Colin | SSgt | 24 | 19.9.44 | Oosterbeek 3.D.9 |
| McMANUS, Vincent Desmond | SSgt | 20 | 23.9.44 | Oosterbeek 3.D.5 |
| McMILLAN, Alexander Crawford | SSgt | 22 | 25.9.44 | Groesbeek Memorial |
| MIDGLEY, Gordon | Sgt | 19 | 24.25.9.44 | Oosterbeek 20.B.3 |
| MILLS, Gordon T | Capt | 27 | 28.9.44 | Rhenen 27.A.1 |
| MILLS, Kenneth S | Lt | 21 | 23.9.44 | Enschede East General 199 |
| MINARDS, A.H. | Sgt | 26 | 19.8.47 | Luton 9.H.18 |
| MOON, Edward Brindle | Sgt | 30 | 23.9.44 | Oosterbeek 21.B.20 |
| MOORCOCK, Dennis Edgar | SSgt | 23 | 25.9.44 | Oosterbeek 3.B.1 |
| MUIR, Ian Colquhoun | Capt | 22 | 25.9.44 | Oosterbeek 3.C.15 |
| MURPHY, Thomas | Sgt | 29 | 19.9.44 | Groesbeek Memorial |
| NADEN, John Ernest Peat | SSgt | 27 | 24-26.9.44 | Oosterbeek 16.C.20 |
| NAYLOR, Cyril | Sgt | 23 | 24.9.44 | Groesbeek Memorial |
| NEALE, Francis J.T. | Capt | 24 | 26.9.44 | Amerongen General 2 |
| NEILSON, Roy Campbell | Sgt | 19 | 19.9.44 | Oosterbeek 15.C.4 |
| NEWARK, Matthew Charles, RAMC | Pte | 35 | 25.9.44 | Oosterbeek 3.B.13 |
| NEWMAN, David Henry | Sgt | 27 | 23.9.44 | Oosterbeek 17.C.2 |
| NEWMAN, Roy Frederick | Sgt | 19 | 25.9.44 | Oosterbeek 3.A.13 |

| | | | | |
|---|---|---|---|---|
| OGILVIE, James G | Capt | 26 | 26.9.44 | Rhenen 27.C.12 |
| OSBORN, Ronald E | SSgt | 26 | 19.9.44 | St. Michielsgestel RC |
| OXENFORD, Arthur Ruthven (Jonah) | Capt | 31 | 8.10.44 | Oosterbeek 24.A.11 |
| Died of wounds Apeldoorn. | | | | |
| PAINTER, Graham | Sgt | 22 | 25-26.9.44 | Groesbeek Memorial |
| PALMER, John | SSgt | 25 | 18.9.44 | Groesbeek Memorial |
| PARKINSON, Henry | Sgt | 28 | 20.9.44 | Oosterbeek 16.C.12 |
| PATTINSON, Lewis Reginald | Sgt | 21 | 19.9.44 | Oosterbeek 17.A.16 |
| PHILLIPS, Arnold | Sgt | 21 | 25.9.44 | Oosterbeek 6.B.14 |
| PHILLIPS, Eric | SSgt | 21 | 18.9.44 | Oosterbeek 3.B.10 |
| PICKFORD, Edwin | SSgt | 25 | 27.9.44 | Jonkerbosch (Nijmegen) 13.A.2 |
| PICTON, Raymond Kenneth | SSgt | 23 | 25.9.44 | Oosterbeek 3.A.10 |
| PIDDUCK, Dennis F | Sgt | 20 | 24.9.44 | Rhenen (Elst) Gen 15.4 |
| PLOWMAN, Thomas Anthony | Capt | 24 | 24.9.44 | Oosterbeek 3.C.2 |
| POWELL, Howard Edward | SSgt | 23 | 25.9.44 | Oosterbeek 3.A.3 |
| RAGGETT, Denis Bernard Frank | Sgt | 24 | 21.9.44 | Oosterbeek 31.A.9 |
| RANGER, Norman John | Sgt | 28 | 24.9.44 | Oosterbeek 18.A.4 |
| REDDING, Francis George | Sgt | 23 | 24.9.44 | Oosterbeek 19.B.11 |
| RICHARDS, Arthur Edward | SSgt | 23 | 24-25.9.44 | Groesbeek Memorial |
| RICHARDSON, Conway Dennis | SSgt | 24 | 25.9.44 | Oosterbeek 28.C.6 |
| RICHARDSON, William Kenneth | Sgt | 26 | 22.9.44 | Oosterbeek 3.B.20 |
| RICKWOOD, Gordon Albert | SSgt | 23 | 18.9.44 | Groesbeek Memorial |
| ROWLAND, Roy R | SSgt | 23 | 17.9.44 | Bergen-op-Zoom 13.C.13 |
| ROYLE, John Popplewell | Maj | | 20.9.44 | Oosterbeek 3.B.9 |
| RUBENSTEIN, Theodore Albert | Sgt | 21 | 22.9.44 | Oosterbeek 3.B.7 |
| SAUNDERS, Reginald Herbert | SSgt | 23 | 26.9.44 | Oosterbeek 3.C.13 |
| SHARP, Harry | Sgt | 21 | 23.9.44 | Oosterbeek 3.C.6 |
| SHARROCK, James Johnson | Sgt | 21 | 22.9.44 | Groesbeek Memorial |
| SHIPP, David H | Sgt | 23 | 25.9.44 | Mook 1.D.11 |
| SHUTTLEWORTH, Donald Harrop | Capt | | 23.9.44 | Oosterbeek 3.A.4 |
| SIMION, Ernest | Sgt | 24 | 20.9.44 | Oosterbeek 3.B.4 |
| SMALLWOOD, William Albert | SSgt | 27 | 24.9.44 | Oosterbeek 3.A.17 |
| SMELLIE, John Frederick | Capt | 30 | 23.9.44 | Oosterbeek 6.A.4 |
| SMITH, Harold Wilson | Sgt | 26 | 22.9.44 | Oosterbeek 22.B.19 |
| SMITH, John Creese | Sgt | 23 | 25-26.9.44 | Groesbeek Memorial |
| SMITH, Sidney R | Lt | 21 | 20.9.44 | Oosterbeek 30.C.4 |
| SMITH, Thomas Montgomery | Sgt | 23 | 18.9.44 | Oosterbeek 3.C.20 |
| SNUSHALL, John Alan Wakefield | Sgt | 30 | | Oosterbeek 3.C.9 |
| SPENCER, Harold Herbert | Sgt | 30 | 18.9.44 | Oosterbeek 3.D.4 |
| STATHAM, William John Garth | SSgt | | 10.3.45 | Durbach (Bad Tolz) 3.D.8 |
| Died after march from PoW Camp, Aschaffenburg | | | | |
| STEWART, Thomas Walter (Jock) | SSgt | 23 | 23.9.44 | Oosterbeek 4.A.19 |
| TARRANT, Harold Alfred Percy | SSgt | 27 | 17.9.44 | Oosterbeek 3.B.12 |
| TAYLER, Cyril Cadle | Lt | 24 | 20.9.44 | Oosterbeek 29.A.7 |
| TAYLOR, Frank William | Sgt | 26 | 25-26.9.44 | Groesbeek Memorial |
| TAYLOR, Henry Charles | SSgt | 24 | 25.9.44 | Oosterbeek 6.B.15 |
| TAYLOR, John Davie | Sgt | 26 | 22.9.44 | Oosterbeek 24.B.6 |
| THOMAS, Emrys James, AFC | Capt | 28 | 22.9.44 | Oosterbeek 3.D.8 |
| THOMPSON, David | Sgt | 27 | 20.9.44 | Groesbeek Memorial |
| THOMSON, James W.R. | Sgt | 23 | 17.9.44 | Rhenen 27.3.6 |

| | | | | |
|---|---|---|---|---|
| TOMLINSON, Edward Bernard Ernest | Sgt | 26 | 25.9.44 | Groesbeek Memorial |
| TOSELAND, Peter | Sgt | 20 | 26.9.44 | Oosterbeek 24.A.19 |
| TURL, John | Sgt | 25 | 25.9.44 | Oosterbeek 23.C.4 |
| WADSWORTH, Lewis | SSgt | 24 | 20.9.44 | Oosterbeek 11.A.15 |
| WALKER, Harry | Sgt | 29 | 29.9.44 | Oosterbeek 24.B.15 |
| Died of wounds Apeldoorn | | | | |
| WALLACE, David Bruce, MM | SSgt | 24 | 24.9.44 | Oosterbeek 27.B.8 |
| WALTERS, John | Sgt | 27 | 25.9.44 | Wijk bij Durstede 1.7B |
| WATERHOUSE, Alfred | Sgt | 27 | 4.10.44 | Oosterbeek 24.A.20 |
| Died of wounds Apeldoorn | | | | |
| WATSON, Laurence Frank | SSgt | 30 | 18.9.44 | Groesbeek Memorial |
| WEST, Ernest Lionel | Sgt | 23 | 21.9.44 | Oosterbeek 3.D.14 |
| WEST, John | Sgt | 25 | 19-20.9.44 | Oosterbeek 3.D.19 |
| WEST, Richard William | SSgt | 21 | 6.10.44 | Oosterbeek 24.A.9 |
| Died of wounds Apeldoorn | | | | |
| WHITE, David Adrian | SSgt | 22 | 17.9.44 | Oosterbeek 1.B.10 |
| WHITE, Alan | SSgt | 22 | 25.9.44 | Groesbeek Memorial |
| WHITE, Raymond Ernest, DCM | SSgt | 27 | 18.9.44 | Oosterbeek 16.B.17 |
| WHITEHOUSE, Norman Kenneth | Sgt | 26 | 19.9.44 | Groesbeek Memorial |
| WHYBORN, Philip Ernest | Sgt | 21 | 20.9.44 | Groesbeek Memorial |
| WILKINSON, Sydney Augustus | SSgt | 30 | 25.9.44 | Oosterbeek 26.A.12 |
| WILLIAMS, Llewelyn Elwyn | Sgt | 19 | 18.9.44 | Groesbeek Memorial |
| WILLIAMS, Norman D | Sgt | 21 | 25.9.44 | Uden 2.F.8 |
| WILTON, Donald Claud | Sgt | 25 | 25-27.9.44 | Groesbeek Memorial |
| WINKWORTH, Charles William | Sgt | 22 | 17.9.44 | Groesbeek Memorial |
| WINSPER, Leslie | SSgt | 27 | 9.12.44 | Oosterbeek 18.C.17 |
| Died of wounds Apeldoorn | | | | |
| WISEBAD, Julius | Sgt | 25 | 18.9.44 | Groesbeek Memorial |
| WITHINGTON, Thomas | Sgt | 30 | 21.9.44 | Oosterbeek 30.C.7 |
| WOOD, Harrold | Sgt | 30 | | Oosterbeek 3.C.5 |
| WOODROW, Ernest Walter | SSgt | 29 | 19.9.44 | Oosterbeek 27.C.7 |
| WOODS, Roy Oliver | SSgt | 24 | | Groesbeek Memorial |
| WORTHINGTON, Bertram Gordon | Sgt | 27 | | Groesbeek Memorial |
| WRIGHT, John | SSgt | 25 | 19.9.44 | Groesbeek Memorial |
| WRIGHT, John Robert | SSgt | 27 | 24.9.44 | Oosterbeek 3.A.12 |
| WYATT, Donald | Sgt | 21 | 21.9.44 | Oosterbeek 30.A.5 |
| YATES, Arthur Gregory | Sgt | 22 | 19.9.44 | Groesbeek Memorial |
| YEATMAN, Frederick James | SSgt | 28 | 24-25.9.44 | Oosterbeek 32.A.3 |

## Operation VARSITY

| | | | | |
|---|---|---|---|---|
| ANKERS, Alfred Michael | Fg Offr | 23 | 24.3.45 | Venray VF.6 |
| ARMSTRONG, Joseph | Tpr | 39 | 24.3.45 | Reichswald Forest 40.B.5 |
| ASTOR, Jeffrey Frederick | Sgt | 19 | 24.3.45 | Reichswald Forest 38.D.6 |
| AUSTIN, Maurice | Fg Offr | 21 | 24.3.45 | Reichswald Forest 2.C.17 |
| BENNETT, John Philip | Sgt | 30 | 24.3.45 | Reichswald Forest 40.A.4 |
| BOND, Dennis Langdown | Flt Sgt | 22 | 24.3.45 | Reichswald Forest 39.A.10 |
| BOWLER, Kenneth W | Flt Sgt | 20 | 24.3.45 | Reichswald Forest 34.A.1-11 |
| BRIGHT, G | SSgt | | 24.3.45 | |
| BRUCE, Edward Osborne | Sgt | | 24.3.45 | Groesbeek Memorial |
| CARR, Angus Montgomery Dingwall | Capt | 34 | 24.3.45 | Reichswald Forest 52.A.12 |
| CATT, Leslie John Teddy | SSgt | 22 | 24.3.45 | Reichswald Forest 42.C.2 |

| | | | | |
|---|---|---|---|---|
| CLARK, Maurice Robert | Flt Lt | 24 | 24.3.45 | Reichswald Forest 21.G.18 |
| COLLINS, Geoffrey H | Sgt | 25 | 24.3.45 | Reichswald Forest 40.A.3 |
| COOK, Edwin | Fg Offr | 21 | 24.3.45 | Reichswald Forest 1.G.12 |
| COOMBER, Herbert Walter | Sgt | 22 | 24.3.45 | Reichswald Forest 40.A.8 |
| CUSWORTH, Frank Horrower | Fg Offr | 23 | 24.3.45 | Reichswald Forest 2.A.18 |
| D'ARCY-CLARK, George John | Lt | 31 | 24.3.45 | Reichswald Forest 38.F.5 |
| DENBY, Herbert Hartley | Sgt | 31 | 24.3.45 | Reichswald Forest 34.B.1 |
| DENHOLM, William Beverley | SSgt | 24 | 24.3.45 | Reichswald Forest 40.A.6 |
| DORMER, Reginald | Flt Sgt | 22 | 24.3.45 | Reichswald Forest 4.F.10 |
| DOUGHTY, John | Sgt | 26 | 24.3.45 | Reichswald Forest 40.E.6 |
| DUNS, George | SSgt | | 24.3.45 | Groesbeek Memorial |
| EDWARDS, Derek Wallace | Fg Offr | 27 | 24.3.45 | Reichswald Forest 21.G.8 |
| ELLERINGTON, Claude | Sgt | 20 | 24.3.45 | Reichswald Forest 42.A.6 |
| ELLISON, John Lawrence | SSgt | 25 | 24.3.45 | Reichswald Forest 39.A.11 |
| ESSEN, Malcolm Frederick | Flt Sgt | 21 | 24.3.45 | Reichswald Forest 1.D.17 |
| EVANS, George Richard | Sgt | 24 | 24.3.45 | Reichswald Forest 38.F.8 |
| FOWLER, Hubert Alexander | Fg Offr | 28 | 24.3.45 | Reichswald Forest 1.G.8 |
| FREEMAN, John William | Fg Offr | 20 | 24.3.45 | Runnymede Memorial 266 |
| GORDON, Harry Jack | Sgt | 26 | 24.3.45 | Reichswald Forest 40.B.4 |
| GRAEFE, Reginald Lionel | Lt | | 24.3.45 | Reichswald Forest 32.B.4 |
| GRAHAM, Gordon Noel | Sgt | 24 | 24.3.45 | Reichswald Forest 21.G.15 |
| GRANT, Geoffrey John Cardross | Flt Sgt | 20 | 24.3.45 | Reichswald Forest 1.D.18 |
| GRAY, Robert | Flt Lt | 27 | 24.3.45 | Runnymede Memorial 265 |
| HAIG, John Sutherland | Flt Lt | 20 | 24.3.45 | Reichswald Forest 39.A.7 |
| HANSON, Geoffrey Bernard | Fg Offr | | 24.3.45 | Runnymede Memorial 267 |
| HARRISON, Douglas | SSgt | 26 | 24.3.45 | Reichswald Forest 38.E.3 |
| HARRISON, Laurence | Lt | 23 | 24.3.45 | Reichswald Forest 38.D.1 |
| HAYMAN, William | Sgt | 20 | 24.3.45 | Reichswald Forest 21.G.16 |
| HEADS, Robert | Flt Sgt | 21 | 24.3.45 | Runnymede Memorial 271 |
| HEDLEY, Frank | Sgt | | 24.3.45 | Groesbeek Memorial |
| HUTCHENS, David Leslie | Sgt | 22 | 24.3.45 | Runnymede Memorial 275 |
| HYDE, Percy Nicholas | Flt Sgt | | 24.3.45 | Runnymede Memorial 271 |
| JAMIESON, Robert William Charles | Fg Offr | 21 | 24.3.45 | Reichswald Forest 1.G.17 |
| JARVIS, Eric Lionel | SSgt | 23 | 24.3.45 | Reichswald Forest 32.B.1 |
| JOHNSON, Kenneth Maurice | Fg Offr | 22 | 24.3.45 | Reichswald Forest 42.D.9 |
| KELSALL, Kenneth Albert | Sgt | | 24.3.45 | Reichswald Forest 1.D.16 |
| KENNARD, Douglas Charles | Lt | 22 | 24.3.45 | Reichswald Forest 37.F.7 |
| KNOWLES, Edwin James | Fg Offr | | 24.3.45 | Groesbeek 22.B.11 |
| LAIDLAW, Thomas | Flt Sgt | 23 | 24.3.45 | Reichswald Forest 21.G.12 |
| LEAVY, Joseph Patrick | Fg Offr | 21 | 24.3.45 | Reichswald Forest 21.G.11 |
| LEDBROOK, Arthur Sydney (Tiny) | Fg Offr | | 24.3.45 | Reichswald Forest 42.C.8 |
| LOGIE, Alexander Randolph | Sgt | 26 | 24.3.45 | Reichswald Forest 1.G.10 |
| LOVE, Andrew Bell Coliville | Sgt | 21 | 24.3.45 | Reichswald Forest 4.F.13 |
| LOWMAN, William Samuel Edgar | Sgt | 20 | 24.3.45 | Reichswald Forest 4.F.11 |
| McLAREN, Patrick Alastair | SSgt | | 24.3.45 | Reichswald Forest |
| MADDOCK, Geoffrey William | Fg Offr | 22 | 24.3.45 | Reichswald Forest 21.G.14 |
| MANSELL, Stephane Peter Anthony | Fg Offr | 20 | 24.3.45 | Reichswald Forest 13.F.7 |
| McGREGOR, Andrew | Fg Offr | 29 | 24.3.45 | Reichswald Forest 37.C.8 |
| McINNES, William George | Flt Sgt | 21 | 24.3.45 | Reichswald Forest 21.G.7 |
| McLEAN, Samuel | Fg Offr | 21 | 24.3.45 | Reichswald Forest 1.G.16 |
| MONTGOMERY, David Roger | SSgt | | 24.3.45 | Reichswald Forest 40.A.7 |
| MURPHY, Walter Francis | Sgt | 33 | 24.3.45 | Reichswald Forest 1.D.15 |

| | | | | |
|---|---|---|---|---|
| NASH, John Kenneth Patrick | Fg Offr | 20 | 24.3.45 | Reichswald Forest 31.C.18 |
| NEILSON, James | SSgt | | 24.3.45 | Groesbeek Memorial |
| NORTON, Harold Martin Rex | Capt | | 24.3.45 | Reichswald Forest 37.B.9 |
| NUTTALL, Douglas | Sgt | | 24.3.45 | Reichswald Forest 39.C.6 |
| O'SULLIVAN, John Mortimer | Flt Sgt | 22 | 24.3.45 | Reichswald Forest 41.A.11 |
| PARKINSON, Thomas Anthony | Sgt | 21 | 24.3.45 | Reichswald Forest 2.A.17 |
| PAUL, William Henry | Fg Offr | 26 | 24.3.45 | Reichswald Forest 2.C.18 |
| PAVITT, William Charles | SSgt | | 24.3.45 | Reichswald Forest 40.A.10 |
| PODMORE, Roland | Sgt | 25 | 24.3.45 | Reichswald Forest 30.F.1 |
| READ, Philip James | Sgt | | 24.3.45 | Groesbeek Memorial |
| RICHARDSON, Gordon Knight | Sgt | | 24.3.45 | Groesbeek Memorial |
| ROBERTS, Stanley | SSgt | | 24.3.45 | Reichswald Forest 40.A.2 |
| ROBERTSON, Andrew Clelland, ACC | Pte | | 24.3.45 | Reichswald Forest 34.C.8 |
| ROCHE, Christopher Verdun | Sgt | | 24.3.45 | Reichswald Forest 40.F.9 |
| ROSS, William Lynch | Sgt | | 24.3.45 | Groesbeek Memorial |
| ROWLEY, Reginald Albert | Sgt | 21 | 24.3.45 | Reichswald Forest 41.B.4 |
| SCRASE, Robert Alfred | Fg Offr | | 24.3.45 | Reichswald Forest 21.G.13 |
| SHEPHERD, Robert James | Flt Sgt | 22 | | Runnymede Memorial 272 |
| SHERWOOD, John Richard | Flt Lt | | 24.3.45 | Reichswald Forest 31.F.18 |
| SHORE, James Alphonsus | Sgt | 25 | | Runnymede Memorial 276 |
| SKELDON, Angus Wallis | Sgt | 20 | 24.3.45 | Reichswald Forest 2.A.16 |
| SMITH, John Frederick | SSgt | | 24.3.45 | Reichswald Forest 42.A.2 |
| SMITH, John Kenneth | Sgt | 23 | 24.3.45 | Reichswald Forest 21.G.6 |
| SPARKES, Kenneth Charles | Sgt | 20 | 24.3.45 | Reichswald Forest 4.F.14 |
| SPOWART, Jasper Blake | SSgt | 25 | 24.3.45 | Venray 8.F.10 |
| STEVENS, John Henry | Sgt | 22 | 26.3.45 | Reichswald Forest 38.F.3 |
| STEVENS, Thomas John Alfred | Sgt | | 24.3.45 | Reichswald Forest 21.G.17 |
| STRATHERN, Kenneth Fairley | Capt | | 24.3,45 | Reichswald Forest 41.B.3 |
| STUBBINGS, Jack William | Sgt | 21 | 24.3.45 | Reichswald Forest 30.F.10 |
| SUMMERS, Frank | Sgt | | 24.3.45 | Reichswald Forest 38.D.9 |
| TAYLOR, Frederick Arthur | Sgt | 23 | | Runnymede Memorial 277 |
| TYSON, William John | Sgt | 20 | 24.3.45 | Reichswald Forest 1.G.18 |
| WARREN, Kenneth John | Sgt | 20 | | Runnymede Memorial 277 |
| WATES, William John | Fg Offr | 20 | 24.3.45 | Reichswald Forest 2.A.15 |
| WELPLEY, James Victor Alton | Fg Offr | 20 | 24.3.45 | Reichswald Forest 17.A.6 |
| WHITELEY, Tom | Sgt | 20 | 24.3.45 | Reichswald Forest 21.G.4 |
| WRIGHT, Herbert | SSgt | | 24.3.45 | Reichswald Forest 4.F.12 |

Casualties other than those on operations, 1942-45

| | | |
|---|---|---|
| CHADDAWAY, E. | Cpl | 25.3.42 |
| Flying accident Dalling Lees | | |
| ALLAN, J.H. | Cpl | 1.4.42 |
| Flying accident EFTS Derby | | |
| GOSS-ROBINSON, F.A.MC | Maj | 6.5.42 |
| Flying accident 2 GTs, | | |
| Weston-on-the-Green | | |
| SCUDAMORE, W.J. | Cpl | 8.5.42 |
| Flying accident EFTS Derby | | |
| BORTON, R.H. | Sgt | 16.5.42 |
| Flying accident Hurn | | |
| GRAHAM, S.J. | Sgt | 5.6.42 |
| Flying accident Abbotts Bromley | | |

| | | | |
|---|---|---|---|
| ROSCOE, A.D. | | 2Lt | 14.6.42 |
| Flying accident Innsworth | | | |
| KEENAN, J.H. | | Cpl | 18.6.42 |
| Flying accident nr Kidlington | | | |
| HINE, A.C. | | Cpl | 1.7.42 |
| Flying accident Weston-on-the-Green | | | |
| TERRY, G. | | Sgt | 3.7.42 |
| Flying accident Taplow | | | |
| SMITH, J.E. | | Sgt | 7.8.42 |
| Flying accident Netheravon | | | |
| BEEVERS, E.S. | | Cpl | 17.8.42 |
| McQWEEN, N.G. | | Cpl | 17.8.42 |
| Flying accident Stoke Orchard | | | |
| HALL, Robert E. | | Cpl | 1.9.42 |
| Flying accident EFTS Derby | | | |
| BROWN, P.E. | | Cpl | 4.9.42 |
| Flying accident Booker | | | |
| PALMER, W.C. | | Cpl | 4.9.42 |
| Flying accident Boddington | | | |
| ELLIDGE, T.E. | | Cpl | 4.9.42 |
| Flying accident Upper Heyford | | | |
| CORKE, H.W.C. | | Cpl | 14.9.42 |
| Flying accident nr Croughton | | | |
| ATKINSON, R.F. | | Cpl | 24.9.42 |
| Flying accident Chesterton | | | |
| ROCK, John Frank | | Lt Col | 27.9.42 |
| Flying accident Shrewton | | | |
| ASHWORTH, G.G. | | Cpl | 2.10.42 |
| Flying accident Stoke Orchard | | | |
| BASKETT, A.H.R. | } ★ | Sgt | 2.10.42 |
| DENWOOD, J.E. | | Cpl | 2.10.42 |
| ★Flying accident Kidlington | | | |
| GULLEN, J.N. | } ★ | Cpl | 2.10.42 |
| QUARRELL, F. | | Cpl | 2.10.42 |
| ★Flying accident Kidlington | | | |
| BOWERMAN, A.J. | | Cpl | 3.10.42 |
| Flying accident Clyffe Pypard | | | |
| BURKE, R.J. | | Lt | 23.10.42 |
| Flying accident Liverpool | | | |
| YEOMANS, S.R. | | Cpl | 26.10.42 |
| Flying accident Booker | | | |
| McALEER, G. | | Sgt | 6.11.42 |
| Flying accident Shobden | | | |
| MALCOLM, G.S. | | Sgt | 26.11.42 |
| Flying accident Netheravon | | | |
| BURNS, F. | | Cpl | 8.1.43 |
| HOSTED, E.I. | } ★ | Cpl | 8.1.43 |
| URWIN, D.I. | | Cpl | 8.1.43 |
| ★Short shell from ranges struck Tilshead | | | |
| DEVONPORT, J. | | Cpl | 6.2.43 |
| Road accident Shobden | | | |
| BURGESS, F.J. | | Lt | 1.3.43 |

| | | | | | |
|---|---|---|---|---|---|
| Flying accident Slade Farm SLG | | | | | |
| RENFREY, R. | | Cpl | | 26.3.43 | |
| Flying accident Weston-on-the-Green | | | | | |
| KELSEY-WILKINSON, C.W. | | Cpl | | 2.4.43 | |
| Flying accident Hurn | | | | | |
| REYNOLDS, Geoffrey E. | | Sgt | | 17.4.43 | |
| Flying accident Chilbolton | | | | | |
| DAVIES, F.J. | }★ | Sgt | | 16.5.43 | |
| SUNTER, R.D. | | Sgt | | 16.5.43 | |
| ★Halifax crash at Hurn | | | | | |
| GLADMAN, G.H.G. | | Sgt | | 1.6.43 | |
| Flying accident Netheravon | | | | | |
| PRATT, J.C. | | Sgt | | 11.6.43 | |
| Flying accident Stoke Orchard | | | | | |
| DIXON, T. | | Sgt | | 18.8.43 | |
| SHAMBROOK, F.M. | }★ | Sgt | | 19.8.43 | |
| ELMS, V.P. | | Sgt | | 19.8.43 | |
| ★Flying accident Zeals | | | | | |
| BROWN, J.B. | }★ | Cpl | | 1.10.43 | |
| VINCE, J.L. | | LSgt | 25 | 1.10.43 | Marlow (Trinity Ave. Bucks) |
| ★Flying accident Booker | | | | | |
| DORNING-NADEN, R.E. | | Cpl | | 13.10.43 | |
| Flying accident Princess Risborough | | | | | |
| WESTON, N.M. | | Cpl | | 22.10.43 | |
| Flying accident Shobden | | | | | |
| HYDE, W.D. | }★ | Sgt | | 15.11.43 | |
| PENNY, D.M. | | Sgt | | 15.11.43 | |
| ★Flying accident nr Denham | | | | | |
| JEFFS, E.A. | }★ | SSgt | | 7.12.43 | |
| TAYLOR, P.D. | | Sgt | | 7.12.43 | |
| ★Flying accident Collingbourne Ducis | | | | | |
| GOWER, T.C. | | Sgt | | 12.12.43 | |
| Road accident Boscombe | | | | | |
| TYLER, C.J. | | Cpl | | 28.12.43 | |
| Flying accident Stoke Orchard | | | | | |
| BATES, R.G. | | Sgt | | 20.1.44 | Chesham (Bellington Rd., Bucks) |
| HAGUE/HAYNE, E.A. | | Cpl | | 7.2.44 | |
| Flying accident Lyneham | | | | | |
| CUTHBERT, William | | Tpr | 48 | 25.2.44 | Brookwood Memorial |
| BRIM, Leonard | }★ | Sgt | | 31.3.44 | |
| FIELDEN, Alan T. | | Sgt | | 31.3.44 | |
| ★Flying accident nr Hanging Langford | | | | | |
| JOEL, Henry | }★ | SSgt | | 4.4.44 | |
| WALKER, W.G. | | Sgt | | 4.4.44 | |
| ★Flying accident nr Petersfield | | | | | |
| LEVY, B.J. | }★ | SSgt | | 12.4.44 | |
| FRENCH, Noble | | Sgt | | 12.4.44 | |
| ★Flying accident Brize Norton | | | | | |
| KIRTON, P.M. | | Tpr | | 13.4.44 | |
| Flying accident Wroughton | | | | | |
| ELLSON, J.R. | | Capt | | 13.4.44 | |

| | | | | |
|---|---|---|---|---|
| Road accident Wroughton | | | | |
| CLARKE, W. | | SSgt | 19.4.44 | |
| Flying accident Fairford | | | | |
| NEDDLEMAN, J. | } ★ | SSgt | 28.4.44 | |
| BROWN, Frederick Charles | | Sgt | 28.4.44 | |
| *Flying accident Coombe | | | | |
| CHARRETT, S.H. | } ★ | Tpr | 29.4.44 | |
| McEWAN, H. | | Tpr | 29.4.44 | |
| *Road accident Rollestone | | | | |
| LOWE, Eric H. | | SSgt | 4.5.44 | |
| Flying accident Keevil | | | | |
| CUNLIFFE, W. | | Tpr | 7.5.44 | |
| Road accident Stratton | | | | |
| DYER, J.C. | } ★ | SSgt | 8.5.44 | |
| COE, G.D. | | Sgt | 8.5.44 | |
| *Flying accident Sleap | | | | |
| BLACKBURN, E. | | Sgt | 13.5.44 | |
| Flying accident Tarrant Rushton | | | | |
| FLETCHER, Sidney | } ★ | SSgt | 9.6.44 | Manchester Southern |
| HEBBERD, L. Roy | | Sgt | 9.6.44 | Teddington |
| *Flying accident Fairford | | | | |
| SIMPSON, F.W. (Jock) | } ★ | SSgt | 4.7.44 | |
| SHAW, Dennis | | Sgt | 4.7.44 | Calder, Lanark |
| *Flying accident Netheravon | | | | |
| DOWDS, H.M. | | SSgt | 10.7.44 | Groundsable Cemetery, Grangemouth (Stirling) |
| ANSELL, Herbert James | } ★ | Sgt | 10.7.44 | Longside Cemetery, |
| *Flying accident Maud, nr. Peterhead | | | | Aberdeen |
| FRYER, MC | | Lt. Col | 11.7.44 | |
| Flying accident Stoke Orchard | | | | |
| POLLARD, H. | | Tpr | 15.10.44 | |
| Road accident Bournemouth | | | | |
| BROWNE, H.R. | | SSgt | 10.11.44 | |
| Flying accident Sleap | | | | |
| WESTON, J.B. | | Lt. | 27.11.44 | |
| Flying accident Chelmsford | | | | |
| STARTUP, Frank Joseph | | SSgt | 29.11.44 | Groesbeek Memorial |
| Flying accident Earls Colne | | | | |
| WORMLEIGHTON, C.J. | | SSgt | 29.11.44 | Coventry (London Rd) |
| Flying accident Chelmsford | | | | |
| ANDERSON, A.S. | } ★ | Sgt | 5.12.44 | Mazargues 3.C.55 |
| BARCLAY, Frank Horace, MC (Bull) | | Capt | 5.12.44 | Mazargues 3.C.38 |
| | | | | |
| CROOT, Robert Shirley, TD | } ★ | Maj | 5.12.44 | Mazargues 3.C.36 |
| COX, A.J. | | Lt | 5.12.44 | Mazargues 3.C.59 |
| DAWKINS, G.P. | } ★ | Sgt | 13.12.44 | Mazargues 3.C.41 |
| GIBBS, A.J. | | Sgt | 5.12.44 | Mazargues 3.C.37 |
| HORROCKS, G. | } ★ | Lt | 5.12.44 | Mazargues 3.C.35 |
| LAWTON, D.J. | | Sgt | 5.12.44 | Mazargues 3.C.50 |
| NORMAN, E.H.W. | | Lt | 5.12.44 | Mazargues 3.C.53 |
| PALMER, R.V.D. | } ★ | Capt | 5.12.44 | Mazargues 3.C.58 |
| TELFER, R.D. | | Capt | 5.12.44 | Mazargues 3.C.39 |

| | | | | |
|---|---|---|---|---|
| WAKEFIELD, E. | } ★ | Sgt | 5.12.44 | Mazargues 3.C.56 |
| WALSH, J. | | Sgt | 5.12.44 | Mazargues 3.C.49 |
| WATT, William | } ★ | WO2 | 5.12.44 | Mazargues 3.C.51 |
| WOODWARD, J. | | Sgt | 5.12.44 | Mazargues 3.C.40 |

*Flying accident en route India

| | | | |
|---|---|---|---|
| HOBBS, W. | Sgt | 23.1.45 | |
| Flying accident Broughton | | | |
| BEARD/BAIRD, R.S. | Sgt | 24.1.45 | |
| Flying accident Broughton | | | |
| WILLIAMS, K.J. | Sgt | 11.2.45 | |
| Flying accident Tarrant Rushton | | | |
| BATTERSBY, J. | Sgt | 3.3.45 | |
| Flying accident whilst on practice para drop nr Giola, Italy | | | |
| EGAN, J.R. | Sgt | 12.3.45 | |
| Flying accident Exeter | | | |
| FAULKNER, P.M. | Sgt | 25.3.44 | |
| Flying accident Exeter | | | |
| DOORN, H.J. | WO2 | 27.3.45 | St Patrick's RC, Leytonstone |
| Road accident Braintree | | | |
| HUNT, D.J. | Sgt | 4.5.45 | |
| Flying accident Keevil | | | |
| BOWER, J.B.W. | Fg Offr | 8.5.45 | |
| Road accident Golders Green | | | |
| BREBNER, J.L. | Fg Offr | 11.5.45 | |
| Road accident Bournemouth | | | |
| HARDY, E. | Sgt | 25.5.45 | |
| Flying accident Honiton | | | |
| COLLINS, F.F. | Lt | 17.6.45 | |
| Accidentally drowned | | | |
| COOK, N. | Sgt | 21.6.45 | |
| Meningitis | | | |
| PETTIT, E.T. | Sgt | 22.6.45 | |
| Road accident Witney | | | |

Post-War casualties
Berlin Airlift 1948-49

| | | | |
|---|---|---|---|
| TOAL, Joseph | Sgt | 16.7.49 | Berlin 1939-45 G.16 |
| Flying accident Tegel | | | |

Operation FIREDOG, Malayan Emergency

| | | |
|---|---|---|
| GAY, W.D. | SSgt | 13.3.52 |
| PERRY, J. | Sgt | 21.1.54 |

Non-operational

| | | | |
|---|---|---|---|
| HONEYWELL, Arthur Noel, MM | Sgt | 26.4.46 | |
| Flying accident Elsham Wolds | | | |
| SHERRY, T. William (Bill) | Sgt | Feb. 47 | Stoke |
| Flying accident Fairford | | | |
| CHADD | Sgt | 17.5.47 | |
| COOPER, Cyril Lewis | Sgt | 22.9.49 | |

# ROLL OF HONOUR

| | | |
|---|---|---|
| NORGROVE | Tpr | |
| MANSFIELD, J.J. | SSgt | 21.7.51 |

# APPENDIX II

## HONOURS AND AWARDS

| Award | Name | Rank | |
|---|---|---|---|
| AFC | COOPER, Astley John | T/Maj | Op BEGGAR |
| AFC | THOMAS, Emrys James | T/Capt | Normandy |
| AFM | ANTONOPOULOS, Sotiris | A/Sgt | Op BEGGAR |
| AFM | HALL, Denis Arthur | A/Sgt | Op BEGGAR |
| AFM | MEATON, R. | Sgt | |
| BEM | BELL, A. | Sgt | |
| BEM | JOHNSTONE, Samuel Findlay | SSgt | Arnhem |
| CGM (Flying) | TURNBULL, Lawrence William | WO2 | Rhine Crossing |
| Croix de Geurre | BAACKE, F.W. | SSgt | Normandy |
| Croix de Guerre | BOLAND, Oliver F. | SSgt | Normandy |
| Croix de Guerre | BRAMAH, Maurice Alexander, MM | SSgt | Normandy |
| Croix de Guerre | GUTHRIE, Leonard | SSgt | Normandy |
| DCM | GARRATT, Edward Ivan | Sgt | Sicily |
| DCM | TILLEY, Russell Frederick | Sgt | Arnhem |
| DCM | WHITE, Raymond Ernest | SSgt | Normandy |
| DFC | ASTON, F.C. | Capt | Rhine Crossing |
| DFC | ATKINSON, G. | Fg Offr | Rhine Crossing |
| DFC | BARRIE, William Nicholson | Lt | Sicily |
| DFC | BARTLETT, Hugh Tryon | T/Maj | Rhine Crossing |
| DFC | BLATCH, John Frank Bernard | T/Maj | Arnhem |
| DFC | BOUCHER-GILES, Arthur Francis | Lt | Sicily |
| DFC | DALE, James Alexander | Lt | Sicily |
| DFC | DODWELL, Christopher Bradford | T/Capt | Arnhem |
| DFC | DOWNWARD, Peter A. | Capt | Korea |
| DFC | GRIFFITHS, Stewart Cathie | T/Maj | Arnhem |
| DFC | HOLT, Bertram Richardson | WO2 | Rhine Crossing |
| DFC | INCE, E.K.P. | Flt Lt | Rhine Crossing |
| DFC | JACKSON, Burton Henry Peter | T/Maj | Rhine Crossing |
| DFC | LODGE, J.E. | Flt Lt | Rhine Crossing |
| DFC | LOVE, J.T. | Plt Offr | Rhine Crossing |
| DFC | METCALF, Vernon K. | Capt | Malaya |
| DFC | MEW, Kenneth | A/WO1 | Rhine Crossing |
| DFC | ODLUM, M.J. | Plt Offr | Rhine Crossing |
| DFC | PICKWOAD, Aubrey Earle | Lt | Normandy |
| DFC | PRIEST, Maurice William Dallow | T/Capt | Rhine Crossing |

| DFC | STOKES, George Rose Innes Masters | Lt | Arnhem |
|---|---|---|---|
| DFC | TAYLERSON, Thomas Whitby | Lt | Normandy |
| DFC | TOLER, Thomas Ian Jodrell | T/Maj | Arnhem |
| DFC | WILSON, Peter F. | Capt | Korea |
| DFC | YOUNG, David Tyne | Lt | Malaya |
| DFC –<br>bar to DFC | DALE, James Alexander, DFC | T/Maj | Normandy |
| DFM | ANDREWS, Harold Norman | SSgt | Sicily |
| DFM | BAKER, Ernest John | SSgt | Normandy |
| DFM | BANKS, Richard | SSgt | Normandy |
| DFM | BARKWAY, Geoffrey Sidney | SSgt | Normandy |
| DFM | BAYLEY, William John | Sgt | Italy |
| DFM | BONE, Stanley George | SSgt | Normandy |
| DFM | BOWMAN, Albert | SSgt | Rhine Crossing |
| DFM | CALDER, Ronald Reid | A/SSgt | Arnhem |
| DFM | DANCE, Albert Victor | SSgt | Arnhem |
| DFM | DOUGLAS, Robert Gordon | A/SSgt | Arnhem |
| DFM | EDWARDS, John Ewart | SSgt | Rhine Crossing |
| DFM | ENGLAND, Edgar | SSgt | Normandy |
| DFM | EVANS, Ivor Wyn | SSgt | Rhine Crossing |
| DFM | FORD, John I.A. | SSgt | Malaya |
| DFM | GALPIN, Dennis Patten | A/WO2 | Sicily |
| DFM | GRAY, Thomas | SSgt | Rhine Crossing |
| DFM | HERBERT, William Charles | SSgt | Normandy |
| DFM | HOBBS, Philip Allan | SSgt | Normandy |
| DFM | HOWARD, Roy Alan | SSgt | Normandy |
| DFM | HUTCHINGS, James W. | SSgt | Malaya |
| DFM | ISAACS, Samuel Gregory | A/SSgt | Arnhem |
| DFM | JENKINS, Geoffrey D. | WO2 | Malaya |
| DFM | KERR, David Fisher | SSgt | Normandy |
| DFM | MASSON, William, MM | A/WO2 | Sicily |
| DFM | MATHER, William | SSgt | Arnhem |
| DFM | McCULLOCH, A. | SSgt | South of France |
| DFM | MINALL, Laurence James | SSgt | Rhine Crossing |
| DFM | MOORCRAFT, Gerald Eric | SSgt | Rhine Crossing |
| DFM | PEARSON, Stanley | SSgt | Normandy |
| DFM | PROTHEROE, Harold George | SSgt | Sicily |
| DFM | RASPISSON, Edgar | SSgt | Rhine Crossing |
| DFM | RICHARDS, Frank Alan | SSgt | Rhine Crossing |
| DFM | ROLLEY, John C. | SSgt | Malaya |
| DFM | RYANS, Desmond | SSgt | Rhine Crossing |
| DFM | RYE, Joseph Aloysius | SSgt | Arnhem |
| DFM | STREMES, George Frederick | SSgt | Arnhem |
| DFM | TAYLOR, John R. | SSgt | Rhine Crossing |
| DFM | TWIGGS, Cyril Wilfred | SSgt | Arnhem |
| DFM | WALLWORK, James Horley | SSgt | Normandy |
| DFM | WATKINSON, Charles Rollet | A/SSgt | Arnhem |
| DFM | WHITE, Frank Herbert | SSgt | Sicily |
| DFM | WRIGHT, Leonard | SSgt | Rhine Crossing |
| DFM –<br>bar to DFM | ANDREWS, Harold Norman, DFM | SSgt | Arnhem |
| DSO | CHATTERTON, George James Stewart | T/Lt Col | Sicily |

| | | | |
|---|---|---|---|
| DSO | DAUNCEY, Michael Donald Keen | Lt | Arnhem |
| DSO | MURRAY, Iain Arthur | T/Lt Col | Normandy |
| DSO – | MURRAY, Iain Arthur | T/Lt Col | Rhine Crossing |
| bar to DSO | | | |
| Dutch Bronze | CORRIE, Michael Taylor | T/Capt | Arnhem |
| Cross | | | |
| Dutch Bronze | SWIFT, Walter Hemmerton | Sgt | Arnhem |
| Cross | | | |
| Dutch Bronze | WAINRIGHT, Thomas James | T/Capt | Arnhem |
| Cross | | | |
| Dutch Bronze | BRIODY, M.J, MBE | WO2 | Arnhem |
| Lion | | | |
| Dutch Bronze | CROOT, Robert Shirley, TD | Maj | Arnhem |
| Lion | | | |
| KB | HAYWARD, Jack Arnold | Flt Lt | |
| KW | BARCLAY, Frank Horace, MC | Capt | |
| KW | LESCHALLAS, E.H. | Capt | |
| MBE | ANDREWS, Kenneth James Stuart | T.Maj | Arnhem |
| MBE | BRIODY, M.J. | WO1 | |
| MBE | FLETCHER, Peter Noel | Capt | |
| MBE | HARDING, Patrick Graham | T/Maj | |
| MBE | LANCASTER, Ivan | Sqn Ldr | |
| MBE | TURNER, A.C.G. | Lt | |
| MBE | WHITE, J.B. | WO2 | |
| MC | BARCLAY, Frank Horace | Capt | Sicily |
| MC | CARN, Walter James | Lt | Sicily |
| MC | HALSALL, Bernard Holt | Lt | Sicily |
| MC | LYNE, John Francis | Maj | Sicily |
| MC | McMILLEN, Thomas Dermot | Capt | Sicily |
| | Brockbank | | |
| MC | MURRAY, Francis Anthony Stobbard | T/Maj | Sicily |
| MC | ROBSON, Foster | Lt | Sicily |
| MID | ADAMSON, R. | Sgt | Malaya |
| MID | ANDREWS, Kenneth James Stuart | T/Maj | Arnhem |
| MID | ATTWELL, D.O.E. | SSgt | |
| MID | BADGER, M.G. | Capt | Malaya |
| MID | BALDWIN, A.C. | Sgt | |
| MID | BELSEY, A.L. | Cpl | Malaya |
| MID | BOWLES, Robert Wallis | SSgt | Malaya |
| MID | BRADBROOK, B.H. | Capt | Malaya |
| MID | BRAZIER, Peter John | Lt | |
| MID | BRIDGEWATER, W.G. | SSgt | |
| MID | BROWN, A.S. | SSgt | Rhine Crossing |
| MID | BROWN, A.T.C. | Capt | Korea |
| MID | CAMPBELL, G. | SSgt | Rhine Crossing |
| MID | COLLINS, A.L. | Lbdr | Malaya |
| MID | COULTHARD, G.A.R. | T/Maj | South of France |
| MID | ELLIOTT, L. | Cpl | Korea |
| MID | FANE, J.H.M, MBE | T/Capt | Greece |
| MID | FISH, | Cpl | Korea |
| MID | GARNETT, R.H. | T/Capt | |
| MID | GWINN, Malcolm Ian | Sgt | Arnhem |

| MID | HALL, R.E. | SSgt | Korea |
|---|---|---|---|
| MID | HALLER, B.J.F. | Sgt | Rhine Crossing |
| MID | HARRIS, Owen William | SSgt | Malaya |
| MID | HARTSHORN, C.G. | LAC | Korea |
| MID | HENDON, S. | Sgt | Greece |
| MID | HOBBS, Philip Allan, DFM | SSgt | Ardennes |
| MID | HOOPER, J.H. | T/Capt | Rhine Crossing |
| MID | HORSEY, B.A. | Sgt | Malaya |
| MID | IVINS, | Cpl | Korea |
| MID | KILLER, D.E.S. | Sgt | Malaya |
| MID | LOW, Angus Feredith W. | T/Capt | |
| MID | MAHONEY, P.J.D. | Sgt | Arnhem |
| MID | MANN, John Robert | Sgt | Arnhem |
| MID | McARTHUR, Ian A. | A/Maj | Rhine Crossing |
| MID | METCALF, V.K. | Capt | Malaya |
| MID | MILLS, Gordon T. | T/Capt | Arnhem |
| MID | MOORE, W.G. | SSgt | Rhine Crossing |
| MID | MORRISON, W.B. | Sgt | Greece |
| MID | MOUSLEY, Samuel | Sgt | Malaya |
| MID | MUIR, Ian Colquhoun | A/Capt | Normandy |
| MID | MYERS, P.K. | Capt | Malaya |
| MID | NADEN, John Ernest Peat | A/SSgt | Arnhem |
| MID | NASH, S.G. | LCpl | Malaya |
| MID | NEALE, Francis J.T. | T/Capt | Arnhem |
| MID | NYE, G.H.E. | SSgt | Rhine Crossing |
| MID | PALFREEMAN, C. | Sgt | Rhine Crossing |
| MID | PARE, G.A.F. | CF4 | Arnhem |
| MID | PHILLIPS, Eric | SSgt | Arnhem |
| MID | PLOWMAN, Thomas Anthony | T/Capt | Arnhem |
| MID | PUGSLEY | LAC | Korea |
| MID | PULLEN, Harold Neil Desmond | Capt | Malaya |
| MID | REDWAY, G. | SSgt | |
| MID | RICHARDSON, C.D. | SSgt | Normandy |
| MID | ROYLE, R.J. | Capt | Malaya |
| MID | SHUTTLEWORTH, Donald Harrop | T/Capt | Normandy |
| MID | SMITH, J.J. | LCpl | Malaya |
| MID | TAPPING, J.R. | Sgt | Malaya |
| MID | TAYLER, Cyril Cadle | Lt | Arnhem |
| MID | TIGHE, J.P. | Capt | Malaya |
| MID | TURNER, A.G.C., MBE | A/Capt | Rhine Crossing |
| MID | WAINWRIGHT, Thomas James | Capt | Arnhem |
| MID | WETHEY, A.B. | Sgt | Rhine Crossing |
| MID | WHITEHEAD, Stuart R. | Capt | Malaya |
| MID | WINT | Sgt | |
| MM | AINSWORTH, John Alfred | SSgt | Sicily |
| MM | BLACKWOOD, Ian James | WO2 | Arnhem |
| MM | BRAMAH, Maurice Alexander | SSgt | Normandy |
| MM | HAIG, Lewis | Sgt | Arnhem |
| MM | HOLLOWAY, Eric John | Sgt | Arnhem |
| MM | MOORE, Thomas Raymond | SSgt | Sicily |
| MM | WALLACE, David Bruce | SSgt | Arnhem |
| OBE | CHATTERTON, George James Stewart | Brig | |

| | | | |
|---|---|---|---|
| Perak DCM | HICKEY, Shirley Michael Wright | Capt | Malaya |
| TD | BOTTOMLEY, John B | Capt | |
| US Bronze Star | WATT, William | WO2 | |
| US Silver Star | JACKSON, Burton Henry Peter, DFC | T/Maj | |
| US Silver Star | STRATHERN, Kenneth Fairley | T/Capt | |

# APPENDIX

# III
---

## Colonels Commandant

12.11.42 to 22.7.45 General Sir Alan Brooke (later Field-Marshal Viscount Alanbrooke, KG, GCB, OM, GCVO, DSO★, DCL, LLD.)

23.7.45 to 1.9.57 Lieutenant-General Sir W.J. Eldridge, KBE, CB, CBE, DSO, MC.

## Commanding Officers

|  | |
|---|---|
| 1942 | Lieutenant-Colonel J.F. Rock. |
| 1942–45 | Honorary Brigadier G.J.S. Chatterton, DSO. |
| 1945–46 | Lieutenant-Colonel J.F. Lyne. |
| 1947–48 | Lieutenant-Colonel F.A.S. Murray, MC. |
| 1948–50 | Lieutenant-Colonel C.J. Deedes, MC. |
| 1950–52 | Major R. King-Clark, MC. (later Lieutenant Colonel, MBE, MC.) |
| 1952 | Major J.W. Stonor, MBE. |
| 1952–55 | Major G.H. Wotton. (later Lieutenant Colonel, OBE). |
| 1955–57 | Major P.A. Downward, DFC. (later Major General, CB, DSO, DFC.) |
| 1957 | Major M.W. Sutcliffe. (later Brigadier, OBE.) |

## Battalion/Wing/Squadron Commanders

| Year | Place | Designation | Officers | | RAF Squadrons |
|---|---|---|---|---|---|
| Feb. 1942 to Oct. 1942 | Tilshead | 1st Bn. | Lieutenant-Colonel J.F. Rock. | C.O. | – |
| | | | Major G.J.S. Chatterton | 2 i/c | – |
| | | | Captain E. Leschallas | Adj. | |
| Aug. 1942 to Oct. 1942 | Tilshead | 2nd Bn. | Lieutenant-Colonel G.J.S. Chatterton C.O. | | – |
| | | | Major M. Willoughby | 2 i/c | – |
| | | | Captain A.J. Cooper | Adj. | – |
| Oct. 1942 to Feb. 1943 | Tilshead | Regtl. HQ | Lieutenant-Colonel G.J.S. Chatterton C.O. | | – |
| | | | Major B.H.P. Jackson | Adj. | – |
| Oct. 1942 to Aug. 1943 | Bulford | 1st Bn. ) | Major M. Willoughby | C.O. | – |
| | | 2 Wing ) | Captain N. Denholm | ) Adj. | – |
| | | | Captain B.H.P. Jackson | ) | |
| | | 1 Sqdn. | Major P. Cooper | | – |
| | | 2 Sqdn. ) | Major E. Leschallas | | – |
| | | ) | Major F.A.S. Murray | | – |
| | | 3 Sqdn. | Major J.A. Dale | | – |
| | | 4 Sqdn. | Major P.F. Stancliffe | | – |
| | | 5 Sqdn. | Major G.A.R. Coulthard | | – |
| Oct. 1942 | Tilshead and Fargo Camp | 2nd Bn. ) | Major I.A. Murray | C.O. | – |
| | | 1 Wing ) | Major J.P. Royle | 2 i/c | – |
| | | | Captain J.B. Bottomley | Adj. | – |

|            |                |                | 1 Sqdn.   | Major K.J.S. Andrews                      |       | –        |
|------------|----------------|----------------|-----------|-------------------------------------------|-------|----------|
|            |                |                | 2 Sqdn.   | Major S.C. Griffith                       |       | –        |
|            |                |                | 3 Sqdn.   | Major T.I.J. Toler                        |       | –        |
|            |                |                | 4 Sqdn.   | Major J.F. Lyne                           |       | –        |
|            |                |                | 5 Sqdn.   | Major R.S. Croot                          |       | –        |
|            |                |                | 6 Sqdn.   | Captain R. Sinclair-Scott                 |       | –        |
|            |                |                | X Sqdn.   | Captain K.J.S. Andrews                    |       | –        |
|            |                |                | HQs Sqdn. | Major Greville-Williams                   |       | –        |
| Apr. 1943  | North Africa   | Regtl.         |           | Lieutenant-Colonel G.J.S. Chatterton      |       | 295      |
|            |                | HQs            |           |                                           | C.O.  |          |
|            |                |                |           | Captain J. Hooper                         | Adj.  | 296      |
|            |                |                | 2 Sqdn. ) | Major E.H. Leschallas                     |       |          |
|            |                |                |         ) | Major F.A.S. Murray                       |       |          |
|            |                |                | 3 Sqdn.   | Major J.W. Place                          |       |          |
| Sept. 1943 | Italy          | 2 Wing         |           | Lieutenant-Colonel J.W. Place             | C.O.  | –        |
| 1943       | Netheravon     | Regtl.         |           | Colonel G.J.S. Chatterton                 |       | –        |
|            |                | HQs.           |           | Commander Glider Pilots                   |       |          |
|            |                |                |           | Major P.G. Harding                        | SO2   | –        |
|            |                |                |           | Major K.J.S. Andrews                      | Ops   | –        |
|            |                |                |           | Captain I.A. McArthur                     | SO3   | –        |
|            |                |                |           | Captain G. Rostworowski                   | I.O.  | –        |
| 1944       | Various        | 3 Sqdn.        |           | Major G.A.R. Coulthard                    |       | –        |
|            |                | re-named       |           |                                           |       |          |
|            |                | 1 Ind.Sqdn.    |           |                                           |       |          |
| 1944       | India          | 10 Ind.        |           | Major P.F. Stancliffe                     |       | 670      |
|            |                | G.P. Sqdn.     |           |                                           |       |          |
| 1944-45    | Fargo Camp     | 1 Wing         |           | Lieutenant-Colonel I.A. Murray            | C.O.  | –        |
|            |                |                |           | Major J.P. Royle                          | 2 i/c | –        |
|            |                |                |           | Captain P. Fletcher                       | Adj.  | –        |
|            |                |                |           | Captain J.B. Bottomley                    | I.O.  | –        |
|            |                |                |           | Lieutenant E.E. Nichols                   | Q.M.  | –        |
|            | Harwell        | "A" Sqdn.      |           | Major S. C. Griffith                      |       | 295, 570 |
|            | Brize Norton   | "B" Sqdn.      |           | Major T.I.J. Toler                        |       | 296, 297 |
|            | Fairford       | "D" Sqdn.      |           | Major J.F. Lyne                           |       | 190, 620 |
|            | Fairford       | "G" Sqdn.      |           | Major R.S. Croot                          |       | 190, 620 |
| 1944-45    | Fargo Camp     | 2 Wing         |           | Lieutenant-Colonel J.W. Place             | C.O.  | –        |
|            |                |                |           | Major J. Blatch                           | 2 i/c | –        |
|            |                |                |           | Captain D. Shuttleworth                   | Adj.  | –        |
|            |                |                |           | Captain Maltby                            | I.O.  | –        |
|            |                |                |           | Captain Maher                             | Q.M.  |          |
|            | Tarrant        | "C" Sqdn.      |           | Major J.A. Dale                           |       | 298, 644 |
|            | Rushton        |                |           |                                           |       |          |
|            | Down           | "E" Sqdn.      |           | Major B.H.P. Jackson                      |       | 48, 271  |
|            | Ampney         |                |           |                                           |       |          |
|            | Broadwell      |                |           |                                           |       |          |
|            | & Blakehill    | "F" Sqdn.      |           | Major F.A.S. Murray                       |       | 233, 271 |
|            | Farm           |                |           |                                           |       |          |
| 1945-46    | India          | 671 Sqdn.)     |           | Major W. McNeill                          |       |          |
|            |                |          )     |           | Major W. Tallentire                       |       |          |
|            |                | 672 Sqdn.)     |           | Captain J. Hyson                          |       |          |
|            |                |          )     |           | Major J.E. Lockett                        |       |          |
|            |                | 673 Sqdn.      |           | Major F.A.S. Murray                       |       |          |

|  |  |  |  |  |  |
|---|---|---|---|---|---|
| 1945 |  | 670 Sqdn. | Major H.B. Haeffner |  |  |
|  |  | 1 Wing | Lieutenant-Colonel S.C. Griffith | C.O. |  |
|  |  | 2 Wing | Lieutenant Colonel B.H.P. Jackson |  |  |
|  |  |  |  | C.O. |  |
|  | Harwell & | "A" Sqdn. | Major H.J. Bartlett |  | 295, 570. |
|  | Rivenhall |  |  |  |  |
|  | Earles Colne | "B" Sqdn. | Major T.I.J. Toler |  | 296, 297. |
|  | Tarrant | "C" Sqdn. | Major J.A. Dale |  | 298, 644. |
|  | Rushton & |  |  |  |  |
|  | Woodbridge |  |  |  |  |
|  | Fairford & | "D" Sqdn. | Major J.F. Lyne |  | 190, 196, |
|  |  |  | S/Ldr. S.C. Kent |  |  |
|  | Shepherds |  |  |  | 299, 620. |
|  | Grove |  |  |  |  |
|  | Down Ampney | "E" Sqdn. | Major B. Murdoch |  | 48, 233, |
|  | & Birch |  | S/Ldr. White |  | 271, 437. |
|  | Broadwell & | "F" Sqdn. | Major F.A.S. Murray |  | 271, 512, |
|  |  |  | S/Ldr. Reynolds |  |  |
|  | Gosfield |  |  |  | 575. |
|  | Fairford | "G" Sqdn. | Major M.W.D. Priest |  | 190, 233, |
|  | & Gt. Dunmow |  |  |  | 271, 437, |
|  |  |  |  |  | 575, 620. |
|  | Keevil | "H" Sqdn. | Major M.W.D. Priest |  | 196. |
|  |  | "I" Sqdn. | S/Ldr. Reynolds |  |  |
|  |  | "J" Sqdn. | S/Ldr. Avery |  |  |
|  |  | "K" Sqdn. | S/Ldr. Huntley |  |  |
|  |  | "L" Sqdn. | S/Ldr. S.C. Kent |  |  |
|  |  | "M" Sqdn. | (S/Ldr. J.R. Patient DFC |  |  |
|  |  |  | (S/Ldr. K.L. Ashurst OBE |  |  |
|  | Netheravon | "N" Sqdn. | Major B.H.P. Jackson (later C.O. |  | – |
|  |  |  | No.2 Wing) S/Ldr. White |  |  |
|  | Fargo Camp | Regtl. | Lieutenant-Colonel K. Greville |  | – |
|  |  | HQs | Williams | C.O. |  |
|  |  |  | Captain B. Halsall | Adj. |  |
| 1946 | Aldershot | Depot Sqdn. | Major I.W. Stonor |  |  |
|  |  | (later Trng. | Major J.B. Bottomley |  |  |
|  |  | Sqdn.) |  |  |  |
| 1946-47 | Egypt & |  | ) Lieutenant-Colonel J.F. Lyne |  |  |
|  | Palestine | 1 Wing | ) Lieutenant-Colonel R. Gaitley |  | – |
|  |  |  | ) Lieutenant-Colonel F.A.S. Murray |  |  |
|  |  | "D" Sqdn. | Major A. Murdoch |  |  |
|  |  | "A" Sqdn. | Major F.C. Aston |  |  |
|  |  | (with det. |  |  |  |
|  |  | from "G") |  |  |  |
| 1948 | Aldershot | Regtl. | Lieutenant-Colonel C.J. Deedes | C.O. | – |
|  |  | HQs |  |  |  |
| 1947-49 | Oakington & | "D" Sqdn. | Major F.C. Aston |  | Two |
|  | Waterbeach | (later "A") |  |  | Flights |
|  |  |  |  |  | det. |
| 1947-49 | Netheravon | "N" Sqdn. | Major R.H.D. Riggal |  | Wunstorf |
|  | & Fairford | (later "B") |  |  | and |

| | | | | Schleswig-land |
|---|---|---|---|---|
| 1949-50 | Booker & Aldershot | "A" Sqdn. | Major D.C. Lyall | |
| 1950 | Aldershot | 1st Ind. Sqdn. | Major R. King-Clarke | – |
| 1951 | Middle Wallop | 1st Ind. Sqdn. | Major I.W. Stonor | – |
| 1951 | Middle Wallop | Regtl. HQs | Major G.H. Wotton | – |
| 1954 | Middle Wallop | Regtl. HQs | Major P.A. Downward | – |
| 1957 | Middle Wallop | Regtl. HQs | Major M.W. Sutcliffe | |

# BIBLIOGRAPHY

Chatterton, George, *The Wings of Pegasus*, Nashville, Tenn., The Battery
       Press
Dank, Milton, *The Glider Gang*, London, Cassell
Devlin, Garard M., *Silent Wings*, London, W. H. Allen
Morrison, Will, *Horsa Squadron*, London, William Kimber
Mrazek, James E., *The Glider War*, London, Robert Hale
Seth, Ronald, *Lion With Blue Wings*, London, Victor Gollancz
Wright, Lawrence, *The Wooden Sword*, London, Elek Books

# INDEX

Barbara Cartland · 1931 p. 2

Horsa. 25 men.
Hotspur 7–8 m p. p. 13
Hengist 15 men 3, P. 16

Hamilcar 40m – p. 16
  Waco   13 men   p. 47  Wing span 83'–5" p 50.
(Hadrian)


Both R.E.C.°
Glider Pilot Regiment p. 25
Sicily p. 57  145 Waco. 19 Horsa.

Portsmouth to Sile 1400 miles p. 1400 miles p 48